Hunger Like a Thirst

Hunger Like a Thirst

From Food Stamps to Fine Dining, a Restaurant Critic Finds Her Place at the Table

....

Besha Rodell

CELADON
BOOKS

NEW YORK

www.celadonbooks.com

Grateful acknowledgment is made for permission to reproduce from the following:

"Welcome to Los Angeles: You're So Ugly!!!," first published in *LA Weekly*, May 23, 2012.
"40 Ounces to Freedom," first published on *Punch*, October 28, 2013,
courtesy of Vox Media, LLC.
"The City That Knows How to Eat," first published on *Eater*,
December 19, 2016, courtesy of Vox Media, LLC.
"Review: The Agrarian Kitchen Eatery & Store in New Norfolk, Tasmania,"
first published in *The New York Times*, December 21, 2017.
"Outback Steakhouse Review: Please Don't Call This Food Australian,"
first published in *LA Weekly*, June 13, 2013.

All art on part titles by Shutterstock

The Library of Congress Cataloging-in-Publication Data is available upon request.

ISBN 978-1-250-80712-0 (hardcover)
ISBN 978-1-250-80713-7 (ebook)

Our books may be purchased in bulk for promotional, educational, or business use.
Please contact your local bookseller or the Macmillan Corporate and
Premium Sales Department at 1-800-221-7945, extension 5442,
or by email at MacmillanSpecialMarkets@macmillan.com.

First Edition: 2025

10 9 8 7 6 5 4 3 2 1

For the ghosts.
And for Felix.

Contents

Author's Note   *ix*

Amuse-Bouche

A Note from the Critic   3

Appetizer

Food = Good: Stephanie's   11
Food = Sex: Goldie's   16
Food = Love: Ryan   26
New York City   31
North Carolina   45
The Truffle   53

Entrée

Who Writes?   61
Billy   69
From Our Desk to Your Eyeballs   76

Owner's Disorder and Other Aberrations   90
The GOAT   100
Interlude: The Celebrity Shepherd   122

The Part of the Meal Where I Take Notes in the Bathroom

We Are What We Eat   133
We Are What We Drink   146
To Serve and Be Served   162

Palate Cleanser

The City That Knows How to Eat   175

(Bittersweet) Dessert

LAX–MEL   189
Ian   201
A Day on the Road   208
Michelle   219
Billy II   232
Epilogue: Tony   242

Acknowledgments   253

Author's Note

This is a book of my memories and experiences; as we all know, memory is a fickle beast, but I have done my best to reflect those experiences as accurately as possible. Some names and identifying details have been changed for privacy purposes.

Hunger
Like
a Thirst

Amuse-Bouche

A Note from the Critic

The hotel I'm sitting in is shaped like a crocodile. Reception is in the beast's maw; the awning over the driveway is held up by pointy teeth. Rooms are along its sides; to find the pool, you head toward the belly. The circular parking lots to the side represent crocodile eggs. The hotel lies in a serpentine sprawl at the center of Jabiru, the township inside Kakadu National Park in the far north of Australia, a park bigger than Connecticut, as big as Slovenia.

I am in the restaurant, located approximately in the creature's brain, sipping something from a martini glass called Yellow Waters. It's a gruesome name for a cocktail but not without justification: it honors the popular tour offered in Kakadu, wherein you take a boat at dawn out onto Yellow Water Billabong in order to spot birdlife and, yes, crocodiles. I'd taken the cruise that morning, the boat skimming over wetlands, the peachy-orange sunrise reflected in the water's mirrorlike surface, interrupted occasionally by massive crocs that eyed us hungrily, their snouts barely breaking the surface.

I'd traveled for days to get here, on two planes and then in a rental car, to one of Australia's most remote and sacred places. Indigenous Australians have been living on this land for sixty thousand years or more. There are paintings at Ubirr, a rock formation that juts out over the Nadab floodplain, of animals that are thought to have gone extinct thousands of years ago. On a horizontal overhang far above the ground, paintings of Mimi spirits, spindly and ethereal fairylike creatures, decorate the rocks. There's no logical explanation for how humans might have managed those paintings, so high above the ground—legend says that the Mimi spirits themselves made the paintings and brought the rocks down to earth to do so.

I am here as a journalist, but not to write about the cultural significance of the park or its people, or to report on any particular controversy. I'm here for the curry.

At the entrance to Ubirr sits a small shop called Border Store. It acts as a rest stop for busloads of tourists, a place to grab a drink before or after visiting the heritage site, and to use the bathroom. (Though caution is advisable; the day I was there, one of the doors to a stall had a piece of paper taped to it that read, "Snake in the toilet. Beware!") Border Store is only open for part of the year because the wet season, from November to April, makes the roads out here impassable. Border Store sells postcards and chips, sunscreen and Popsicles. It also serves a full menu of Thai dishes, thanks to the couple who lease the space from the Aboriginal traditional owners of the land. Michael Brown, the husband, is Anglo-Australian, but his wife, Rattana Mana, is from Phayao Province in Thailand. In Kakadu, where the food options are limited, full-time residents wait anxiously every year for Border Store to open, for Mana's noodles and curries and soups.

Which is why I'm here. I've come all this way to write about how a blended family took over a tourist rest stop in this far-flung place and became indispensable to the community thanks to the traditional Thai food they serve. I'm spending my nights sipping terrible cocktails in a crocodile-shaped hotel, and my days sitting on a plastic chair in the heat outside Border Store, gobbling fiery jungle stir-fry, slurping curries made with paste that Mana hand-pounds.

How did I wind up here? It's a question I ask myself constantly.

· · ·

A few years ago, I was driving from southern Virginia toward Charlotte, North Carolina. I had a plane to catch back to Los Angeles, where I lived at the time. I was with my sister Ruby, who is fourteen years my junior, and we were driving a very rusty black Mitsubishi that had been my car when I'd lived in Atlanta and that I'd gifted to her when I left for LA, not sure it would survive the journey if I tried to drive it out west.

Ruby and I were coming from Lambstock, a party on a farm thrown annually by this dude who is basically a celebrity sheep farmer. I was writing a story about the farmer and Lambstock and had brought Ruby along for company. For four days, we'd been camping in a sheep field and drinking bourbon and moonshine and cooking over fires with a bunch of bartenders and line cooks and other restaurant types. We hadn't showered, and the rusty Mitsubishi was crammed with all our camping gear, as well as half of Ruby's possessions, her being somewhat between lives at the time.

Somewhere between Statesville and Charlotte on I-77, a police cruiser pulled into my blind spot and then stayed there for fifteen miles before flipping on his lights. When we pulled over, the officer asked me to get out of the car and took me a few feet away so another officer could question Ruby separately.

I was wearing a men's white undershirt, a black bra underneath, very dirty jeans, and muddy rain boots I'd bought at Walmart on the way in when we'd realized it was going to be soggy out in the sheep fields. The police officer asked me where I was going, and where I'd been, and if he could search the car. I told him no, we didn't have time for that, that I had a plane to catch. I asked him why he'd pulled me over, and he said, "Erratic driving." It was clear he thought we had drugs in the car, and I'm not sure I blamed him given our appearance and the state of the car. But I wasn't going to sit there while they pulled old Rusty apart, and besides, I *did* have a plane to catch, and also there may have been a couple of bottles of moonshine in the trunk.

After about thirty minutes of questioning me, and then Ruby, and then comparing notes and looking flummoxed, I finally said to the cop,

"Look, if I was out here doing something illegal, if I really was just some girl running meth down the highway, do you think *this* is the story I'd come up with? That I'm a restaurant critic from Los Angeles who just came from a party full of chefs in a sheep field? That I'd have made up the concept of a party called Lambstock? That I'm writing a story for a magazine about a celebrity shepherd? I understand we look a bit unusual, but you find me a North Carolina druggie that good at bullshitting, and I'll tell you what, I'll buy them a ticket to Hollywood, 'cause that's where they belong."

The guy glanced at his partner, who shrugged. Then he let us go.

When I was in high school, I had a boyfriend who believed I made up my entire life story, down to my name: Beshaleba River Puffin Rodell. "All that shit about how you were born in a bungalow on a farm called Narnia?" he said to me a few years ago, when admitting that he never trusted even the most basic facts of my life. "It was all so fantastical. There was no way it could have been true."

I was a little flattered, to be honest. Imagine being sixteen and having the kind of ingenuity to come up with such things. I was, in fact, a liar at sixteen, but lying is different from creating fantastical fictions. My lies were the sort engineered to get me out of trouble. They were occasionally exaggerations, self-aggrandizements, glaring omissions. I was not then, and am not now, talented enough to attempt pure fiction.

But I have sympathy for his assumption of fabrication. The circumstances of my life are so unlikely and have only become more improbable as time has gone on. I am a child of hippies, born in Australia on a farm called Narnia, named Beshaleba. I am a restaurant critic whose first real assignments came when I was living on food stamps off a rural highway in North Carolina. I am the daughter of a history professor, who cared nothing for that topic until I became obsessed with the history of eating and drinking. I am the daughter of a journalist, the granddaughter of a playwright, who rejected the call to pursue writing professionally until

I figured out a way it could support my addiction, not to drugs or sex or gambling but to fancy restaurants.

How did I get here?

And, perhaps even more baffling, how did we all get here? To a place where food is important enough that some publication or other might foot the bill for my wild adventures, where eating became important enough to the zeitgeist that there would be any such thing as a celebrity shepherd or that people would care about Thai food in the middle of the Australian outback?

The answers are, appropriately and improbably, gorgeously entangled.

Appetizer

Food = Good

Stephanie's

Yes, there was a trip to France. A tower of profiteroles at Les Deux Magots. Breakfasts that included flaky, buttery croissants and fine porcelain cups of le chocolat chaud, so thick and creamy it has taken up residence in my sense memory as a paragon of deliciousness. But my journey into a life in food did not begin there. It began in Melbourne, Australia, at a restaurant called Stephanie's.

Stephanie's was Melbourne's grandest restaurant at the time, housed in a majestic old home in Hawthorne and run by Stephanie Alexander, a chef who is credited with changing the way Australians ate. She trained many of the cooks who went on to become the country's most prominent chefs. The name *Stephanie's* was synonymous with the finest dining.

In 1984, I was aware of none of this, because I was eight and living with my American mother, my Australian father, and my three-year-old brother, Fred, in a share house in Brunswick, an inner neighborhood of Melbourne.

The hulking old terrace where we lived—white, with black wrought iron framing its verandas—had previously housed an elderly order of nuns. When my parents rented it, with the idea of filling it full of other like-minded hippie/academic/journalist types, its sweeping staircase and stained-glass windows and high-ceilinged rooms were filthy. They scrubbed it, claimed its grandest bedroom upstairs, and advertised the downstairs rooms for rent.

Some of the first housemates they attracted were a single mother and her daughter, Sarah, who was about my age. Sarah was small, with dark hair and freckles and a gap-toothed grin, the opposite of my pudgy, blond, self-conscious self. She quickly became the leader of our gang of two, bossing me into compliance, though I did manage to inspire some awe with my firm belief that I was the queen of the fairies. (At night, while she slept, I flew away to fairyland, where I lived in a rosebush with my many fairy princess daughters. This is the subject for a different book entirely.)

The central mythology in Sarah's young life had to do with her father, who was mostly absent. He was, she told me, handsome and rich and lived in a fancy house with his beautiful new wife. (The narrative was quite different when Sarah's mother told the story.) About once a month, Sarah would disappear for the weekend to her father's house and come back with fifty-cent pieces that he had given her—more proof that he was "rich," since our parents would never have bestowed such lavish wealth upon us. I distinctly remember after one such weekend, Sarah leading me dramatically to the milk bar near school and pointing to the wall of candies at the counter. I could pick whichever one I wanted, and she would buy it with her paternally acquired riches. (Did I mention my parents were hippies? Candy was not part of my usual diet.)

When Sarah turned nine, her father proved the point of Sarah's mythology by taking both of us for a celebratory birthday meal at the fanciest restaurant in town: Stephanie's.

I have almost zero recollection of the food. There was a huge, beautiful chocolate soufflé that haunts me to this day, but other than that, I cannot recall a thing I ate. I remember the brocade seating and deep red curtains, which gave everything a feeling of grandeur. I remember the lighting, the tinkle of glasses, the swoosh of the waiters, the mesmerizing, intense luxury of it all. I remember feeling *special*, truly special, that I was allowed into this room where people were spending ungodly amounts of money on something as common as dinner.

Quite honestly, I can't remember much about that year or my life at that time, other than the fact that my mother started sleeping with men other than my father and he moved into a different bedroom and cried a lot and then eventually she moved out of the share house and into a tiny, crappy house somewhere else with the guy who would end up becoming my stepfather. But. I remember Stephanie's.

My family did not frequent restaurants like Stephanie's, and in fact I do not remember any specific restaurant meal in my life prior to the one that occurred there, although I'm sure there were a few.

I didn't need an education in food. I grew up with fantastic food, some of it just as good—and in some ways better!—than what was served at Stephanie's. My father was an academic and an occasional farmer and a gardener and a devotee of Julia Child. I was reared on homegrown fruits and vegetables, rich cream sauces, chocolate mousse made with egg whites and heavy cream and not a lick of gelatin.

My mother had melded her American upbringing with her hippie sense of exploration. She spent her earliest years in Hollywood, where my grandfather was a screenwriter and many of his friends were Syrian. Rice and yogurt became staples of her childhood meals, a tradition she never gave up. My father did most of the cooking while they were together, but when she cooked, lemon juice was added to everything: chicken livers, broccoli with butter, salads full of olives and feta bought from the Greek stalls at the Queen Victoria Market. No, I did not need an education in food. I needed—or more accurately, I desperately *wanted*—an education in luxury.

After my meal at Stephanie's, I began haranguing my parents on my own birthdays. No longer satisfied with the family tradition of picking a favorite home-cooked dish as a birthday meal, I told them I wanted to eat at restaurants instead. They tried. My mother and my new stepfather took us out—now with a baby sister, Grace, in tow—to a neighborhood Lebanese restaurant for my eleventh birthday, an expense that I'm sure they could not afford. I was disappointed. The food was good, but the luxury was lacking.

This instinct, this need for extravagance where it is wholly unearned, runs in my family. Wealth has come and gone on both sides of my lineage, but it has never settled in and stayed. My paternal grandfather owned Malties, a cereal company that was one of Australia's most popular brands in the early twentieth century. Then he had a heart attack and died, leaving my grandmother with five children and no idea how to run a business, and before long, the cereal company and the grand house in Eltham were lost. My maternal grandfather grew up exceedingly wealthy in Philadelphia and spent his life squandering that wealth on fancy cars and trips to Europe and multiple divorces, including two from my grandmother, all the while fancying himself some sort of genius playwright. Both of my parents grew up resenting the lack of luxury that should have been their birthright. I somehow absorbed that, but from a very early age, the thing I thought I ought to have, in a just world, was meals at fancy restaurants.

Money was a constant stress when I was growing up; I'd be lying if I said it hasn't remained a constant stress in my own adult life. And yet my mother has a thing for vintage cars, French soap, French underwear, Chanel perfume, tiny pieces of luxury that she should not be able to justify given that she is the type of woman who carries an extra canister of gas in her car because she runs out of gas so frequently because she never has the money to fill her tank. (I know this makes no sense; you need not explain that to me.)

In fact, the trip to France was a case in point. When I was thirteen, my mother came into a small amount of money and decided to whisk me off for an around-the-world trip, even though she and my stepfather were struggling with a mortgage and my sister Grace was a toddler and leaving her alone with my stepfather for months in order to take me to France and America was a wholly ridiculous thing to do. But this is my mother we're talking about, who drove a vintage red MGB convertible rather than a normal car, who believed her teenage daughter *must* see

Paris in order to understand the brand of sophistication she believed we deserved to inhabit.

I have endeavored, in my life, to be more pragmatic. I have mostly failed. If I thirst for designer clothes, I know how to find them in thrift stores. I do not long for money, other than the kind that relieves you of the deep, existential dread that accompanies poverty. What I long for—what I've longed for since I was eight years old, sitting wide-eyed in that grand restaurant—is the specific opulence of a very good restaurant. I never connected this longing to the goal of attaining wealth; in fact, it was the pantomiming of wealth that appealed.

I did not belong in that grand room! And yet there I was! It was intoxicating.

I have been chasing that feeling ever since.

Food = Sex

Goldie's

n 1999, unhappily in love and living in a tiny house in North Carolina, I realized that the best way for me to satisfy my lust for fine dining was to get a job in a restaurant that had foie gras on the menu.

My boyfriend at the time occasionally made an exception to his wannabe proletariat stance and accompanied me to the French restaurant in town for anniversaries and birthdays. But he hated every minute of it—he rejected anything he deemed too bourgeois (while also letting his wealthy dad pay his half of the rent). I had to find new ways to satisfy my lust for luxury.

By the time I was in my early twenties, I had moved back and forth between America and Australia numerous times and then all over the USA. My mother decided when I was fourteen that she wanted to return to America and brought all of us—me, my brother, my stepfather, and my (now two) sisters—with her. We were all reluctant, other than Ruby, the youngest, who was only two months old. My mother had graduated from Harvard and was a journalist, and her ambitions demanded the opportunity to write for world-respected publications—not just Melbourne newspapers. We landed first in Denver, then moved to Connecticut—the shit, depressing, armpit-of-the-universe inner city of

Hartford, Connecticut, not the quaint, cute, *Gilmore Girls* Connecticut. In Hartford, my mother and stepfather broke up, and I became a proper delinquent. From there we went to Tarrytown, outside of New York City, where I graduated high school (barely), and my mother finally got what she wanted: a job at *The New York Times*.

You want to know what it does to you to be taken from your friends and father at fourteen, to be jostled around to five different high schools (one of them a truly shitty American inner-city nightmare of a school), to live through the second parental divorce in under a decade? It turns you into an asshole. Or at least that's what it did to me.

My mother's time at *The New York Times* was short-lived. That's her story to tell, not mine, but I will say that she worked under Howell Raines and it was not fun. She began an affair with an alcoholic small-town lawyer, who was also *her* brother's brother-in-law, who lived in North Carolina, and she eventually found a plausible reason to move south. While this move was happening, I embarked on a never-ending road trip with my proletarian boyfriend in his 1984 Toyota Corolla, and over the course of a summer, we lived and worked on an island off the Georgia coast that was deserted except for old, falling-down mansions, spent some time in Mississippi, and then ran out of money while heading north again. We drove to my mother's house in the woods of North Carolina and pitched a tent on her lawn, got jobs, and then moved into town.

I had briefly dabbled in the hospitality industry in suburban New York, where I'd worked as a barista at a café run by the Albanian mafia, but North Carolina was where I went all in. For two years, I was a manager in the café of a gourmet supermarket that had recently been acquired by Whole Foods. I found out the beloved elderly woman Peggy, who had worked the steam table for over a decade, was still making less than eight dollars an hour, tried to unionize the place, failed, and got fired or quit—I can't remember which. Then I talked (lied) my way into my first true waitressing job at one of the Triangle's longest-standing nice restaurants, where I was constantly in trouble for my thrift store–acquired white button-down shirts being so very oversize and often wrinkled.

The first workplace terror in my hospitality career was not a raging chef throwing pans or a sleazy line cook or even a demanding customer. It was the pastry chef, a woman named Michelle. With her long red hair wrapped in tight braids around her head, her towering six-foot-tall frame, and her tattered band T-shirts, she glowered at me from behind the pastry line and muttered about my ineptitude loudly. She radiated the kind of energy that intimidated almost everyone. I dreaded the days she was in the kitchen. "Just get it right" was her mantra, and as I began to get it right, to fuck up orders less, to move quickly and with efficiency, she began to tolerate me. It was my first good lesson in the values of the kitchen.

Across the street, another restaurant was opening, one unlike anything I'd seen in North Carolina at that point. Goldie's was small, and dark, and looked impossibly cool. The staff, who were all incredibly hot, wore flat black—not the frumpy khaki pants and white shirts that I was expected to wear. Decent music played in the dining room, not the flaccid soft jazz that was piped into the other nice restaurants in town.

One day, I worked up my nerve and stuck my head in the door in the late afternoon, clutching a résumé in my hands. A stylishly bald man in a perfectly slick suit wearing thick-rimmed glasses took it and looked me over. He asked me some questions, showing little emotion. He told me he'd call me if he had an opening.

A few days later, he did call, offering me a job as a hostess. I was over the moon. This restaurant had everything I'd always craved: buzz, energy, and foie gras on the menu. (A tiny foie gras club sandwich, to be exact, which sounds ridiculous, and was ridiculous, and was also fucking delicious.) It was late December, and my new boss invited me to stop by the restaurant to meet everyone on New Year's Eve (1999!) when they were having a staff party.

I barely remember the party, and I didn't stay long, needing to move on to other parties. But I do remember feeling like: *This is it. I'm finally with my people.*

The cast of characters who worked at Goldie's was too perfect, too

cool, too straight-out-of-central-casting. My boss, the manager and maître
d', oversaw everything with a smooth nonchalance, moving rapidly to
contain any mishap, giving orders sharply and professionally, and flashing a disarming, brilliant smile at customers and worthy staff members.
He had an encyclopedic knowledge of wine, of music—particularly the
punk and indie rock bands that North Carolina was known for—but
also of poetry and politics. He had a law degree that he had used sporad-
ically, but he preferred nighttime hours.

The bartender was an all-American muscled blond hunk of a dude
named Jason. His best friend, Derrick, was a taller, lankier brunette who
rode a motorcycle and was the most assured waiter I've ever known.
The two of them boasted endlessly about their sexual conquests, their
irresistibility to women, but we all suspected they were in love with each
other, and this repartee was actually elaborate foreplay.

There was a waitress named Gloria, with cropped hair and the aura of
Marlene Dietrich, all flashing eyes and growling banter and witty asides.
She also had the largest ass I've ever seen on a small-waisted white
woman, and it was the subject of about 60 percent of the jokes from the
kitchen crew. She took it in stride, always with a withering comeback or
a naughty wink. She was in on the joke—as if she had any choice.

There was Angie, tall and blond and goofy, one of the sunniest and
least pretentious women I've ever known, her wide smile instantly appealing to customers—and the rest of us, too. And Jenny, who had been
playing in bands in town since she was in high school, effortlessly awesome with her gap teeth and sly humor. I loved them both immediately.

The restaurant was small, intimate, and the kitchen was tiny. The crew
back there was also tiny, and included Andy, the tall, quiet, muscled sous-
chef; Sarah, the young, hilarious, beautiful grill cook; Miguel, the dishwasher, who was barely nineteen and newly arrived from Mexico and
breathtakingly sweet; and Ryan, the shaggy-haired, skinny sauté cook
who was rumored to be a local rock star, though his band had broken up.

And in the basement, making the desserts? There was Michelle. She'd
also made the jump across the street when she saw the opportunity. She

was like a benevolent beast down there in her basement lair, growling if you got in her way, but also funny and hyper, being on a constant sugar high from the amazing desserts she was creating.

A few months in, a guy named Matt joined the upstairs kitchen crew as grill cook. Matt was burly and tough, with greasy hair and a goatee. He talked endlessly about all the heroin he used to do, the bands he used to see, and all the excellent food he'd one day make. He was the first line cook I knew who treated cooking the way everyone I knew treated music—obsessively, with the passion of the true fan. He and Ryan formed an instant bond—the kitchen version of the rock and roll high school clique. And then there was the chef: Dave.

Dave was in his midthirties, bald but handsome, with a twinkle in his eye and his soul that was immediately appealing. He was the kind of dude who had run with the bulls, had spent a year traveling around Mexico learning Spanish and drinking mezcal and befriending old ladies with his charm, convincing them to give up their culinary secrets. His stories were wild, his focus intense, and his food . . . was really fucking good. He usually worked as expediter, and he could be scary as hell. I saw him throw things and yell, but mostly his power came from people wanting to please him, as well as a quiet focus that brought all banter to a stop, that made everyone put their heads down and work.

Dave was newly married to a woman who owned an art gallery in town. She was from money; he was not. She was perfectly blond, and perfectly perfect, and icy cold. They never seemed to fit, and there were rumors about how and why they came to be, rumors that made sense to me but were so vague and pedestrian that I can't even recall them. I do know that it was her money, along with a couple of partners, that bought him the restaurant. Without her, there was no Goldie's.

I also know that, among many other things Dave taught me—a love of Riesling, the potential for Southern food to be fancy and delicious, the pushing of limits for how many ways the word *fuck* might be employed in one sentence—he taught me the universal sadness of the chef sitting at the end of the bar of his own restaurant (during service), drinking wine after wine, "going over numbers." I see it still. Constantly. It's almost an archetype. The guy at the end of the bar, drinking the inventory, putting off the inevitable: home.

For me, those early months at Goldie's were magical. I learned so much. I loved every second. The dirty banter was *constant*, the boundaries were always blurred. But I relished it.

At some point during that year, I went to visit my mother where she lived, in the North Carolina countryside, and found my sister Grace in distress. At thirteen, she was having a rough time at school and at home. My youngest sister, Ruby, nine at the time, had very obviously been my mother's favorite since the day she was born. They looked exactly alike, and there was a bond between them that none of us could penetrate. For a while, when all of us lived at home, this was okay. There were so many of us. But then I left home, and eventually my brother, Fred—who hated North Carolina from the minute they moved there—decided to forgo his senior year of high school and move back to New York, where his friends were. He finished his high school diploma at a community college and then went to a university upstate.

Grace was alone in the house with Ruby and my mother, and felt like an outsider. I told her that if she ever wanted to come and stay with me, to get a break, she was welcome. Grace, the bubbliest and best of us, the smallest and most straightforwardly pretty, the most positive, the dancer, the one who made friends easily. In my family, those qualities are apt to make you feel like a stranger.

When I relayed this to my mother—that I'd told Grace she could spend time with me if she wanted to—she balked. We were sitting on her bed after the girls had gone to sleep, and I wasn't prepared for her to tell me that she wasn't comfortable with me looking after her thirteen-year-old for a night every now and then. I had helped to raise these kids. It never occurred to me that I wouldn't continue to help, even though I hadn't lived with them for years.

"You're not doing a great job of looking after yourself these days, Besh," she said. "I'm not sure how I feel about you looking after Grace."

"What do you mean?" I asked, genuinely confused. I had a job, was paying my own rent—had always paid my own rent, had never had any help once I left home.

"You're just kind of drifting. Waiting tables? Going to bars?"

"I'm twenty-four. What should I be doing?"

"Going to college?"

I rolled my eyes. This was rich—I had gotten into college but couldn't afford to go, because no one would help me with tuition and my father's income in Australia made me ineligible for financial aid. I had *wanted* to go to college. But I had rent to pay.

My mother acknowledged the eye roll but continued. "Doing something with your life? Art, music? Even when I was just bumming around in my early twenties, I was always passionate about *something*—theater, politics, something. I was interested in something."

"Ma," I said, "I am passionate. I'm passionate about restaurants. I'm passionate about food and wine. I'm *interested* in waitressing."

Now it was her turn to roll her eyes.

It would be unkind of me to pretend that her lack of enthusiasm or understanding was wildly snobbish. Historically, the social standing of cooks, chefs, and even waiters has ebbed and surged. There was a time during the early 1900s when working as a waiter in certain upscale hotels was seen as a respectable career; in big cities, maître d's had plenty of social clout throughout much of the twentieth century; and Europeans have treated restaurant work as honorable throughout history. But, for the most part, and especially in America, service has never been respected, and restaurant work had almost zero social cachet outside the confines of its own insular community in the 1990s and early 2000s. What my mother saw was that same asshole teenager, now fixating her punk rock attitude onto a career with few prospects for intellectual or financial opportunities. That she was wrong and I was right—that food and restaurants would soon become enough of a cultural force that a satisfying career would become possible—was pure luck on my part.

The sense of camaraderie and silliness and fun at Goldie's never turned bad. (For me.) Until it did.

I worked there as a hostess (second-most-underappreciated job in restaurants), a back waiter, a waitress, and an expediter. The expediter gig (first-most-underappreciated job in restaurants) paid the worst, but I loved it the most. It was like the hostess gig—playing chess with the dining room—but with less face-to-face customer interaction and far more camaraderie and drinking on the job. It was in this capacity that I held an honorary place as part of the kitchen crew and because of that wound up helping at an off-site event one Sunday at a fancy country club. The event was sold as "an evening with master chefs" and included a different course from five of the region's best chefs, to be paired with Australian wines.

The restaurant was usually closed on Sunday, and none of us were being paid any extra to be there. In order to compensate for this, Dave had brought a huge cooler full of wine and beer for us to consume while we worked. In fact, when I arrived an hour after the rest of the kitchen crew, they were already all sloshed. They were missing ingredients because the booze had seemed more important to fit into the car—my first task was to drive back to the restaurant and gather those ingredients.

When I got back to the country club, I could tell Dave and the crew were in way over their heads. Goldie's sat about sixty people, and this was an event for seven hundred. We had never delivered anything like that before, and as far as I knew, Dave was winging it along with a stupidly inebriated group of cooks.

Other crews from other restaurants looked on with embarrassed horror, their crisp white uniforms gleaming in comparison to our disheveled selves. Ryan and Matt were wearing old band T-shirts, Matt in his favorite L7 shirt that read SMELL THE MAGIC, with a woman gleefully presenting her pussy to a man with his head between her thighs; I was in a white men's undershirt. (Honestly, I hadn't really expected to work the event at all and had mainly shown up to hang out and drink—but when things started to deteriorate, Dave called my name without looking up, and I jumped to attention.)

As Dave's course drew near, we all became quieter, Dave barking out orders. Even in our drunken state, we clicked into gear: working alongside one another with adrenaline-spiked focus. I moved down the rows of plates adding garnishes and taking orders from Dave and Andy, weaving between Matt and Ryan and Sarah like we were cogs in a machine.

When the course finally went out, we collapsed in giddy relief. It had been touch and go, but we did it. And Dave's food was better than the other stuffy nonsense the older and more established places were serving. He seized on the Australian theme, incorporating Vegemite in a sauce somewhat like red-eye gravy, served with grilled quail and grits garnished with pomegranate seeds. We had more fun and did it despite our rough appearance. Here again, I was somewhere I wasn't meant to be, getting away with being included in this fancy thing while maintaining that punk rock sense of outsider status. It was thrilling.

At the end of the dinner, each chef was asked to go into the gaudy, gilded dining room and say a few words to the patrons about their dish. Unlike the other chefs, Dave insisted on bringing his whole crew with him, all of us in our disheveled glory, pointing down the line at each of us and thanking us by name. As we stood there in front of some of the wealthiest people in the state, I felt a sense of pride and belonging that I'd never felt at work before.

We spent an hour or two sitting in the parking lot afterward, finishing off the contents of the booze cooler. When that was gone, we headed back to the restaurant to raid the bar. Phone calls were made, and other staff members came by. Angie, the lanky blond waitress, was walking past the back door after exiting a nearby bar and joined the party. I left at about 3:00 a.m., at which point most of the kitchen crew had left—we'd been drinking since about 11:00 a.m.—but Dave was still going strong.

The rest of the night, I only heard about in second- and thirdhand whispers, but from what I know, it went something like this:

Everyone but Dave and Angie left. At some point, he kissed her. At about 6:00 a.m., when he still hadn't gone home, his wife came looking for him and found him pressed between Angie's legs in the kitchen, where she was propped on the pass, half naked. His wife literally chased Angie around the restaurant screaming—Angie eventually locked herself in the bathroom sobbing.

And then, once she was able to escape the building and go home, Dave's wife chased Angie out of town. Called and harassed her daily. Called everyone she knew—and being a wealthy socialite in a small town, she knew everyone—and told them if they hired or housed Angie, she would ruin them.

On the phone, Angie sobbed to me, "It was so stupid . . . but, Besh, he told me he *loved* me."

The pall that fell over the restaurant was awful, immediate. Nothing was ever the same again. Dave suffered some humiliation, and his marriage stuttered but did not expire—his wife kept her husband, and Dave kept his restaurant. He muttered an apology to me in the basement a week later, saying something along the lines of, "I was so drunk, I didn't know what I was doing. And I sure *hope* she didn't know what she was doing either." The blame was implicit.

He was ten years older, her boss, and a charming motherfucker. He never called to check on her, despite her having lost her job and basically her whole life.

And it was then, dear reader, that I knew: I had to get the fuck out of this industry.

Food = Love

Ryan

I still have the waitressing dream. The one in which I don't know the menu, my section is filling up at an alarming rate, I don't know how to use the POS system, the chef is yelling at me, there are apparently tables outside for which I'm responsible but I haven't even seen. A thick, cold sludge runs in my veins, making me move at quarter speed. Everyone is angry, everyone is hungry, everyone is leaving because I'm just so, so very slow.

For a few years, there was a particularly cruel version in which one of the customers I somehow could not get to was my father—who lived in Australia, whom I missed terribly, whom I only saw every few years and only for a precious few days. He looked at me longingly from across the room but also with the righteous frustration of a hungry customer who had been sitting for forty-five minutes without service. I never did get to him.

It has been more than fifteen years since I've worked in a restaurant, and almost twenty since I waited tables regularly. But the dream lingers.

Suffice to say, it took a long time after my Dave-related epiphany for me to extricate myself from the industry. I couldn't go back to making eight dollars an hour in retail. I had no other salable skills. I was still in love with the food and wine that working in nice restaurants afforded me, as well as the conversation that surrounded it.

And also: I fell in love with the sauté cook.

My relationship of five years with the wannabe-proletarian boyfriend was collapsing. He kept admitting to crippling crushes on my best friends. Our too-much-wine lifestyle was morphing, for him, into a habit of sitting up all night drinking whiskey and smoking cigarettes and growing ever more belligerent. One night, after a party, we fought, and he lashed out at me like a frustrated toddler, fists flying. I woke up with a dark bruise on my chest. I explained it away, as the cliché requires: he had always been so sweet; he was physically weaker than I; he posed no real threat; if I needed to defend myself, I could; he'd never done this before; blah blah. Somewhere in my heart, I knew it was over.

So I applied to college in New York. At twenty-four, I was finally able to declare financial independence for the purpose of student loans and grants (despite the fact that I'd been financially independent for years at that point). The boyfriend applied to a summer music program in Boston, his latest career goal to become a professional guitarist after years of solitary strumming in our living room. I was going to free myself from the restaurant industry and my increasingly toxic relationship in one swoop, by moving to New York and becoming a writer.

(I was a dedicated journal-keeper but had resisted writing as a profession, thinking of it more as a family curse than an inherited talent. My mother is a journalist, her father was a playwright, I resented the notion that I was just one more link in a long line of self-serving Rodell navel-gazers. And yet . . . here we are! Have you seen my navel?? It's very interesting and fucked up and complicated, and yet I find a weird beauty in its blah blah blah.)

I was set to leave in early September. The boyfriend left for Boston in June, our relationship not officially terminated but only because I was a coward who couldn't manage the task. Over the summer, I worked at Goldie's and saved money and relished having my small house to myself. At night, after the shift ended, a crew of us would decamp to one of the nearby bars, drinking $1.50 Miller High Lifes (the champagne of beers!) and smoking cigarettes. More and more often, the night would wind down, Matt and the others would go home, but I would stay, along with Ryan, the ex–local rock star and skinny sauté cook.

Ryan had an open, childish sweetness about him, though he hinted at a troubled past that was only barely in the rearview mirror. He made it clear that Dave had taken a chance on him, that he had been vouched for by my boss, the slick maître d', and that he meant to prove that he was reliable. When Matt boasted loudly about his druggie escapades, Ryan laughed knowingly but didn't join in.

When the bars closed, we'd wander around in the summer nights, the college town emptied of students, the Southern air thick and heavy. We'd talk for hours, and I slowly learned Ryan's story, about being in a band, being on the road, about the drugs and how they slowly took him down. We could have walked and talked until the sun came up, but he always reluctantly went home around 3:00 a.m., saying that he had to be up early. I never knew why.

On a night off, we went to an Indian restaurant, ordering a bottle of Riesling like we knew what we were doing. He wore a suit that was slightly too big for him. I wore a dress. Despite working in one of the nicest restaurants in town, the act of going out and spending money on food still felt wildly fancy. We ate curry and sipped the too-sweet wine and laughed a lot. It felt giddy. It felt like a date.

One weekend, I decided I needed to see the ocean and talked a few coworkers and Ryan into driving to the beach after work on Saturday night. I knew a crappy beach motel near the South Carolina border that would cost us barely anything. At first, Ryan hesitated at the plan. "I have to see if I can," he hedged. When I pressed him, he told me that his early mornings were to drive to a methadone clinic in Raleigh. But, he thought, he may have gained enough trust for them to give him the couple of doses he would need to go away for two nights. He came to work on Saturday triumphant, and we drove that night the three hours to the beach, along with a couple of other waitresses.

When we arrived, we ran to the water, peeling off our clothes in the moonlight. After swimming and laughing for an hour, we went back up to fetch our clothes but couldn't find them anywhere. It took us an hour of running up and down the beach naked before we finally found them, then returned to the motel room exhausted.

Ryan and I shared one of the double beds for those two nights but never touched. When we got back to town, we continued our nighttime walks, but sometimes we'd spend the night together, still not touching. I knew about his early mornings, and it was just easier to fall asleep at his house or mine. One Sunday, we bought a ton of cheese and bread and a bottle of wine and found a small park near his house. "No one would ever have done this with me before," he told me as we sat on a picnic blanket and ate Époisses and Stilton on hunks of crusty baguette. "No friends I've ever had before cared about the thing I do for a living."

That night, we cooked tuna steaks on the small grill on his front porch. I made a mango salsa with chili and ginger and lime that felt very sophisticated to me, and Ryan, the actual cook, indulged my fantasy of this sophistication. We ate while looking up at the full moon. When we went inside to watch TV, he took my hand. His roommate came home, and Ryan didn't flinch or pull away from me, he just sat relaxed with his hand in mine, talking to his roommate as if this were the most natural thing ever.

And then he took me to bed.

At work, we tried to play it cool, to act as though nothing had changed. But people started to catch on. We'd sit on the back steps and smoke cigarettes, and Matt would say, "You guys look as though there are magnets pulling you together. Just touch already."

One day, I was in the basement to grab some bottles of wine to restock upstairs, and Michelle the pastry chef backed me into a corner, towering over me. "What are your intentions with that boy?" she demanded. Michelle had known Ryan for years, from working with him in restaurants but also because they both played in bands in the same indie/punk scene that brought Michelle to North Carolina. Her band was a feminist power trio called the Knights of Her Majesty's Secret Cervix.

"He's a good boy!" she said, peering above her cat-eye glasses. "Do not hurt him!"

That was in mid-July. I left for New York in early September. The six weeks we had together were amazing, but I tried to believe it was just a fling (and hoped that Michelle would not hunt me down and kick my ass if Ryan felt as though it were more). I was leaving. He was on methadone, fighting a heroin addiction that was still a physical reality. I hadn't even properly, officially ended the relationship I had been in for the previous five years.

But when I got to New York, I realized I was not done with Ryan. I was lonely and terrified, but it was more than that. Looking for work, looking for an apartment, starting classes, riding the subway, I thought of him constantly. I took the train to Boston to make the final break with my boyfriend, and when I got back to New York, I called Ryan from a pay phone at Grand Central. "I miss you too much," I cried into the phone. "I wish you were here with me."

"Well then," he said, "we'll figure out a way that I can be."

It took a year. Of going back and forth. Of visits. My housing in New York fell through, and I went back to North Carolina to be with Ryan and save money and help him through the last parts of weaning himself off methadone. He was so determined to be able to have the life he wanted, to be able to have me. I've never seen anyone do anything so hard, with such strength and conviction.

I took online classes and worked the brunch shift at Crook's Corner, the legendary Southern restaurant, as a waitress (so much shrimp and grits—they show up in the dream regularly, after months of Sundays slinging countless bowls) and took a job as a line cook in another restaurant in town a few days a week. We saved money, staying with a friend. And when I finally went back to New York, he came with me.

That was over twenty years ago. I still have the waitressing dreams. And I still have Ryan.

New York City

Traveling with my family is like crossing the interstate with four deaf,
dumb, and blind people. Danger whizzes by, nearly hitting us. Planes
are barely caught, children almost lost. Tragedy is always right behind
us or in front of us. I try to steer them through, coaxing them away
from disaster, but half the time, they don't even notice I'm doing it.

So began one of two creative nonfiction essays I spent my entire
college career workshopping. Can you feel the angst, the self-
importance? Don't worry, there's a twist at the end that lets the
reader know how wrong I am to feel this way . . . but only barely. May
God have mercy on my pretentious twenty-four-year-old self.

There was no way in hell I was going to sit in Sociology 101 classes
with a bunch of eighteen-year-olds, which is what would have been required of me at most universities. I went to the New School because it
sold itself as a university for people who were mature enough to build
their own degrees without the confines of requirements.

That was mostly the case, and I was able to fill my schedule with writing and literature classes, but I soon realized that the school's business
model—which allowed for both degree-seeking and casual learners to
take any class—meant that many people took classes as one-offs. There

were a lot of bored Upper East Side housewives with novelist ambitions in these writing classes, and not a lot that built on previous knowledge. The nice thing about Sociology 101 classes is that there's a 102 class if you're interested, and so on. Apart from a few history and language classes, most of what I learned at the New School was designed to be taught in one semester.

This meant I was able to workshop two "short stories" for most of my college career. The excerpted one above was about a trip I'd taken with my mother and siblings to Miami and how much I loved and related to the cabdriver who took us to the airport. I may have had my own proletarian-wannabe tendencies now that I think about it. (Another choice line from this grand work: "Ma, there is nothing wrong with being a working-class person.")

I didn't learn a lot in college, and what I did learn was mainly in religion and philosophy classes, not writing classes. Descartes convinced me I should probably stop shoplifting, a habit I'd had since I was seven years old. For a time, I became obsessed with shamanism. The religion classes gave me a base in human history that would serve me well years down the line. But the real lessons I got over those years, the invaluable education I received, came from the city itself.

I have called so many cities "home" that I'm not even sure what the word means. No matter where I am, I'm always homesick for somewhere else. But New York is different, for me, and probably for most people who have lived there. I felt a sense of belonging there that I hadn't felt since leaving Australia.

Ryan and I lived at first in a sublet in Fort Greene, which was outrageously cheap but came with an untrained golden retriever / shih tzu mix named Pup Pup, whose fur came off in great golden drifts all over the apartment, who stole people's sandwiches in Fort Greene Park, and who generally made our lives miserable.

Ryan got a job as the sauté cook at Montrachet in SoHo, one of the city's best French restaurants at the time. I paced the streets of Brooklyn, dropping off a résumé that had zero New York restaurant experience, and eventually got a job as a waitress at a tiny Brooklyn fine diner, at the very beginning of that borough's culinary rise. It was run by a couple—Charlie the chef and Sharon the pastry chef and manager of everything else. Their relationship and its problems bled into the essence of the restaurant in every way, meaning that it felt like being in a family, and it was also as toxic and fucked up as any dysfunctional family. Being from a mildly toxic and dysfunctional family myself, I felt immediately at home. And the food was good. Charlie cooked the kind of food that's just two steps above home cooking: sautéed squid with black risotto; a goat cheese ravioli with a roasted beet sauce that almost every table ordered. And Sharon made a fudgy, crunchy chocolate fig cake with figs from the huge tree in the restaurant's backyard that I still think about regularly.

Ryan worked six-day, eighty-hour weeks at Montrachet, and I took a full schedule of classes at the New School, waited tables four nights a week, did freelance work as a reader for some literary agencies, and took on the odd internship as well.

Three months after we arrived, while we were still trying to adjust to what it even meant to live in this wild city, we awoke one morning to the phone ringing and ringing. I heard the ex-boyfriend's voice on the answering machine begging me to call him to let him know I was okay, and I knew something was very wrong. He did not call now that I was living with Ryan. Next to call was my father in Australia, whom I also rarely heard from unless it was my birthday or something was wrong.

It's hard to make sense of the timeline in retrospect, but those phone calls happened after the first plane hit the first tower, and we were outside among a crowd at the top of Fort Greene Park, blinking in the sunshine of that glorious September day, in time to see the second tower fall. I remember the silence interrupted by a guy in a delivery company uniform answering his cell phone and saying, "New Jersey!? Tell that motherfucker the Twin Towers fell down. I ain't going nowhere."

Ryan couldn't go back to work because Montrachet was too close to Ground Zero, but his crew was quickly absorbed by the consortium of chefs, led by Daniel Boulud, who were working to feed first responders every day. At first, they took boats from Midtown to a facility near Ground Zero, and Ryan somehow got assigned to the serving team rather than the cooking team. For once, he was happy to be seeing the faces of the customers, covered in ash, grateful for the food.

I went back to work on September 14, which was a beautiful Friday evening in Carroll Gardens. Charlie, the chef, prepared a sit-down staff meal before service of homemade pasta and green salad, and told us all that he knew many of us were far from our families but that he hoped we felt like we had a family at the restaurant.

I've since learned to take the "restaurant as family" shtick with a grain of salt.

When service started, the backyard dining area was packed. There was still white stuff falling from the sky in that part of Brooklyn. I couldn't stop thinking about all those people, just across the river, under all that rubble. But people wanted to come out and eat, to get back to normal, I suppose. I couldn't fathom it.

My first table was a couple of Wall Street bros who ordered Belgian beer and then threw a tantrum when I served it to them in stemmed glasses. "This isn't a beer glass," one of them spat at me. I went and cried in the walk-in. It was the first time since the planes hit that I'd cried.

New York had so many lessons for me. Lessons about wine, and food, and humanity. And the limits of humanity. And more than any other place in the world, I came to understand the city as a sentient being, with moods and proclivities, like some sort of ancient Greek goddess—a magical trickster. Some days she loved me and sent multiple blessings my way. Some days she turned on me, shunning me and making me question everything.

In the days following 9/11, I felt for the first time like I was responsible for the city, not the other way around. I wanted to love New York and comfort it, to wrap myself around it. The public displays of grief and chest-beating anger both felt off to me, though I hesitated to judge anyone for whom those coping mechanisms worked. It was the quiet looks people gave one another on the street, the nod of sadness and commiseration that felt the most impactful to me. And it was the many New Yorkers who turned back into entitled jerks the second they stepped into a restaurant again that broke that spell, the illusion that we were a city united. I had hoped, perhaps, that the act of serving, the care involved, the giving of joy, might bolster that precious sense of togetherness that existed in the few days after 9/11. But if anything, for many New Yorkers—at least the ones who felt ready to eat out so soon after such a seismic collective wound—getting back to normal meant returning to an attitude in which you don't have to see restaurant workers as human.

Ryan and I were broke, always. And yet, we lived large in so many ways. We blew rent money on eating at every new restaurant in Brooklyn, which was just coming into itself as a serious place to dine. We took the subway to Queens to eat Egyptian chicken hearts cooked on a griddle. I spent months searching the city's bakeries for the best almond croissants, the best hamantaschen. We read the *Times* reviews every week, written then by William Grimes, and debated his takes and tastes. I chased that Stephanie's fancy restaurant high like it was my job, and Ryan gleefully participated. At Montrachet, they served foie gras terrine in perfectly round slices—he kept the scraps, and we used it to stuff our Thanksgiving turkey. (That was some good gravy, my god.)

We learned that the main benefit of working in high-end restaurants is the way hospitality people treat one another. When Matt, the burly line cook from Goldie's, and his girlfriend, Amy, came to visit us, we put on the fanciest clothes we could find at the thrift store and booked a table at Bouley. The four of us were nervous, sitting among the diamond-bedecked customers, but as soon as we'd ordered, the maître d' arrived at our table and demanded, "Okay, which of you are cooks?" I suppose our appearance plus our extravagant/adventurous ordering tipped him off—that and the inherent clairvoyance of a very good service professional. After that, the night turned magical. Champagne arrived immediately. Free courses were sent out. That maître d' stopped by and chatted, demanding at one point that each of us really question what we wanted to do in the food world, how we might define our own excellence. We left giddy and full and inspired.

One night, Ryan and I had a booking at the Tasting Room on the Lower East Side, a restaurant that was known for championing American wines and cheeses and generally pushing forward the notion of modern American cooking. We really didn't have the money to be eating out, and over drinks before dinner at Mars Bar, the legendary dive bar that was close by, we bickered about the state of our finances.

The Tasting Room was one of those restaurants where the tables are so close together, it's almost impossible to ignore the small dramas taking place around you. Next to us, a young blond woman and an older man (who looked—and talked!—very much like Mr. Burns from *The Simpsons*) seemed stalled in their conversation, and they began chatting with us about the things we ordered: sautéed morels with pea greens and foie gras sauce; wild ramps with scrambled eggs; rabbit stew with hominy. When the man got up to use the bathroom, the woman turned to us. "Oh, thank god," she said. "This is the worst blind date I've ever been on. You guys have saved me."

When the guy came back, we pushed our tables together and shared food. The man, whose name was Greer, was delighted with the fact that we cared so much about the food and wine and began peppering us with questions. What did we think about the wine? What were our favorite restaurants? How did we even know what a wild ramp was?

Before dinner was over, he gave me his card. When they got up to leave, the woman leaned down and whispered a thanks for our intervention and company. A few minutes later when we asked for the bill, bracing ourselves for its impact, the waiter informed us that Greer had paid for our dinner before he left.

Of course, I emailed to thank him. He responded that he found our company delightful—he didn't know many people who cared about food and wine the way we did. He invited us to go to dinner with him again.

And so began our brief, weird time with Greer, who was basically a no-sex version of a sugar daddy. Every month or so, he'd invite us out to dinner. He always included the blonde as well, perhaps to make the whole situation seem less strange, though she told us those were the only times they saw each other. He took us to some of New York's best restaurants: Veritas, Gramercy Tavern, places we might never have afforded otherwise. Greer, a divorced Wall Street broker who lived on the Upper East Side, usually showed up late and a bit drunk. He'd pass me the wine list, these giant magnificent tomes that I barely understood, and insist I choose the wine—price was no object. I'd consult with the sommelier, bluffing my way through, and learning as I went. It's hard to understand good wine unless you've tasted great wine, and Greer provided that opportunity for me. We always tried to help with the bill when it came, and he never let us.

Did we have anything in common? Would we have been spending time with this dude if he weren't buying us high-priced dinners? Increasingly, these questions bothered me. I decided that if we were to continue, we needed to reciprocate in some way. We offered, for months, to cook dinner for him, at our house or his. He always refused. Ultimately, the setup felt too odd for me. Were we using him? Was he using us? Either way, I didn't like it. I stopped answering his emails other than to say: *When can we cook for you?* And eventually, he stopped emailing. But I credit Greer and his generosity for a huge part of my restaurant and wine education, as well as my growing obsession.

I got fired a number of times from the small restaurant in Brooklyn. I loved the job—the intimacy of the dining room, the chance to really learn about the food and wine—but like many restaurant jobs, I was basically in an abusive relationship with my workplace. Working for a couple is always hard. Charlie, the chef, was the type of dude who might come out to the table and yell at a customer if she asked for salt—you might imagine what he'd do if he were mad at an employee. Sharon, his partner in life and business, was controlling and could be spiteful—to us and to Charlie. She handled the money, and I suspected she skimmed our pooled tips, but worse, we were always stuck in the middle of their small and large dramas as a couple. I'd push back too hard, and they'd tell me to leave. Then a month or so later, Charlie would call and say, "You're a total pain in the ass, but you're also one of the best servers we've ever had. You want some shifts?"

Occasionally, I'd try to level up. Wylie Dufresne was in the midst of building his new restaurant that would become wd~50, and I spoke to him in the construction zone, hoping for a job when they opened. I dropped my résumé at Blue Hill, Dan Barber's original New York restaurant, more than once. And for a short while, I worked at Savoy, Peter Hoffman's Mediterranean restaurant in SoHo.

As a server, I hated the pace of Manhattan dining—you were always in the weeds, and other servers liked it that way (more money for all). I was used to taking my time with tables, figuring them out, having real conversations with them. At Savoy, I barely had time to take orders and get them in—there was no time for my usual charm offensive. I pretended to know more about wine than I did when I was hired—there was an actual written test, but I'd seen a copy of it tucked behind the host stand when I dropped off my résumé, so I went to the interview with a cheat sheet. I muddled through when trying to help customers with the large wine list, but it was obvious I was in over my head in more than one way. But the way Hoffman thought about food thrilled me, particularly how he combined a cultural and historical curiosity with the things he served.

I was especially blown away by the feasts he would serve for Passover: each year, he explored a different aspect of Sephardic dishes from around the Mediterranean. The year I worked at Savoy, Passover was based on the testimony of household workers during the Spanish Inquisition. Many Jewish families aimed to pass as Christians to adhere to laws forcing conversion and to avoid expulsion. Much of the inquisition proceedings was geared toward proving that these people were still practicing Jewish traditions, including keeping kosher. And so, much of the testimony was around what was eaten in their homes.

Hoffman had studied these testimonial transcripts and devised recipes based around them—re-creating the things Jews in Spain might have eaten in the 1400s. There was a chickpea stew that some Jews added pork to, in order to fool the authorities, earning them the name Marranos, or "pork eaters." This was a level of nerdery that I'd never conceived of and gave me a glimmer of understanding about the places that food obsession might take me beyond pure gluttony and satisfaction.

There were other lessons to be learned at Savoy. A gazpacho made from bread, nuts, and garlic got me thinking about the ways in which the discovery of the New World changed the food of the Old World. Italy without tomatoes! The UK without potatoes! Switzerland without chocolate! I looked for books on the subject but couldn't find any, outside of dense academic texts that weren't particularly concerned with recipes or culture but focused on commerce and colonialism.

I was eventually fired from Savoy. I had spread myself too thin, working multiple jobs and taking classes, and I missed a mandatory staff meeting, the timing of which had fallen out of my brain because there were too many other things crowding it to the point of breaking. School assignments, a pile of manuscripts to read for the literary agency where I was working, early mornings in class and late nights at the restaurant. And a coveted internship at *Time Out New York* that held the first glimmer of a career that might blend my two great loves—food and words.

The internship mainly consisted of compiling and fact-checking the magazine's huge section of listings, but occasionally, I'd get a chance to write a small blurb or contribute to a larger story. They sent me to a couple of cafés for one of their guides, which was, in retrospect, the first time I dabbled in restaurant criticism of any kind. Themed issues were often gimmicky, and for the Cheap Eats issue, the editors decided it would be cute to send me out to places they thought "cheap" people might hang out and ask them where they got inexpensive food. I was required to barge into Supercuts and demand to know where customers bought their lunch. I may as well have been stopping people on the street and saying, "You're obviously poor, where do you eat?" It was mortifying. They wanted me to go to a plasma donation center, the joke being that people desperate enough to sell their bodily fluids would absolutely know where to get a great deal on a sandwich. I only avoided it by discovering that it's illegal to pay people for plasma in New York City.

Toward the end of my internship, two jobs came open at the magazine. One was for a front desk receptionist, something I'd done as an intern to cover lunch breaks, so I already knew the job. It was a common way for interns to transition to employees, the accepted path from free to paid labor. The other job was a staff food writer. I wrote an impassioned letter to the editor in chief, explaining that while I knew the receptionist job was a more realistic career path, food writing was what I wanted to do. I hoped they might consider me, despite my lack of experience—perhaps passion could make up for that.

At the annual staff Christmas party, held on the top floor of a Manhattan skyscraper, one of the staff writers cornered me and drunkenly told me that the food editor objected to me even being considered for the food writing job. "In meetings, she keeps saying, 'She's just an intern!'" he told me, talking a little too closely for comfort. "But the big boss wants her to put you in the mix of candidates." One of the younger women editors sidled up and asked to introduce me to someone—once we were out of earshot, she said, "You've got to watch out for that guy. He can be handsy."

"Don't worry," I told her. "I've been dealing with line cooks for years."

"Yeah," she said, "but line cooks can't give you a byline."

The food editor did eventually find me in the office and explained what I'd need to do in order to be considered. It was a massive amount of work—sample articles, ten or so story ideas, fleshed-out pitches for themed issues. I learned later that the deadline for turning in this package was rolling, and she had given me the earliest possible deadline. I worked like crazy on it, turned it in on time, and then waited for a response.

I'm still waiting. Who knows? Maybe I got the job and she forgot to tell me.

In the meantime, I'd begun to spend a lot of time on eGullet, the forum-style website devoted to eating. And eventually, I dipped my toe in the water of criticism, just for the hell of it, via the online food forum. Behold, my very first restaurant review, posted on eGullet in mid-2002. Please forgive the cockiness, the slight undertone of misogyny. I was but a child.

BISTRO SAINT MARKS

We went for Lobster Night. A full menu of lobster dishes, plus the regular menu.

"Two, please," we said at the door.

"Okay," said the host, "but I have to tell you that we're out of lobster."

We sat anyway.

We had been here before, egged on last summer by a wonderful review in the *Times*, which said among other things that Bistro Saint Marks had a level of service rarely seen in the boroughs. We had been pleasantly surprised by the restaurant's attempt at Brooklyn haute cuisine, although it was obvious that the floor manager also waited tables and understaffed on purpose in order to bring in more tips for himself. This time, the schmoozy French manager/waiter was gone, and our waitress was one of those girls who is so beautiful that she's never had to do anything well in her life.

We sat and waited for her for a long time.

The wine list was short. When our beautiful waitress finally blew in, I asked her about an Italian white. "That's a crowd-pleaser," she said, nodding enthusiastically.

"Have you tried it?"

"No, but people really like it."

"What about this Riesling? Is it dry?"

"Um, yeah, it's a dry Riesling, but sometimes if we have no dessert wine, we serve that instead. So it's kinda dry and kinda not."

Although I was not in the mood for anything cloying, it's rare for me to meet a decent Riesling that I don't get along with, as opposed to Italian crowd-pleasers, which could mean anything. We decided to go for that, then tried to order.

"We'll start with the oysters," Ryan started.

"We're out of oysters," the waitress interrupted.

"Okay, um . . . we might need a minute to figure out what we want to do, then," Ryan tried.

The waitress was not so easily scared off. "You might want to try the carpaccio," she said, leaning over with her pen and paper.

"Yeah, we were going to have that too, but . . ."

"Good," she said and started writing. "What else?" She wasn't even being a bitch. She was that clueless.

"Let's just do what we were gonna do without the oysters," I said. I just wanted her out of there.

"Well, maybe you should get the cod instead for your entrée," Ryan suggested.

"We're out of cod," the waitress said.

"And you're out of all the lobster dishes?" I asked, just to make sure, pointing to the top section of the menu, where seven or eight lobster dishes appeared in half or whole portions.

"Everything but the lobster sandwich. But it's not worth it anyway," she said dismissively.

"Okay, fine," I said. "We'll start with the carpaccio, then we'll split a half order of the chicken livers."

"Do you want that to come with the carpaccio?"

"No, in the middle. Then we'll each have an order of the tuna."

"Okay, good." She snatched our menus and was off. Ryan was furious. I was worn out already.

The wine came, then the scallop carpaccio on a b&b plate. The scallops were tender and fresh, and seasoned with a lovely herb oil, or at least I think that's what I remember from the bite and a half that was my share. We finished it and were only a few sips into our wine when the chicken livers and two tunas we ordered were dumped in front of us. We had been there for thirty minutes, spent ten waiting for the waitress, ten squabbling with her about what we could or should or shouldn't have, and here we were, ten minutes later, with the last two courses of the three we ordered already crowding our table. I pushed the tuna over to the side, took a deep breath, and started on the livers, which had been advertised as livers and figs on the menu, but was more like a big plate of pasta with a few livers on top. Figs can be one of my favorite foods, but when they're cooked, they need to be macerated beforehand in order to keep their flavor. These seemed to have simply been thrown in with no prior attention and were a bland waste as a result.

When we go out to eat, we like to sit and drink and eat a lot. We'll usually go through a bottle and a half of wine, spend a lot of money, and tip very well for a place putting up with us settling in for a couple of hours. By the time I moved my (by now cold) tuna entrée over, I was only a sip into my second glass of wine, and I felt like crying. We don't have the money to do this all the time. If I'm not enjoying myself, it's my one true joy of the week down the toilet.

When we first ate here, I had the tuna entrée, which I loved. Seared tuna over strips of shaved fennel root, with the tuna itself smothered in a fennel leaf oil. The absolutely overboard with the fennel routine worked for some reason, worked well, and I think I dreamed about it at one point. Well, I don't know what happened, but it's different. The dish now has a more Asian lean to it, with the addition of pickled ginger, and a LOT of vinegar. Ryan, the cook, loves vinegar and spends most of his free time in the kitchen pickling whatever he can get his hands on. But after a valiant effort, he finally pushed his plate away. "I just can't eat that much vinegar," he said sadly.

In a second, our plates were whisked away and dessert menus dropped. We decided we were still hungry and would go for the cheese plate, which would be hard to fuck up. At the bottom of the menu, it claimed that we could have tawny or ruby port. When the waitress appeared, I asked her what kind of port it was. "Um, well, as far as ports go . . . I mean, I'm not sure." She looked at us. We stared at her. "Do you want me to ask?"

"Yeah, that'd be great."

In a minute, she came back and said very seriously, her pretty eyes open wide, her head nodding, "It's port wine." When that wasn't enough, she turned to the man behind the bar and whined, "They still want to know what kind it is." When she came back, she had two bottles of port in her hands, which she dumped on the table.

"Okay," I said, "we'll have two glasses of the tawny and the cheese plate."

"We're out of the cheese plate," she said.

"Baby," Ryan said as we walked out the door, "I feel like we've been chewed up and shit out."

North Carolina

A year later

I spread a blanket on the overgrown grass underneath the clothesline and laid the baby on the blanket. It was difficult to carry him plus the blanket, plus the basket of wet diapers, but I put him in a sling against my body and managed it. Walking was still a little bit hard, but those first few days of motherhood are full of finding ways to overcome your own physical limitations in order to care for a new person.

I was hanging the diapers on the line—I had no dryer, and besides, the sun is the best bleach for cloth diapers—when I saw my neighbor hobbling toward me. She was well into her eighties. We'd not met before; our houses were semirural, and I'd only lived there for a few months.

"Is the little one yours?" she asked, holding on to the fence with gnarled hands, nodding toward the bundle on the blanket.

"He is," I said, confessing motherhood aloud for the very first time and also suddenly self-conscious that I was outside in my nightgown.

"How old is he?" she asked.

"Three days old."

"Three days! Honey, what are you even doing out of bed? Isn't there someone who can help you?"

"I guess not," I said.

The tiny, yellow, four-room house was between Chapel Hill and Durham in North Carolina. It sat in the middle of a scrappy patch of land, its paint chipping and the ledges around the windows rotting. There were four of us living there: me; my seventeen-year-old sister, Grace; Ryan; and our newborn son, Felix.

Less than a year earlier, I'd been living in Brooklyn, going to class, working numerous jobs, filling my belly with all New York had to offer. One of those jobs was a promising position in one of the city's best respected literary agencies, handling rights and permissions. It wasn't a writing job, but it was close enough to the writing world that it felt like a potential career. But I kept returning to the Brooklyn restaurant to wait tables, partly for the money and partly because I could never quite divorce myself from the food world.

When my birth control failed and I became pregnant, I had not had a day off in months. I was a year away from graduating from the New School, and there was no real end in sight to this frenzied schedule that allowed me to both pay my rent and work toward a future. The apartment we'd been subletting in Carroll Gardens was being sold, and the timing was bad: trendy young Manhattanites were moving to Brooklyn in droves, and rents were skyrocketing. I saw the pregnancy as a divine intervention of sorts, a sign from the universe to get off this warp-speed ride, slow down, spend some time with my family, create a family of my own.

The pregnancy was also, unavoidably, a litmus test for my relationship. I was twenty-six; Ryan and I had been together for two years. We had the kind of romance most people my age had: committed but light, more based on having a good time than building any kind of tangible future. He was thrilled about the prospect of a baby, but I was terrified of that level of commitment and responsibility. I wanted to go on as we had, young and broke and cobbling together a life, and see where it might take us eventually. But our situation forced a reckoning: I suspected the relationship would not survive an abortion. Ryan would see it as an allegory for my hesitance to commit to him, and he would have been right.

For a few fraught days, I weighed my options. Ryan put no pressure on me but made sure I knew his preference. He wanted me, he wanted us, he wanted our kid. I wasn't ready to let go of him. So I decided to commit—to Ryan and to a baby. I called him on the kitchen line at Montrachet between lunch and dinner service. "Let's do it," I said. He arrived home that night ecstatic, a bouquet of bodega roses in his hands.

One of the first phone calls we made was to Matt and Amy in North Carolina. "I can't wait to see the awesome person you guys make," Matt said.

But we had to leave New York. A cursory apartment hunt was depressing and terrifying. If I was going to have a baby, I needed my mother, and my mother was in North Carolina with my two younger sisters, Ruby and Grace. I had helped her raise them through her years as a single mother—everything I knew of babies and parenting was thanks to her. I sat on the F train as it rumbled under the river between Brooklyn and Manhattan and watched young women struggling with their strollers and toddlers and bags of groceries. I put up my emotional force field in order to protect myself from the crush and madness and occasional abuse that New York City delivers and tried to imagine expanding that force field to encompass a small, soft human. I knew enough about new motherhood to realize how impossible that would feel. I imagined an easier path in North Carolina, with my mother and Ryan's family there to help us, a car and a house rather than a cramped apartment and the crowded subway. It seemed like the only way.

And so, trembling, I told my bosses at the literary agency that I was pregnant and would be leaving. They looked at me like I had three heads. Almost all my friends reacted similarly. It felt as though I were sixteen and not twenty-six. Young, hip, twenty-six-year-old New Yorkers in my orbit did not have babies.

Still, our friends showed up for a long celebratory farewell lunch at Blue Ribbon Brooklyn. My brother, Fred, came down from college in Binghamton to help us move, and we took a break from the hauling and cleaning to go eat lunch at Union Pacific, where Ryan and I had wanted to go for months. New York was smiling on us that day—the weather was gorgeous, the hostess somehow knew who Ryan was (he had risen to sous-chef at Montrachet by that point), and champagne appeared on the table as soon as we sat down. Fred, who sported long, greasy hair and a lip ring, reveled in the confused stares from the other customers, all much fancier than we were, as we were lavished with attention. We had our minds blown by Rocco DiSpirito's layered cauliflower soup, its velvet consistency made without the use of any dairy.

Before we left, I wrote a passionate essay about everything I'd miss in the city. The sticky buns at Balthazar Bakery, the tripe at Al Di La, the kielbasa I bought in sticks at the market in Grand Central. I wrote it for no one but myself, and it's now lost to the graveyard of old laptops, but I remember promising in that essay—and to anyone who would listen—that we'd be back. I'd have this baby, take some of my classes online, save some money, and return to New York and to the life we'd made there. I never expected it to be the end of my New York story. Some days, I still hope it wasn't.

When we arrived in North Carolina early in the summer, after driving a U-Haul from New York, my fantasy of an easier path to motherhood seemed possible. The house, just off a secondary highway, was falling apart but had its own charm: a big kitchen with sloping wooden floors, a wild, overgrown yard full of flowers, a dusty old screen porch off the bedroom. The small second bedroom would be the nursery. My mother gave us her old silver Camry station wagon to drive. Ryan went to work immediately as the chef de cuisine at Goldie's, under our old pal Dave.

I nested and spent time with my mother and young sisters. I drove Ruby and Grace, twelve and sixteen, along the winding green country roads and pulled over for blackberries, scrambling in and out of ditches to pick fruit until I was too huge and pregnant to do so. Then I directed the girls from beside the car. Their reward was endless blackberry pies. Ryan worked constantly, and we were incredibly tight on money, but for a while there, things seemed to be going according to plan.

And then, the plan changed. My mother announced that she was

being courted for a job as an editor at a newspaper in West Virginia. She
had been living for years in a house way out in the country, working for
a publishing company over an hour away in Greensboro, raising the girls
alone. It was an extremely hard juggling act, and this new job paid better,
was more rewarding, would allow her a breath of respite. I couldn't even
really fathom what was happening—I had moved all this way to be with
her when I became a mother. She didn't seem to comprehend my anxiety.
One day, we were driving, and I said, "If you take this job, you'll need to
come here for Christmas." She got inexplicably angry with me, told me I
was being a brat and trying to control the situation in ways that weren't
fair to her.

Years later, when looking back on it, she told me, "I couldn't imagine
you needing me for anything. You'd been trying to prove to me that you
didn't need me at all since you were seven years old."

Grace, who had just turned seventeen and was on the cusp of her senior year of high school, was horrified by the idea of a move. My mother
saw a solution: Grace could move in with us. I could become her legal
guardian. My mother would send child support, from her new, better
salary, and also some of the money she got from Grace and Ruby's father. I agreed, for Grace's sake, and probably my own. She was just a kid,
but she was family, and I was about to lose the rest of the family I was
counting on.

And that's how I got a newborn baby and a confused teenage girl in
the space of a few months. My mother moved to West Virginia eight
weeks before Felix was born.

My water broke on a Saturday, the strange sensation of going to pee in
the morning and the pee not stopping when my bladder was empty. I
stood up and climbed into the bathtub as the trickle continued, calling
out for Ryan.

My labor didn't start in earnest until midnight, which meant it was
enough time for my brother, Fred, and his girlfriend to drive all the way
from upstate New York, arriving after twelve straight hours on the road,

and plenty of time for my mother and Ruby to get to us from West Virginia. My annoying habit of becoming eerily calm in a crisis failed me that night—when I called the birthing center to tell them I needed to come in, that it was time, the midwife on the other end of the line told me she was trained to hear the right level of distress in a laboring woman, and I was nowhere close. "If you come in, we'll probably just send you home," she said. I made Ryan drive me to the center anyway, where a nurse met us and told us the midwife was taking a nap—it was 3:00 a.m., after all. The nurse tried to rub my shoulders through a contraction, so I locked myself in the bathroom.

I had assumed I'd want a team of helpers, midwives and sisters surrounding me, encouraging and supporting me, laying their hands on me. When the time came, I wanted to be left the fuck alone. I understood the instinct, encouraged in some cultures, for a woman to wander out into the woods by herself to labor, squatting when the time came.

By the time I breathlessly asked Ryan to go wake up the midwife, just before 6:00 a.m., Felix was only a few minutes away.

He had a shock of blond hair and plump, ruddy cheeks and, once he'd been wrapped and handed to me, a steady and quiet gaze. "Hello, little boy," I said, reeling from the odd sensation of meeting a stranger who was also undoubtedly the most important person in my life.

Sometime after, my mother washed me in the birthing tub I'd not had time to use. She told me I was beautiful, and I felt like a baby, not a mother. My mind understood that she was leaving, but my body didn't.

Even nomads travel in family groups. Only shamans, or soldiers, or princesses traded away in marriage for the sake of the clan went out into the world alone. Having a child will make you understand these things in your bones.

When Ryan took the job at Goldie's, it came with a promise that he'd get a week off when the baby came. But Felix arrived ten days early, and Dave was on vacation with his family out of state, and another cook had just quit suddenly. Dave declined to come home early, and Ryan went back to work. My mother stayed for two days. She cooked chicken livers with rice and yogurt, insisting the iron would help me regain my strength. She helped me change those first few diapers, helped teach me how to breastfeed. And then she was gone. And I was alone, most of the day.

Grace was in high school, dancing at a ballet studio most afternoons, and in the midst of a devastating breakup with her first love. Ryan got home late and slept until just before it was time to leave for work. Felix slept in the room with us—Grace now had the room that was going to be his nursery—and Ryan helped when he woke in the night. But mostly, it was just Felix and me.

I was desperately lonely in those first few months. The friends I'd had in North Carolina, back in the Goldie's days, had either left town or were still in twentysomething-year-old party mode. Part of me was ashamed, to be the one with the baby, the one who wasn't fun anymore. The one who left for New York in order to make my life bigger and had returned to a life so small I could barely fathom it. I retreated.

It was especially weird that we hadn't seen Matt since we returned to North Carolina. He was working as the chef de cuisine at a restaurant that was widely considered the best restaurant in the state—one of the best in the South—at that point. So he was busy. But there was something else. Ryan had seen him one night at Goldie's, when Matt had stopped by. He seemed off, sweaty, shifty. It only occurred to us in retrospect that if Matt were using again, Ryan would be the one person most likely to know. He was avoiding us.

One night just before Christmas, Ryan called me at home from the Goldie's kitchen. He was panicked. Matt was dead.

We still don't know why or how he died. His family never released the autopsy results, to us or anyone. We do know he'd been using in the months leading up to his death. But the circumstances were strange, and he was found with a great amount of blood surrounding him—it wasn't a simple overdose, and no gun was involved. His father had died of a massive hemorrhage, and the simplest explanation was that something similar had happened to Matt.

Two days later, Ryan and I took Felix to Matt's house, which was being cleared out. Amy, now his fiancée, was going back to Maine, where she was from. It was a strange scene, with friends of Matt's we didn't know digging through his things. Amy asked if there was anything of his I wanted. I asked for his giant, old, ratty Ramones T-shirt. Amy also gave us his wine fridge, saying he'd want us to have it—no one else in his life cared much about wine. At one point, I looked around for Ryan and couldn't find him. I eventually spotted him in the backyard, digging up Matt's rosemary bush, tears streaming down his cheeks. At one time, they had plans together. Some of it was just the loose talk that happens in kitchens, but some of it was more. They shared so many passions: for music, for food, for wine, for ambition. For drugs. They talked about moving beyond that, to open something, to be great together.

In the weeks that followed, a memorial for his restaurant friends was organized at a local restaurant. We drank and told stories and cried. There was a book to leave memories. When I flipped through it, I found Ryan's barely comprehensible scrawl on one page.

"Matt. Remember the future?"

The Truffle

Ryan's grandfather, who lived long enough to know he was going to be a great-grandfather but not long enough to meet Felix, was a dentist in North Carolina and a man of mythical charms. His practice in downtown Durham catered to much of that city's population in the '50s through the '70s, including the many tobacco workers who were employed by the cigarette companies that kept the region's economy afloat.

It's hard to overstate the importance of tobacco in North Carolina, from an economic standpoint, obviously, but tobacco is also baked into the mythology of many families, including the one I eventually married into.

The story goes that Dub, as Ryan's grandfather was known (as well as John Henry, and a slew of other nicknames), kept packs of every brand of cigarette in his desk drawer. When he encountered a new patient, he'd ask what tobacco company they worked for. Whatever answer they had, he'd pull out that specific cigarette brand from his drawer and say, "That's what I smoke!" And then they'd share a cigarette together pre-extraction.

By the time we arrived back in North Carolina in 2003, just months after Dub's death, the state was in the process of an agrarian reinvention. When Ryan was growing up in Durham in the '80s, schools still took students on excursions to tobacco farms—so important was the crop to the economy and identity of the state that it seemed appropriate to educate grade schoolers on the wonders of the mighty cigarette.

But the '90s and 2000s brought huge changes to the industry. Big tobacco companies were being sued by states in order to recover the public health costs of treating smokers.

Here's the thing about tobacco farming: it doesn't take a whole lot of land to be profitable. In 1987, the average tobacco farm was only 4.6 acres—small enough to be run as a family business. Regulation by the U.S. government historically protected these small farms, allowing them to remain profitable even as cheaper overseas tobacco flooded the markets.

Deregulation caused industrial-scale farming to gobble up much of the share of the market that was once supplied by family farms. In 1998, a legal agreement between major tobacco companies and forty-six states was put into effect. The Master Settlement Agreement had those companies agree to pay $206 billion to the states over the course of twenty-five years. In North Carolina, some of that money went to a fund to help small tobacco farmers experiment with other crops, particularly crops that can be grown on small acreage.

Why is this relevant? Because all of the above is the context for the first real assignment I ever got. It's also how I wound up standing in an orchard on a cold January morning in 2004 with a dog named Pierre, holding a freshly dug truffle—one of the first Périgord truffles to be grown in the United States.

Good Christ, we were poor. Poor enough to be occasionally hungry, to be always late on bills, to stress about rent every single month. The monthly money my mother promised us—essentially child support—to help with Grace came once and then never again. Ryan's salary was laughable, especially given that he was working sixty hours or more a week. The four of us living on less than $32,000 a year was, well, poverty.

I'd been broke like that before. In my first months living in New York,

I'd had a strict $5-per-day budget after rent, which usually meant one can of black beans, one lime, one sketchy tallboy of beer from Eastern Europe bought from the bodega for $1.50—to help flavor the beans and take the edge off the hunger. But this was different. I was responsible for people now, and I felt I was failing them. It's acceptable to be broke when you're twenty-four and a college student. Not so much when you're the mother of a baby and the guardian of a teenager.

The only salable talents I had were tied to restaurants and restaurant hours, and none of that made sense with a newborn. I felt lost, and desperate, and ashamed. We were eligible for WIC, the federal program for pregnant people and parents of infant children that provides food relief in the form of vouchers—basically food stamps. But where food stamps generally allow the holder to buy anything edible in the supermarket, WIC only allows for certain items: specific (cheap) brands of milk, bread, juice, cereal, and canned goods; the basics. This, in part, is where the term *government cheese* comes from—there's cheese you're allowed to buy on WIC and cheese you're not. There's a special humiliation to having a supermarket clerk check your cheese to make sure it's in compliance. I'm not complaining. I'll take the humiliation over hunger any day.

When I think about those months just after Felix was born, I understand that I was in shock. Shock at the change in my life, shock at my mother leaving so abruptly, shock at the lack of control I felt I had. I had tried to register for online classes at the New School, in order to finish the diploma I wasn't far from. But when I told them I'd need a week off in September or October in order to give birth, they talked me out of continuing, knowing better than I how overwhelming a newborn would be. And so I found myself consumed with that baby, but also desperate for a better way to care for him. I knew I needed to do something, anything, to move away from the trap of a life that felt small and desperate.

I don't mean to imply that there was no joy in those months. Ryan embarked upon a mission to teach Grace everything she needed to know about music. Having grown up in my mother's house, where NPR and the soundtrack to *O Brother, Where Art Thou?* reigned supreme, Grace was thrilled with all the Outkast, Nick Cave, Built to Spill, 102 Jamz that became the soundtrack of that tiny household (the early 2000s were a golden era for 102 Jamz). We were, all of us, madly in love with the obscenely fat and happy baby who took center stage in our lives. We made up stupid songs to sing to Felix, to the tune of 50 Cent, about taking a bath. "When I'm up in the tub . . ." When my WIC card came, Felix's name was misspelled: my Felix Kingston Stewart became Pelix C. Stewart, an error that led to us calling him Pelix and then Peely, a nickname that remains to this day, along with its variants Peeler, Peeler-Wheeler, and Peely-head. "Go, go, go Peely, it's your bathtime, we're gonna party like it's your bathtime."

Felix never learned to crawl, because there was no room to put him down, and the only heat was a woodstove in the middle of the floor in the crowded living room, so I couldn't risk him getting burned. He was always on one of us—our little koala baby.

We stretched our WIC-subsidized groceries into meals that were delicious. One roast chicken became chicken stock and soup and casserole. We drank cheap wine and six-packs of PBR, and before you tell me we shouldn't have been drinking when we were taking government assistance, let me stop you and say: fuck you, poor people deserve pleasure, too. Babies deserve to have parents who have pleasure in their lives. Our pursuit of edible and drinkable pleasure was at the center of who we were, who we are, as a family.

And then, incredibly, out of the blue: an assignment, one for which I was thoroughly unprepared. The editor of the local alt weekly called me. The previous year, my mother had sent him the review of Bistro Saint Marks that I'd posted on eGullet. He loved it. He already had a food writer, but he'd never forgotten the piece. And now his food writer was gone, and he had a tip about a cool story: some of that government funding to help tobacco farmers diversify their crops was going to help them set up truffle farms. Would I be interested in chasing it up, to see if there was anything there?

I tried to control the shake in my voice as I responded, "Sure, let me take a look into it and get back to you." I put down the phone and shrieked.

The result of that phone call was a 2,300-word cover story in the *Independent Weekly* with the title "Black Gold" and the byline *Besha Rodell*. A dude named Franklin Garland had successfully cultivated black Périgord truffles in an orchard in Orange County, North Carolina—he was the first person in the United States to do so. And he had convinced the North Carolina Tobacco Trust Fund Commission to put $235,000 toward helping tobacco farmers set up truffle farms of their own. No one knew if it would work, if Garland's success with the truffles was likely to be replicated. Only one other person in the state, the ex-chef at the governor's mansion who liked to go by the name "Chef Bob," had truffle-producing trees. But like tobacco, truffles don't take a lot of land to be profitable—just a lot of patience. It takes at least five years, and often many more, between planting an orchard and seeing your first truffle. Chef Bob didn't have a fully productive orchard yet, but six years earlier, he bought trees from Franklin Garland, and by the time I called him, he was getting a few truffles every week during the season.

It's interesting to me now, to think about how my first real assignment was about history and agriculture and the ways in which the push and pull of culture and commerce affect the things that wind up on our plates.

As part of my reporting, I went out to see Chef Bob and watched as his dog, Pierre, dug up two large black truffles in the frosty morning. Bob insisted on giving me one, reasoning that if I was going to write about the birth of truffle farming in North Carolina, I should know what those truffles tasted like. These days, I'd never accept a gift from a source, particularly one worth that kind of money (in 2004, the retail price for Périgord truffles was $2,000 per pound). But I liked his logic. And despite my poverty—*because* of my poverty—I still craved edible luxury.

I took the truffle home and presented it to Ryan. We put it in a jar of arborio rice so the scent would imbue future risottos. We shaved truffle into a bottle of vodka in order to make truffle Bloody Marys. We put truffle on everything: truffle on our scrambled eggs, truffle in our gravy, truffle on the mac and cheese I made with hunks of government cheese, thanks to WIC. Its nutty, earthy, otherworldly scent and taste imbued our lives for about three weeks.

Some days, I think that truffle saved my life. It reminded me that there was more than one way to get what I want. It put luxury back into my life. But more than anything else, it made me a food writer.

Entrée

Who Writes?

He's an older guy, a serious journalist from a family with enough wealth that he doesn't have to rely on paltry journalism wages to fund his appetite for three-martini lunches and trips to Europe to eat around Paris and Rome. He is cultured, well read, thick-skinned, possessed of the kind of self-assurance that allows him to declare the Way Things Should Be without a hint of introspection or acknowledgment that his ideas of proper culture come from a deeply ingrained sense of Western superiority. At some point, the restaurant critic job at his newspaper or magazine came open, and he was getting weary of the slog of hard news. All those three-martini lunches and trips to Paris and Rome made him somewhat of a dining expert—he certainly has strong ideas about how the city he lives in could be better suited to his good taste. Maybe his journalism background includes a stint as a foreign correspondent, making him somewhat of an expert in some kind of foreign cuisine. Perhaps he spent some time covering real estate, which gave him an inside track on the movers and shakers in high-end development—a benefit when looking to understand the restaurant landscape of a city. He is white.

During my burgeoning restaurant obsession, some version of the above described almost every important restaurant critic in America. Of course, there were exceptions—a few women, the occasional scrappy writer who started in restaurants, then rose through the ranks of alt weekly writer, finally making it to a major daily paper. There was Gael Greene, who served as the restaurant critic for *New York* magazine for forty years. But when I looked to the profession I coveted, there was no one who looked like me: young, female, broke.

In New York, I tried unsuccessfully to break into food writing in places that seemed better suited to the audience I thought might appreciate my perspective (mainly line cooks, to be honest). There was the *Time Out* fiasco, obviously. The eGullet thing was a way of dipping my toe into the budding community of internet food obsessives, some of whom were gaining followings of their own. But that world felt alien to me, too, being extremely focused on nerd-laws of authenticity (there were endless minor squabbles about the MOST authentic Mexican and Asian food, and it was a terrible faux pas to admit to getting pleasure from food that existed outside of these strict standards), bragging rights, intense gluttony (if you haven't eaten every dumpling in Flushing in one afternoon, do you even food, bro?), and yes, unabashed machismo.

My closest friend, Mary, whom I've known since high school, was living in the East Village during my New York years and still dating her college boyfriend, who was an editor at what was then an up-and-coming culture magazine called *Vice*. This was right after *Vice*'s founders had bought the magazine back from an early Canadian investor and moved its offices to Williamsburg, and its entire vibe was snide heroin scumbag with an expensive liberal arts degree. Mary's boyfriend fit that description pretty accurately. He knew I wanted to be a writer, and he threw me a few (unpaid) album reviews, which were fun to write and allowed me to put *Vice* on my résumé under the "Freelance Writer" heading. But I knew I wasn't a music journalist. I remember following him around their sunny apartment one day, trying to convince him to let me write about food. "It won't be like the food coverage you're used to," I told him. "I don't want to write about the places where rich people eat. I want to write about the weird little places serving cool, cheap things.

I want to write about dive bars. Have you ever met a line cook? They're like, the ultimate *Vice* reader. Or they should be."

"Our audience just isn't interested in food," he said, and that was the end of it. (Years later, I told this story to the head of Munchies, *Vice*'s massive food vertical, over dinner in Los Angeles, and she laughed and laughed.)

It in no way should be surprising that the model for restaurant critics was, for years, the wealthy, male, urbane bon vivant, since the people who invented the genre were most, if not all, of these things. Allow me to introduce you to a few of the dudes and institutions that shaped the profession:

The original food critic, Alexandre-Balthazar-Laurent Grimod de La Reynière, was born in the mid-1700s to a wealthy Paris family. He originally was a theater critic, both writing for established publications and self-publishing his own critiques. In the early 1800s, after his estranged father died and he inherited the family fortune, he began publishing an annual almanac called *L'Almanach des Gourmands*, a guide that is considered to be the first example of restaurant criticism.

Many of the accusations and ethical quandaries of modern food writing also plagued Grimod de La Reynière—he was accused of taking bribes and of settling personal scores through the power of his pen. He eventually left Paris and faked his own death to see how many people would turn up to his funeral.

A hundred years later, in 1900, Michelin, the tire company, launched its famous restaurant guidebook in an effort to encourage people to drive across France to seek out great restaurants (and wear down their tires). In 1926, they launched their star rating system, which remains in place to this day.

The first restaurant review in American newspapers appeared on the front page of *The New York Times* on January 1, 1859, titled "How We Dine" and with a byline reading "a strong-minded reporter of the Times." It would be almost another hundred years, however, before *The Times* began running regular restaurant reviews.

Does the name *Duncan Hines* ring a bell? If you're thinking of frosting, you're not wrong, but Hines gained the reputation that would allow him to cash in (selling the use of his name to the company that now bears it) by putting out a national guidebook, beginning in 1935, called *Adventures in Good Eating*. Hines was a traveling salesman, his reviews were brief, and the guidebooks—which were written by Hines and others—were also tainted by the probability of pay for play.

Undoubtedly the most influential figure in twentieth-century American food criticism was Craig Claiborne. When Claiborne took over as food editor of *The New York Times* in 1957 (after doing some PR for food products and contributing to *Gourmet* magazine), he was the first man to run the food pages of a major American newspaper. Until Claiborne, the food pages were run by women and aimed almost exclusively at home cooks and ambitious home entertainers. If a paper had a food section, it was full of recipes, meal planners, and tips on how to throw successful soirées. If there were reviews in newspapers, they were mainly seen as untrustworthy.

Claiborne can in some ways be seen as the archetype of the cultured male critic, and those who came after him—not just at *The Times* but in major newspapers and magazines all over the country—shared many of his characteristics. Another attribute of the classic American food critic: he is likely to be gay, in part because, historically, the food pages were more welcoming to gay men than the news or sports pages. Also, gay men were less likely to have kids, making it easier to dine out every night of the week. Claiborne was gay, but he did not come from money, having grown up in an Indianola, Mississippi, boardinghouse. But he did get a journalism degree (in Missouri) and a degree from the world's most prestigious hotel school (in Switzerland) and served in the U.S. Navy during World War II and the Korean War.

Claiborne invented a system at *The Times* that remained the gold standard for restaurant critics for more than half a century—in some ways, I still view it as such. Here's the Claiborne restaurant critic playbook:

1. Reviews will be done by the same person every week, who will put their name to their work.
2. Critics will aim to dine anonymously, using false names for reservations.
3. Critics will visit each restaurant at least three times and try to eat as much of the menu as possible—some dishes more than once, to assure consistency.
4. The publication will pay for meals—no freebies will be accepted.

Claiborne also introduced the star rating system that *The Times* still uses today, a four-star scale that somewhat mimics the Michelin system, though the stars mean vastly different things. (Particularly given Claiborne's time spent in Europe, deep in the world of high-end food, it's unlikely that he would have gone uninfluenced by the Michelin guides—though the history of restaurant criticism usually positions him in an entirely separate world from the traditions of Michelin.)

When Claiborne died in 2000, his obituary in *The New York Times* acknowledged the huge change he'd made to the world of reviewing: "Mr. Claiborne's reviews for The Times, which concluded by rating a restaurant on a four-star scale after repeated visits, were a striking change for American newspapers at the time, most of which considered restaurant reviewing a feckless adjunct of the advertising department."

Claiborne held the title of food editor at *The Times* from 1957 until 1986 and wrote weekly starred reviews consistently from 1963 until 1972, filling in here and there throughout the rest of his tenure. It is no wonder that he had such a broad impact and that so many of the critics who have come since share commonalities with him—the dashing, whip-smart, pleasure-seeking journalist who can raise the recounting of a few meals to an art form.

It was too bad, I think, that my New York years did not coincide with Ruth Reichl's tenure as critic at *The Times*, which was from 1993 to

1999. It would have done me good to look to the top of the profession I coveted and see a woman, and a bold and unconventional woman at that. Reichl was playful with the genre, valued non-Western food, and tested the boundaries of what kinds of commentary were possible in a review.

My years in New York overlapped with the period of William Grimes, and other than Gael Greene at *New York* and S. Irene Virbila at the *Los Angeles Times*, all the powerful critics in the major cities around the country were men: Michael Bauer, Jeffrey Steingarten, Tom Sietsema, Phil Vettel, Adam Platt, Robert Sietsema (no relation to Tom). I knew what I wanted, but I didn't know who I wanted to do it for or who might allow me to do it my way.

(An aside on Greene, who perhaps should have been an idol of mine but wasn't: She brought a huge amount of fun and sensuality to the form of restaurant criticism, as well as a brand of proud bitchiness that many have imitated. But she's also responsible for the trope that has beleaguered every fictional female restaurant critic ever written: that of a journalist who sleeps with her subjects. In her 2006 memoir, *Insatiable*, she wrote unapologetically about sleeping with Elvis while working on a story about him, as well as the fact that she had multiple affairs with chefs whose restaurants she reviewed. I can't say this had anything to do with why I never considered her an inspiration, but I sure have resented the lady-critic-as-seductress cliché that's been an assumption in movies and real life ever since.)

Years later, in 2014, I did my best to figure out the ratio of male-to-female restaurant critics in the United States, surveying every masthead at daily and weekly papers around the country, as well as magazines. Even then, there were two men for every woman in a staff or freelance position with that title. More telling: at most of those papers, the food editors and cooking columnists were women. The takeaway was that women should be domestic and cover home-related topics, and men should have the power and the opinions.

While I didn't do the same level of analysis based on race (something that would have been harder, as I was mainly going by a name on a masthead), that statistic would have been far, far worse. It's only in recent years that food publications have been focused in any meaningful way on diversity, and there's still so much work to be done on the harder part, which is adequately supporting diverse employees and freelancers once you've brought them on. The hard labor of transforming the culture of media to be truly inclusive always falls to the people hired to symbolize that inclusivity—labor that is never part of any job description, nor compensated as such. I have seen countless friends and colleagues drop out of the game entirely as a result, and who can blame them? I've almost done the same numerous times, and my load is featherlight in comparison.

I'm not sure how the gender divide would break down today. Certainly, some of the top jobs in the country have gone to women in recent years, or in the case of the *San Francisco Chronicle*, to Soleil Ho, who is nonbinary. (At the time of this writing, *The New York Times* has still not had a female critic in its lead role since Reichl.) But the options for breaking into food writing have changed so much in the last twenty years, for better and for worse.

The first major change was the internet and the advent of personal blogs, which widened the scope of who could write—on all kinds of topics—and gain a following. But blogs rarely made anyone any money. Different writers gained some prominence, but the most successful blogs—think *Julie & Julia*—were recipe based rather than restaurant focused (this also allowed for a wider audience—reviews are local by nature). And blogs that *were* restaurant focused were mainly self-funded, meaning written by people with enough wealth to travel and eat out. The other option was to fall into the influencer trap, meaning getting free meals in exchange for positive write-ups—even this required a preexisting audience, which meant . . . you had to be flush enough to pay for the meals to write the content that might attract that audience in the first place. I wasn't internet savvy enough in the early aughts to be a pioneering blogger, nor did I have the money to fund such an endeavor.

And also? I'm a snob. I was raised by journalists. I believed in the fourth estate, even for something as frivolous as dining out. I loved Claiborne's rules and stars and structural methodology. It isn't perfect, and it may be inching toward irrelevance. But it seemed to me to be better than the alternatives.

When the websites came along in the mid-2000s, the Serious Eats and Eaters (and yes, *Vice*'s Munchies), they changed a lot about who had a voice in the food world. If many of them grew from the bro-tastic melee of the forums, they didn't take nearly as long as legacy media to realize that their audiences were diverse, and their writers should be, too. I've always contended that *Eater*'s greatest achievement was to take what was basically real estate news—who is opening what business in what building—and make it sexy. But they also treated food as sport and pop culture and did it in a way that the newspapers—even the alt weeklies—didn't quite manage.

Even so, when *Eater* finally hired restaurant critics in 2014, one national critic and two New York critics, they hired three white men.

If Substack and Twitter were around in 2003, could I have started a newsletter? Gained a social media following and parlayed it into a blog and some freelance gigs and an audience that was willing to pay me directly rather than rely on the hulking, creaky world of legacy media?

I'm really not sure. Especially because, whatever burning passion I had, whatever it was I wanted to say, I wanted to say those things about restaurants. Restaurants are expensive. And fuck, I needed an editor. I still need an editor. But especially then, when I was young and naive and way too enamored with my own point of view, I needed the protection of an institution, to pull me up when I was full of shit, to shield me from my own brazen idiocy.

So there was the old guard, the debonair dudes, some of whom are still writing under the same mastheads they were twenty years ago. (And some of whom I love dearly, both professionally and personally.) And there was the new guard, the bloggers, the newsletter writers. Recently, legacy media has begun to catch up—the voices we read on food today, even the critics, are more vibrant and diverse and thoughtful than ever before.

In between, there was me.

Billy

stepped out of the arrivals hall and into the already humid Atlanta spring air, my slim-fit J.Crew suit jacket's still-affixed retail tags scratching the back of my neck, insurance in case I needed to return the suit. If I got the job, I told myself, I'd keep it. If I got the job, I'd be the type of person deserving of a proper suit.

The truffle story had changed so many things for me. For one, it was good enough that the *Independent*'s editor, Richard, had offered me a monthly column. It wasn't a review column (no budget for eating out), it only paid $200 a pop, but it was a restaurant column. He also gave me two food issue cover stories a year, which paid much more, and had me compile and edit the massive restaurant guide that went into each food issue.

And so, I was a food writer. I was *the* food writer for a newspaper. It came with only a tiny bit of credibility, and even less money, but it was a title.

A few months into the gig, Richard called to tell me that the restaurant critic from *Creative Loafing*, the weekly paper in Atlanta, was coming to town and wanted to take me to dinner. He was working on a story about the best chefs in the Southeast and was coming to Durham to eat at the Magnolia Grill, but he didn't know anyone in North Carolina. His editor in Atlanta knew Richard and called him up asking if there was a food writer who might dine with the critic and give him some context on the food scene.

Richard somehow parlayed this into a crazy Magnolia Grill dinner party, hosted by the Atlanta critic and *Creative Loafing*'s budget. Richard, his wife, Ryan, and I met the critic—a guy named Bill Addison—at a long table at the restaurant, a meal that I could never have afforded, even for just me and Ryan, even as the restaurant writer for one of the region's only newspapers.

Every career has a few pivotal moments that send things spinning in a whole new direction. Two of the most important in mine are that truffle dropping into my hand and Bill Addison walking into the Magnolia Grill.

We feasted on pan-seared foie gras on Vidalia onion marmalade with marinated gold beets, slow-cooked pork osso buco with Creole red beans, and lemon custard cake with strawberries and whipped cream. I wore a ridiculous and wholly inappropriate red tiger-print dress from the '70s that was probably my best thrift store find of all time. Bill was immediately my friend for life.

At that point, I'd not met anyone else with my particular brand of obsession—Ryan came close, but he approached it from the point of view of a cook, not a writer. Bill and I could discuss the strengths and weaknesses of every *New York Times* critic in history. We cared about food but also writing and ethics and gossip. He looked pretty serious in his suit and tie—the son of a politician, and it showed—but he had a wildly filthy sense of humor that matched mine. Had he not been gay (and 100 percent not my type—suits just don't do it for me), the meal might have been an uncomfortable one, since Ryan was sitting next to me and Bill and I were obviously falling madly in love, right there in the open.

Unbeknownst to me, Richard entered the truffle story for a handful of national awards, including the Association of Food Journalists' annual writing awards. I got the notice that it had won a prize one day via email when Felix was sick with a cold and the washing machine had broken (a nightmare for a mother who was committed to cloth diapers, for financial reasons as much as ecological ones—my mother had saved all her own kids' cloth diapers, hauling them in boxes from Australia and keeping them in her attic until one of us needed them).

The awards ceremony was in San Francisco, part of the annual AFJ conference. I got a free ticket to the awards but not the conference, and there was no way I could afford the fees to join the days-long series of talks, meals, and lectures. But Ryan's parents offered to buy my plane ticket so I could go to the awards, and I had a place to stay with Michelle, the pastry chef at Goldie's, who had moved home to California after 9/11. ("If the world's going to end, I'd at least like to be in San Francisco when it happens," she told me at the time.) She and her husband, Franz, had bought an apartment in the Mission District and restored it with excruciating vintage accuracy to its 1930s glory, right down to the stove and fridge in the kitchen. Michelle was working as the pastry chef at Delfina and was fiercely proud of me for my "fancy award," as she called it. I suppose, having done right by Ryan—as in, not broken his heart, and given birth to his son—I was now on the list of people she would defend to the death. It's a privilege I will always treasure and never take for granted, because that bitch is terrifying.

I arrived at the San Francisco Ritz ballroom, collected my name tag that said PRIZE WINNER, made my way to a large, round table full of people who looked like they might belong in a gilded room like this, and tried to keep myself from passing out with anxiety. Then, across the room, I saw a dapper man in a very nice suit talking to a blond, slightly older guy who looked as though he owned the place. It was Bill, and he was talking to Michael Bauer, the critic at the *San Francisco Chronicle*, though I didn't know it at the time.

If our dinner at Magnolia Grill had shown me how gossipy and filthy-minded and funny Bill could be, my night at the AFJ awards showed me his political prowess. He is a Grade A schmoozer, and he pulled me into the warm glow of that talent—which I do not possess—and made sure I met every important person in the room. "This is Besha, an amazing writer from North Carolina and Australia, and she's up for an award to-night!" he'd say while I dumbly shook the hand of yet another writer or editor I had long admired from afar. I was in over my head, but Bill kept me afloat, and my easy banter with him made it seem to the rest of them that I was in fact witty enough to warrant conversation.

The truffle story took second place in its category. I drank too much California zinfandel, gave myself an instant migraine, went back to Michelle's, and flew home the next day only with the help of some Percocet she had stashed in her bathroom cabinet. (In my defense, it only takes two glasses of California zinfandel to give me a migraine that lasts for days, a fact I wish I'd learned on some other occasion, but what can you do?) But now, not only was I a food writer, I was an *award-winning* writer, and one who knew other writers.

(A note here about awards, specifically AFJ awards: Unlike the James Beard Awards, AFJ was judged as anonymously as possible, meaning judges did not see your name or the name of the publication when reading entries. Because of this, it was much easier for smaller, lesser-known publications and writers to be considered for or win awards, while the Beards have the potential for rewarding the known cool kids. It's a fact I've always appreciated and understood as a major factor in my own career.)

In the early summer of 2004, Grace graduated high school and got a job, taking a gap year before going to college, and we moved from the tiny beside-the-road house to a bigger brick house in town. It was soulless, but what a relief to be within walking distance of a playground, to have space. Grace had a huge basement room with its own entrance and bathroom—a dream for an eighteen-year-old kid. Felix got his own bedroom, and I got an office. And Ryan and I saved up enough money to throw ourselves a wedding.

We rented a beach house a couple of hours away on the coast, bought a few cases of wine and a pig to roast. My mother towed a trailer full of buckets of water from West Virginia, stopping on the side of the road to gather wildflowers along the way—much cheaper than a florist. My father flew in from Australia, and, having once been an Episcopalian minister (who long ago lost his religion but not his title), he married us. My brother, Fred, walked me down the aisle (made of tiki torches) to "Wouldn't It Be Nice" by the Beach Boys, and we said the I-dos under Spanish moss–laden trees next to the Intracoastal Waterway. It was a very good party, in part because Ryan and I and my siblings catered the whole thing ourselves—down to a Fred-made giant heart-shaped zebra cake, the kind you make from chocolate wafers and whipped cream.

A year later, we were seriously considering buying a house. It was 2006, when loans were far too easy to come by, and houses in North Carolina were cheap. My ambition was not sated with my monthly column and occasional cover stories, and I'd applied, fruitlessly, to any journalism job in the area for which I could claim to be even vaguely qualified (fashion reporter for the daily paper in Raleigh; associate editor at the literary magazine published out of Chapel Hill). I tried to make peace with the idea of forging a life in North Carolina, with trying to be happy enough with a family and a house and a writing career that bordered on a hobby. I took a part-time job in Raleigh as a restaurant manager to supplement our income. Ryan had just been offered his first executive chef job, at a new restaurant in a building in Durham that had once been owned by his grandmother.

And then, I heard that Bill Addison was moving to San Francisco.

All that schmoozing with Michael Bauer had paid off—Bill had gotten a job as a secondary critic at the *San Francisco Chronicle*. Which meant his job in Atlanta would be coming open. I sent him an email.

It all happened so fast: the email, a phone interview while standing outside the Raleigh restaurant, and the following week a return plane ticket from North Carolina to Atlanta—there first thing in the morning, back home late the same afternoon. The stakes felt immeasurable. The job was food editor and restaurant critic for the biggest weekly newspaper in the Southeast.

And that's how I found myself standing on the curb at the Atlanta airport, waiting for the arts editor to pick me up for a day of interviews, wearing a suit that still had the tags attached because I absolutely could not afford it.

"My god, she's so articulate!" the paper's editor in chief, Ken, said to the arts editor and Bill as the four of us sat around a table at a brightly lit modern restaurant in Atlantic Station, the garish new development that was helping to transform Atlanta's Westside. We were halfway through my day of interviews, and this lunch was my first meeting with Ken— the same dude who had called up Richard to organize the Magnolia Grill meal with Bill. His comment was only slightly condescending, since I was sitting right there, and I wondered what he'd expected. But I also blamed the suit: the suit made everything I said seem smarter; the suit was working.

Ken had asked me what I might order if I were reviewing the restaurant—the most bizarre item on the menu, I told him, and the simplest. I'd want to test their ambition but also how well they could do the classics. I could roast a chicken at home; what about a restaurant version could make it special? We talked about the fact that Ryan was a chef and the potential conflict of interest that might pose. "You just won't review any place where he works," Ken said, which seemed too simple a solution, but I wasn't going to argue. They took me to the office and gave me an editing test, going over the copy of one of the longtime columnists at the paper. I sat at Bill's desk in the large, modern, open-plan office, the desk that might soon be my own, and felt as though my head might pop off. I was surrounded by young, cool, smart people writing about music, writing about politics, writing about bars. It was like I'd been plucked from reality and dropped into my fantasy life.

I'd only been to Atlanta once before, in the months between my New York stints. Ryan and I had driven there on a whim to visit an old friend of mine who lived there, but we hadn't told her ahead of time we were coming, and we couldn't get a hold of her when we arrived. (The pre–cell

phone era was wild, folks.) She was living in East Atlanta, though I
didn't have her address, so we looked for the closest place to stay and
wound up at the Atlanta Motel on Moreland Avenue. There were bullet
holes in the walls and people knocking on our door all night looking to
score, and I refused to sleep on the sheets, pulling clothes out of Ryan's
car to sleep on. Anyone from Atlanta who hears that I once spent the
night at the Atlanta Motel has a hard time believing me.

The Atlanta that Bill showed me on the day of my interview, veering
crazily through the streets in his BMW, was so very different from the
Atlanta I'd experienced on that previous trip. The buildings were big and
shiny, the neighborhoods leafy and grand. I remember looking out his
window at the high-rises of Midtown and thinking: *I could be a part of
this. I could have a piece of the life of this city, this huge, exciting place. I could
make a mark.*

It was grandiose of me, I admit—it's not like they were considering
me for the job of mayor. But the thought of a salary, a job, one with the
word *critic* in the title, was more than I'd dared to dream about in the
previous few months.

They offered me the job before I got on the plane home. I called Ryan
and said, "Go buy a bottle of champagne. I'm keeping the suit."

From Our Desk to Your Eyeballs

RESTAURANT REVIEW:

Recline and Dine

Wednesday, April 5, 2006

By Besha Rodell

I have been with my husband for almost six years. We've shared many intimacies, enjoyable and otherwise. But until recently, I've never had the pleasure of eating from a plate that was four inches from his tube-sock-clad foot.

Thus began the first paid restaurant review of my career, as the critic and food editor for *Creative Loafing* Atlanta, one of the country's oldest and largest alternative newsweeklies. The restaurant was BED, a transplant from Miami that had a location in New York that was once featured in *Sex and the City*. The gimmick was that you dined in bed, a raised platform strewn with pillows in a room that looked more like it was purpose built for orgies than for eating dinner. The setup necessitated sitting cross-legged on the bed with plates between you—no breakfast-in-bed trays provided—resulting in the above-described scenario, wherein your feet were horrifyingly close to your dinner. The waiters greeted you by saying, "I'll be joining you in bed tonight." The food was awful. As fodder for a first review? It was perfect.

Ryan, Felix, our cat, Stella, and I moved from North Carolina in early spring. Grace had started at UNC Greensboro and moved into the dorms. As much as Ryan was excited for me and supported me, the move was bittersweet for him. He was leaving his hometown and his family. He had to walk away from an executive chef job offer, and we both walked away from the farmhouse near downtown Durham we'd been planning to buy. (Looking back, we probably should have bought it anyway. It has quadrupled in value in the intervening years.) It was a lot for Ryan to sacrifice in service of my career, and it was only the beginning.

The job was to write a weekly review and edit the weekly food section: a restaurant column by longtime writer (and former editor of the newspaper) Cliff Bostock, a wine column by the sister of the paper's owner, Ben Eason, and a recipe column. I also needed to produce two food issues annually. The pay was $47,000, which seemed like a lot of money until I took day care into account. My weekly dining budget was $300, which seemed like a lot until I realized how expensive Atlanta restaurants were.

We moved into a huge old house in Ormewood Park that had been built by a doctor and his wife in the early 1900s. It was close to the city but was on an acre of land, which stretched back into a bamboo forest that twinkled with fireflies in the summer. The long-dead couple never had any children, and the people who owned it had never properly cleaned it out, meaning the massive attic was still full of the remnants of the house's original tenants—old dresses, old Christmas ornaments, the receipts from life insurance payments, boxes of condolence cards from when the doctor died, the stubs of life insurance payments made to his wife. The detritus of an entire life.

The place was falling down, somewhat literally, but I have never had a house before or since that I loved more. The living and dining areas were big enough to roller-skate through. We put in a pool table instead of a dining room table and covered it with plywood and a tablecloth when we needed to eat. The wide, screened front porch was rotting but glorious. The yard was full of blackberry brambles, which horrified the neighbors but thrilled me and my pie-making obsession. The kitchen had beautiful red oak floorboards, and a built-in fold-out wooden ironing board in the wall, and glassed-in cupboards and no dishwasher. The place was most certainly haunted, and I felt as though the ghosts were whispering, "Welcome to this house we made just for you."

Ryan got a job working at a big corporate pan-Asian restaurant in Buckhead, a place I'd never need to review. He worked nights, and I had to eat out three or four evenings a week. Everything always felt precarious. Somehow, we were still often broke, between day care and babysitting and bills and covering the parts of my job that the paper didn't cover.

I was achingly lonely, in a new city, with my husband always at work. But my own work was thrilling.

Atlanta didn't quite know what it wanted to be in the early 2000s. It was a big city, growing rapidly, the capital of the South. It had already started its ascent as Black Hollywood, and a decade after Outkast's André Benjamin took the stage in New York City to boos, to accept the Source Award for best new rap group and uttered the famous words, "The South got something to say," Atlanta was undeniably the center of hip-hop culture.

It's a magical city, for so many reasons. It's the place kids from all over the South aspire to go, to be someone, to escape small towns and boring cities, to find community, to find themselves. It's a queer mecca, a place that's full of art and life and fun. And it's so exquisitely lush, so achingly green, its giant old houses surrounded by vines and trees, the type of place where nature will climb up and swallow any building in a matter of months if you let it, even in the middle of the city. When you fly into Atlanta, it looks as though you're flying into a forest, with tall buildings poking out of the middle.

But in terms of dining, I could find no real sense of place. The city's main players were huge groups with venues that appealed to a certain kind of outsize fantasy. The dominant restaurant group, Buckhead Life, had a collection of high-end themed places: one of them was a re-creation of the Oyster Bar in Grand Central Terminal, another could have been in the Greece pavilion at EPCOT Center (if such a thing existed), with its white columns and blue ceiling covered in twinkling lights meant to look like the Greek sky at night.

BED, in all its silliness, fit right in with the Atlanta dining scene of 2006.

One of the first places Bill took me when I arrived was Two Urban Licks, an outrageous and massive room in the middle of an industrial park—you had to drive onto the loading dock to reach the valet station. A wall of windows looked out over the Atlanta skyline, while a giant rotisserie spun in the middle of the room, the open kitchen surrounding it, the carcasses of animals spinning around its flames. It was like a sexy Dante's *Inferno*—a ridiculous notion that nonetheless captures a lot of what Atlanta was trying to be: restaurant as high theater, thrilling and strange and placeless. It was as if Atlanta were trying to be Las Vegas (without the casinos) or Miami (without the beach). It felt exciting but somehow false. And the food was often not nearly as considered as the drama of the décor.

The hard-core food obsessives in town gathered on an eGullet-style forum, which was a fun and odd and bitchy place, and was mostly overrun with dudes looking to "discover" the "most authentic" immigrant-run restaurants along Buford Highway, the now-legendary corridor north of the city that teems with Mexican, Korean, Chinese, and Vietnamese businesses. Shortly after I started the job, I did an ask-me-anything-style Q&A on the forum (which, as far as I can tell, no longer exists on the internet). As an homage to my initial review of BED, the moderators gave me the username Smelly Socks. Users peppered me with questions, about my favorite type of food, about my reviewing philosophy. I think I did okay and won some of them over. I knew that following Bill into the job was going to be tough—he was beloved and had recently been nominated for a James Beard Award, and I was a total unknown. I also had a lot of broad criticism of the city's dining scene as it was in those days and struggled to find restaurants that I was enthusiastic about. That was worrisome, because I think the city at that time yearned for validation, not analysis.

Back then, the idea of food—and restaurants in particular—as important pillars of identity was not as widely accepted. Atlanta had soul food restaurants, old-timey Southern restaurants, but the places that were getting all the attention seemed to have no real identity at all other than some version of imitation or theatricality. It may have been cultural cringe—the sense that the authentic Atlanta wasn't culturally important enough to celebrate in its trendy restaurants. It may have been that the right people just hadn't come along yet—or not enough of them. There certainly were exceptions—Scott Peacock at Watershed, Anne Quatrano at Bacchanalia, and a handful of others. But overall, I yearned for more representation of the vibrant city I saw—on the streets and in the art and music scenes—on the plates of the restaurants I was reviewing.

I don't know how I'd have felt about that time in dining if I'd been a native ATLien, but coming from North Carolina—where farm to table was already king—and New York before that gave me the perspective of an outsider, and it's one that did me well. I had something to say. Where is the modern Southern food? Where are the chefs using the amazing Georgia-grown produce? Most importantly: If the South has got something to say, doesn't that extend to food, too? And as the undeniable capital of the South, who do we want to be as a city?

Before I could begin to tackle those questions, I had to learn the trickier intricacies of the job. That Craig Claiborne standard of criticism is fairly simple in theory. In practice, not so much, at least not when you're at a publication that isn't *The New York Times*. And yet, many, many newspapers, including *Creative Loafing*, claimed to adhere to it.

The standard breaks down to three main components: you dine a minimum of three times for each review; the publication pays for the meal (no freebies); you dine anonymously.

Many critics are lucky. The weekly review is their only responsibility. I, on the other hand, was expected to be in the office from nine to five every day in order to act as the food editor, go to meetings, and get my writing done. Then I had to eat out three to four times a week. Ryan also worked nights. Day care was already so expensive. Nighttime babysitting costs added up quickly.

I'm not sure how we cobbled it all together at first. Felix and I almost never saw Ryan—his days off were Sunday and Monday, and he slept most of the day Sunday, having often worked seventy-hour weeks. The music editor at the paper, a woman named Heather, was a couple of years younger than I was and had a kid the same age as Felix. She was the first parent around my age I'd met since Felix was born. Some nights, I'd watch her son, Jack, when she went to shows; some nights, she'd take Felix when I ate out. During the summer, Grace came from North Carolina, where she was going to college, and was basically Felix's nanny. I found a few babysitters, some of them willing to trade childcare for fancy meals out with me. For a while, Felix spent much of his life in the apartment of a woman who had an illegal day care operation and would keep him until 8:00 p.m. if Ryan dropped him off at 1:00 p.m. on his way to work.

My weeks were a blur. I was constantly behind, I never had enough people to eat with, despite the fact that everyone in town *wanted* to eat with me. But that many meals a week is hard to plan, especially if you hope to not give yourself away as a critic. You can't just show up three nights in a row; you need to space them out over the course of a few weeks or pretend you're in town for a conference and staying just around the corner. And finding decent dining partners is harder than you might think.

Some people are way too excited to be there. They want you to narrate the entire process of reviewing. Some people want you to listen to every opinion they have about everything in the place, taking the opportunity to complain about the service, the room, the food. Friends I've had for years don't really understand that this is, in fact, a job—if they flake last minute, they're screwing me over in a way that extends beyond the social aspect. Vegans, people with food allergies, picky eaters—in some circumstances, these folks can be helpful, depending on the restaurant, but more often, they make the process way more difficult.

Over the years, I've come up with a kind of formula for the three-visit restaurant review. First visit, I invite friends. I try to convince them that it's pretty much a purely social affair (apart from the fact that they aren't allowed to flake, and I get to tell them what to order). I want to know what it's like to just go eat at a place, like any member of the public. I don't think too hard about it. I don't take notes. I want to experience it like anyone else would.

Second visit, I take my family. They know it's a job. They can talk to me about the intricacies of the food and service without getting too giddy about being part of the process and without expecting me to be interested in what they think about it. Unless I want an opinion.

Both Ryan and Felix are secret weapons, in one way or another. Dining out with a kid is always interesting, in terms of how we're treated. Felix used to claim that restaurants were "racist against children." (Yeah, yeah, don't worry, I explained how racism is not the same as bad or condescending service, but you get what he meant.) Ryan is a chef—if something is cooked badly, he can usually tell me what went wrong. Both will put up with me spending the whole meal pretending to text on my phone, when I'm actually taking notes. Neither of them expects me to be a particularly charming dining companion.

Third visit, if possible, I go on my own. I sit at the bar. For this meal, I need to concentrate completely, to begin writing in my head with no distractions. On a couple of occasions, when I thought it wouldn't look too suspicious, I've taken my laptop with me and started writing right there in the restaurant. This feels somewhat evil, but it makes for great copy.

If I struggled with the scheduling and logistics of the three visits, I really struggled with the finances of it. The no-freebies rule is absolutely the only way to keep yourself clean in this game (and by "this game," I mean formal restaurant criticism—if you're getting freebies by some other means that doesn't involve extortion or the dubious promise of "ex-

posure," then good on ya), but a weekly review with a weekly budget of
$300 in a town where most of the new restaurants are super goddamned
expensive is a math problem with no solution. Yes, I was expected to
comment on the cocktails. If I skipped dessert, my editor questioned it.
"You just need to round out the review schedule with cheaper places,"
Ken, the editor in chief, told me when I raised the issue. "What's new on
Buford Highway?"

I tried, I really did, but there just weren't enough $20 meal restaurants
worthy of review (and a star rating) to balance out all the $200 meals
I was eating. Some reviews, at tasting-menu restaurants, cost me well
over $1,000 for those three visits. There were no company credit cards
or stacks of cash handed out to cover my meals (things I've heard about
from critics at daily papers and magazines)—I was always fronting the
paper hundreds of dollars at a time, paying for my own meals, and waiting for them to reimburse me. That first year, when I did my taxes, I cal-
culated that I'd spent about $13,000 of my own money, money that was
never reimbursed, subsidizing the newspaper's dining budget.

And occasionally, when I was recognized, restaurants did try to comp
my meals. Or send free dishes. In those instances, I had to explain that
they were putting my reputation and my job at risk. A couple of times,
when an owner refused to give me a bill, I had to go out and find an
ATM and come back and leave a wad of cash. "Give it to your staff if you
want," I'd say, "but I can't not pay."

The free dish, the "gift from our chef," was harder. I've dined with
critics who have refused such dishes, sending the food back. It's a tactic I
can't bear, though it might be the correct one. But this is the hospitality
industry. Even if the freebie is meant to curry favor, it's also an attempt
to be hospitable. It feels like a self-important humiliation to reject the
gesture, I took to saying, "You really shouldn't have, it isn't necessary,"
then smiling when they insist, then adding the cost of the dish to my tip
at the end of the meal.

Needless to say, this did not help my meager budget.

How often was I recognized? Not much at first. But slowly, it became an inevitability. About a year into the job, when eating with Ryan and Felix at Element, a new restaurant from Richard Blais before he went on to become a *Top Chef* star, the maître d' came up to the table and just straight up asked, "Are you Besha Rodell?"

Which brings us to the final and trickiest part of that Claiborne formula: you dine anonymously. Anonymity is by far the most complicated, and asked-about, and stupidest part of my job. I'll admit that when I was first in Atlanta, I loved it. It made me feel important. These days, my feelings about it are much more fraught.

I am a terrible candidate for anonymity. My hair is distinctive (big, messy, often unbrushed). My accent is distinctive—not quite American, not quite Australian. I have tattoos, some of which might be perceived as job-related (they aren't). Even my ass is distinctive. Occasionally, someone will suggest we take a photo from behind—a photo to use on social media after a radio appearance, for instance, of me standing among my hosts with my back turned. My friends and family will see these photos and laugh. "I'd know that ass anywhere," they'll say.

My name isn't Bill or John, it's Beshaleba. As far as I know, I am the only Beshaleba. My father, a man of many lives and vocations, was primarily a religious scholar in the 1970s. He created my name as an amalgamation of two names from the Bible, Elisheba and Bathsheba. (An ex-boyfriend's grandmother once exclaimed, "Beshaleba! That sounds like some kind of biblical whore." She wasn't far off.) There are other Beshas in the world, including a Brazilian handbag company that bears my name, but they are few and far between. If someone says my name too loudly at a restaurant table, the jig is up. I've been made.

I missed the explosion of social media by a hair—I got a Facebook account in 2007 and never put my photo online. But all of the above still makes it difficult. And the longer you're in a city, the harder it gets. Good waiters know what to look for, they move jobs and remember you from a previous restaurant, they figure it out.

That first time, I lied. "Who's Besha Rodell?" I asked.

"She's the new restaurant critic in town," the guy said. "I heard she has an Australian accent."

"Oh," I said, smiling. "I'm South African."

Usually, being recognized doesn't include such a straightforward interrogation. Usually, it's just a shift in tone, the bartender and the host whispering in the corner, the chef poking her head out from the kitchen and eyeing the table. All of a sudden, the formerly confident waiter will trip over his words. Felix will spy a manager huddle across the room behind my back and sigh and say, "I think they've figured it out."

But even in restaurants where a chef or manager knows me, I often manage to get in and out at least once without being noticed. I put my hair up. I get my guests to arrive first and sit facing outward so I can slip in the door and go directly to my table and sit with my back to the room. I ask them to do the ordering (once I've told them what to order). I try to blend into the background, to be a nobody.

This is a game I've now been playing for what feels like my entire adult life. It's served me well, but it's an awfully long time to have been pretending I'm some kind of spy. Most critics these days have given up on anonymity altogether. Others do it for a while, then have some kind of big reveal—*Look, it's me!*—as if it matters as much to everyone else as it does to them.

But from a professional perspective, I maintain that it's invaluable. Most people immediately think of the potential that dining incognito means I'm more likely to receive bad service or food than a known critic. Which is potentially true, and there have been times when my experience has been vastly different from that of recognizable reviewers and other VIPs. In those cases, it's almost always at the type of restaurant that stratifies its guests based on import. I think I'm smart enough to detect such a thing even if I'm being treated well. I actually find anonymity far more valuable in the opposite instance: when I get treated extremely well despite my non-VIP status.

Back in those early days in Atlanta, I realized that my very authentic sartorial reality was a boon to my profession. I still shopped mainly at the thrift store. My hair was a mess. Half the time, I had a small child in tow. If Ryan and I could show up at the fanciest restaurant in town, looking (and often feeling) as out of place as we had back in our NYC days, and have the staff treat us as well as they treated the obviously wealthy older couples around us, then that was a sign of a truly wonderful restaurant—one that understood that the value of a fancy meal is far greater, the stakes way higher, for someone who can't really afford to be there.

And that happened, a lot. I think, like in New York, people often assumed we were in the industry, and we were treated well as a result. But also, sometimes some fantastic waiter would take one look at us and decide to make our night, simply because we were so out of place.

Not always. At my one meal at Seeger's, the exceedingly self-serious fine dining restaurant that defined Atlanta haute cuisine for years and closed soon after we arrived, my cell phone began ringing in the entrance hall when we arrived. My flip phone ringtone back then was the opening bars of "Get Ur Freak On" by Missy Elliott, and it bounced off the marble walls of the hushed room (Günter Seeger, the chef and owner, famously did not play music in the restaurant so that guests might more fully concentrate on his culinary artistry). The hostess was . . . not amused. We were treated like a smelly rag the whole rest of the night.

I can imagine how that might feel if we were spending our own (massive amount of) money, if this were an anniversary and not an assignment. Pretending I wasn't me allowed for insights that known critics would never experience. The good ones would absolutely take note of what was happening to the table next to them, but I'm not sure the emotional impact of social shunning can be learned through osmosis.

What doesn't suit me about anonymity is the self-importance of it all. Outside of my work life, I'm constantly stepping out of photos, declining event invitations, wondering if I'm going to need to explain why I can't appear in a moms-and-kids photo at Felix's school. I give fake names to baristas, shush friends when they say my name in restaurants, refuse to write my name on name tags at events. When my friend Mary got married and asked me to be her maid of honor, I had to ask if she could live with keeping most of her wedding photos offline. These kinds of situations, and the conversations required, always have a whiff of narcissism about them. They presuppose, in some ways, that people might care about the intricacies of my work.

In fact, no matter how you cut it, almost any stance you choose can easily become a vehicle for self-importance. Many non-anonymous critics love to swan into a restaurant, to see the surprise and panic on the faces of the staff, to bask in the glow of that terror-tinged attention. (I have experienced this plenty of times, and it's one of the most uncomfortable parts of my job. Dining out is supposed to be fun, to be relaxed. Absorbing the anxiety of an entire restaurant crew is miserable.)

On the flip side, remaining staunchly anonymous is to imagine that my dumb job is worthy of such acrobatic deception. I hate the dishonesty of it, of sitting at a bar and coming up with some fake life story for a friendly and chatty bartender, of the guarded way I approach social gatherings.

There may well be a photo of me on the back of this book, and if so, I hope I don't look as uncomfortable as I'll certainly feel. Anonymity has given me so many gifts—the gift of freedom from selfies, from having to present myself as a visual commodity as part of my public persona. To ex-boyfriends, I have existed only as a memory, of my younger, hotter self. This suits me just fine.

It has allowed me to avoid the utterly bizarre push and pull between public relations folks and journalists, in which the literal job of PR people is to woo journalists in the hopes that they'll write about their clients. In North Carolina, naive as I was, I found this phenomenon to be baffling. Does this person who keeps inviting me for drinks and lunch want to be my friend? (Spoiler: they do! But not because they like you!) Once I took on the cloak of anonymity, I was able to sidestep the issue almost entirely.

This acceptance of anonymity as a benefit is not always understood or shared by the publications that critics work for. This is especially true in the era of social media, where personal brand and representing a publication's brand can be seen as far more valuable than the minor advantages of avoiding a free dessert here and there. I was good at Twitter in its early days—it's a medium based on words—and struggled with Instagram initially because (a) I am not a photographer, and (b) I could/would not post glamour selfies coyly slipping some food morsel into my mouth, which seemed to be the lady-food-person paradigm on that platform. To this day, it's mostly my cats and my home-cooked meals on IG, and I'm pretty sure I'd have way more followers if I caved to the self-promoting selfie game. TikTok is totally out of the question—what would I even post?

And events have become more and more important for food publications. Bill Addison (one of the only other critics I know who retained his anonymity throughout his reviewing career) occasionally agreed to appear at festivals in full disguise, applied by professional theatrical makeup artists. I have refused to do so—the whole thing seems too embarrassing, too cringeworthy, too self-important. (I did once appear onstage for a Q&A in a plastic knight's helmet. It was so . . . all of the above.)

Bill agrees with me about the ick factor of the disguise, especially because he's had a harder time than I have avoiding recognition in the towns where he's worked. (I'm not sure why—he did manage to keep his photo off the internet.) So the disguises are perhaps not even useful when he's addressing a crowd full of restaurant folks who may already know what he looks like. But as he said to me about these appearances, "I'm a sensitive soul, and the disguise allows me to speak in those types of situations in a way that feels comfortable."

In other words, the disguise, the anonymity, helps people like us avoid the public nature of our job, a kind of exposure that feels antithetical to who we are socially.

I'm still not sure how much of my demeanor, in the way I relate to social situations, is a product of a life lived this way, or if I chose this profession in part because I'm still that kid who went to five high schools and ended up skulking in the corner at parties, daring anyone who had the nerve to come talk to me, never being open or vulnerable or honest about how lonely I really was. Giving up anonymity would mean giving up my pretext to be an antisocial asshole.

Is it good for my job? Absolutely. Is it also a protection, a cover, a really good excuse? Almost certainly.

Owner's Disorder and
Other Aberrations

I arrived in newspapers at the end of the good times, just as the gravy train was veering wildly off its tracks, sloshing fat-drenched journalists out its windows with alarming ferocity. Print classified ads, which had been the weekly newspaper's bread and butter for decades, died practically overnight thanks to Craigslist and the rest of the internet. Sales teams refused to change their tactics, vastly underestimating the scale of the shift. Many newspapers stumbled onto the internet, slapping up terrible websites with worse (or no) advertising, thinking of them only as a minor supplement to the print product and not a major part of their identity or brand.

I think of the timing of the beginning of my career as both a blessing and a curse. I never got to properly ride the gravy train (those big, ambitious stories that Bill had written, which necessitated him traveling all over the Southeast, throwing dinner parties in expensive restaurants for me and my North Carolina editor? Out of the question), but I also never got a comfortable seat, so I didn't mourn its derailment in the same way many of my colleagues did. From the second I stepped on board, *Creative Loafing* was facing budget cutbacks, layoffs, increasingly ridiculous workloads, and, in addition to the things every other newspaper was facing, a whole heap of family drama.

Started in 1972 by Debby and Chick Eason out of their family home in an Atlanta neighborhood, *CL*, as it was affectionately known, held a spot in the culture of its city similar to alt weeklies all over the country. It was based on listings, on telling people what to do in Atlanta, which was becoming a cultural hub, and it did it better than anyone else. In a 2018 oral history of the newspaper published in *Atlanta* magazine, my friend (and former *CL* colleague) Thomas Wheatley wrote:

> *In its heyday,* Creative Loafing *told a story of Atlanta different from the one chronicled in the* Journal-Constitution, *teased on WSB-TV, or splashed across the pages of* Atlanta *magazine. Here was a weekly paper that championed underdogs, miscreants, punk rockers, garage rockers, boat rockers, beat cops, line cooks, addicts, taggers, inkers, squatters, rappers, strippers. Also, of course, Democrats. And yet, it also reserved column space for conservative pundits such as Neal Boortz and Bob Barr. It was the place where, if you were 24 and your girlfriend had just kicked you out, you found a new apartment and maybe even a new girlfriend. It was the place to discover what bands to see, what restaurants to hit, what politicians to vote for. In the antediluvian age of analog media, it was Atlanta's cultural (and countercultural) bible. It made you smarter, hungrier, grittier, cooler. And it was free.*
>
> *Then, the internet came along and . . . well, you know the rest.*[1]

Thomas went on, in that article, to explain the saga of the newspaper, a lore that I learned through osmosis in dribs and drabs while working there. After its scrappy beginnings, the company eventually grew and launched papers in Florida and North Carolina, an expansion that founder and owner Debby Eason was pushed to take on by her son, Ben Eason.

When I arrived, in 2006, the paper was six years into its first Ben Eason

---

1 Thomas Wheatley, "A Long, Strange Trip: The Oral History of *Creative Loafing*," *Atlanta*, July 26, 2018.

phase. Ben bought the paper in 2000 from his mother, who was the publisher at the time, but it was described to me as a "hostile takeover," as in the son bought the paper out from under his mother against her wishes and then pushed her out.

A year after my arrival at the paper, Ben borrowed $40 million to buy two other alt weeklies, the *Chicago Reader* and the *Washington City Paper*. And that's exactly when the bottom fell out.

Watching a newspaper go through that period was farcical, honestly. At the beginning, the office was plagued with insanely overpaid executives who came from some bullshit marketing background and convinced Ben that they could solve all our problems by putting us in conference rooms and spewing corporate speak at us for hours before letting us go back to our jobs. There was one guy in particular: no one knew what he actually did for a living, but he had a very nice office, and every few weeks, we had to listen to him drone on and on in the large glassed-in conference room, giving speeches that basically sounded like: "When we actualize our strategic position within the marketplace, the synergy from our tactical partnerships will fundamentally objectify our potential to activate our core competencies."

None of us had any idea what he was on about, but we did understand that huge change was afoot and we would be expected to pick up the pieces, scrounging for errant globs of gravy on the periphery. I remember sitting in the conference room with all the other editors the day we were told that each section was expected to start a blog. Heather, the whip-smart music editor, sat with her Converse propped up on the conference table and asked, "Where are we supposed to find the time to do this while also running our regular sections? Will we have any extra budget to pay writers for these blogs? Do you have any plans to monetize them, or is this just a vanity project?"

These questions went unanswered, and the blogs were launched without any fundamentally tactical and strategic actualization of any kind.

Despite the extra workload, the strain on budgets, and the fact that we were pouring more and more time into something that had no monetary

value to the paper (I suggested sponsorships many times; I went un-
heeded), those early days of newspaper blogs were a fairly thrilling time.
Critics were given a new voice, beyond the weekly review, to consider all
the aspects of dining culture that we used to only discuss among ourselves. These days, in retrospect, those conversations sound like clichéd
hot takes: I'm sick of tasting menus; the problems with open kitchens;
small plates are too small; small plates aren't small enough. But it was
the first time these conversations were happening in and with the public,
and they went a long way toward turning dining into a populist sport.

But it also, for a while, created a new kind of online community, one
that lived in the comments section of these blogs. Our *Creative Loafing*
food blog, *Omnivore*, had a particularly loyal and voracious readership,
and the comments section was a combative but mainly fun place where
humor was the most valued asset and the jousting was rarely nasty.

Twitter, too, was in its golden era, a time when you could go on and in-
teract with your favorite authors and journalists and musicians and when
the public had a way to talk to journalists about their work outside of the
false parity of the Letters to the Editor page. Many old-school journalists
hated this new era in which they were expected to step out of their ivory
towers and answer for their work, but again, I never experienced the old
days. While other critics were railing against the indignities of having to
compete with Yelp and other review sites, I was saying, "The more voices,
the better."

Back then, my main work-related worries were not internet trolls or
the pressures of writing and editing and blogging—things that would
all become burdensome in years and jobs to come—but the legendary
temper of my boss, Ken.

Ken, the editor in chief, protected his newsroom fiercely, but he was
also part of the problem. His temper was so outsize that the first time I
experienced it, I laughed—it seemed so out of the blue and dispropor-
tionate to the situation that I couldn't quite take it at face value. He called
me into the conference room because he was angry that I hadn't written
enough wholly positive reviews—it was his opinion that the paper existed

to tell people what to do and not what *not* to do, and I was failing in this task.

He actually turned the lights out before I walked into the room, followed by the new arts editor, who had summoned me and who looked like a dog that knew it was about to get a whipping. I stepped into the room, and Ken was standing with his back to the wall next to the door so that he was effectively behind me in the dark. Before I got my bearings, he bellowed, "Why the FUCK have there been no three- or four-star reviews in the last three weeks?"

That's when I burst into a fit of giggles. Wrong move.

Once I composed myself, I tried to explain that my budget and schedule really didn't allow me to spend time wandering around looking for fantastic places; that I went to the restaurants that were new or had a new chef or location and just let them reveal themselves to me. He wasn't buying it. It was my fault. He pulled that week's review and insisted I find something worthy of at least three stars before the next day.

Ken could be sweet. He sometimes got emotional about his personal life when you were alone with him, and he was a breathtakingly good editor. He taught me so much about writing and newspapers and journalism. But he was known for making people cry. In other words, he could be a shouty asshole, and you never knew which Ken you were going to get. I became so attuned to his moods I swear I could tell which Ken had walked through the door in the morning without even looking his way. His happy or angry energy vibrated through my consciousness before I had visually confirmed that he had arrived.

In that way, working at a small newspaper was much the same as working at a restaurant. Ken was the charming, talented, asshole chef, and the newsroom was the band of merry pirates who feared and loved and wanted to please him. Instead of sweaty line cooks, we had fearless news reporters; instead of sleazy bartenders, we had sleazy nightlife writers. And similarly to Goldie's, *Creative Loafing* and its pressure cooker atmosphere created a crew that was tight, with a cast of characters worthy of a sitcom. It also produced some of the closest and longest-lasting friendships of my life.

The main difference between a restaurant and a newspaper was that if some idiot swoops in and buys a restaurant and runs it into the ground or fires everyone and hires all new staff (and then runs it into the ground), you can just go work for another restaurant. But newspaper jobs are far harder to come by, especially if you can't up and move every couple of years, and especially if your job is highly specialized.

Eventually, Ken did his nuclear bellowing tirade thing to Ben, the owner, and was fired. Around the same time, payment came due on that $40 million loan, and Ben defaulted and filed for bankruptcy. And that's when the real trouble started.

In the decade after I began my newspaper career at *Creative Loafing*, the tradition of the great American alt weekly sputtered and died. Unlike daily papers, they couldn't rely on the big-money advertisers, and because they had always been free, the idea of a paywall on their websites made no sense. You could make the argument that a new generation of websites took their place, outlets like Vice and Vox, which catered to a similar young, left-leaning crowd. But from a journalism perspective, I can't say that I think those outlets have the same function.

The alt weekly is where I got my start, and I'm not sure I would have fit in anywhere else. It's also where many of America's best writers and thinkers were first published: the late David Carr, Ta-Nehisi Coates, Colson Whitehead. They were a place for people with new ideas, ideas that didn't quite fit into mainstream publications, where editors like Ken encouraged people to take chances and gave chances to those of us who were unproven. They weren't perfect by any stretch of the imagination— when I arrived at *CL*, the newsroom was overwhelmingly white in a very, very Black city—but they provided an in for many writers who otherwise might not have found their voices.

It was at *CL* that I found my voice, learned what I wanted to champion, learned where my true interests lay. Within my first year at the paper, I'd been nominated for a James Beard Award for a food issue that profiled Atlanta chefs who were leaning into locavorism. (The actual awards night was one of the more humiliating experiences of my life, culminating with standing among a group of older, tuxedoed men whom I admired hugely while they smoked cigars and guffawed at me because I was naive enough to be still wearing my nominee badge at the after-party.)

A while after that, a daily paper in the Midwest tried to poach me, offering me a much larger salary for a much easier job. But Ryan had just been hired as the executive chef at a bar in our neighborhood, a job I didn't want to ask him to give up. Also: I felt as though I was beginning to find something approximating home in Atlanta.

I'm not sure a daily newspaper or magazine would have allowed me to experiment and fuck up and grow in the way a place like *Creative Loafing* allowed. I was on a steep learning curve, and I had editors who saved me from myself countless times—but where, at a more mainstream outlet, they might have corrected me into a more predictable, safer path, my *CL* editors let me be weird. I wrote reviews in the form of love letters, of one-act plays, I learned the art of the wholly negative review, as well as the rave. Because the newspaper was so tiny, the staff so small, I was also able to take on all kinds of fun stories outside of my regular beat. I interviewed musicians, I was part of the editorial board, I covered the ACC and the NCAA when college basketball came to town. And for a short time, I, along with a couple of my coworkers, ran the paper entirely.

After Ken was fired, Ben quickly lost the paper in the wake of his ill-advised borrowing and subsequent bankruptcy, and *CL*, along with the other papers Ben had bought, were purchased by a large hedge fund. There was a wonderful year or so when Mara Shalhoup, a young woman who had been the news editor and a star writer, was in the editor in chief role. When she left to take over the same job at the *Chicago Reader*, we went for around a year without a leader. I, along with the arts editor (and my longtime editor) Debbie Michaud stepped up, both working multiple jobs to keep the paper running. With the encouragement of Mara and a couple of my coworkers, I applied to be the EIC.

I loved running that paper. And I was good at it. But I had no news background, and I was young and potentially too outspoken, and the publisher ultimately hired a flashy dude from Dallas who had recently lost a bunch of weight, realized he was desirable again, left his wife of decades and their teenage daughter, and started dating someone far, far younger than he was—all facts he liked to talk about loudly. His cover letter was full of quips and hyperlinks, and in the interview process, he impressed all of us with his pop culture sensibility.

He was less impressive when he started the job. I swear he never really even moved from Dallas to Atlanta. He was gone all the time. Debbie and I basically still ran the website and edited the cover stories, and if that's what you think an editor in chief does, then you'd be correct.

We no longer controlled the budget, however. And one day Dallas Douchebag did show up for an all-staff meeting, and while everyone else gathered in the conference room, I, along with our senior news writer and our longtime film and theater critic, was taken to the back of the office, sat at a table, and DD told us we were being laid off. I assume he was told to cut the budget, looked at the payroll, and just picked the three salaries that would let him stop thinking about it so he could get back to his girlfriend.

Am I bitter? Fuck yeah. Losing my job at *CL* was one of the biggest blows of my life. I loved that paper, loved that city. My entire identity was wrapped up in being an editor and critic there. And the food there had grown so much—Atlanta was becoming what I always hoped it would be. Places like Miller Union, and Holeman and Finch, and Home Grown were reveling in the city's Southern-ness and doing it extremely well. Covering the scene at that time was an absolute joy.

But also? Debbie and I, and really the entire editorial staff, had spent years after Ken and then Mara left trying to hold the place together, scrambling to put out a funny, passionate, smart newspaper that did justice to the art and food and music and culture of Atlanta. And then this dude comes in and in my opinion basically decimates much of what we'd worked for, just because he didn't want to spend the time to figure out a budget that might save jobs.

DD was likely counting on the fact that I would be lost without my title, because he seemed pretty confident that I'd want to continue as the restaurant critic on a freelance basis, making less than a quarter of what I'd made as a staff member. I told him I was too mad to properly consider it at the time, then sent an email a couple of days later that simply said, "No thanks."

He quit soon after and went "back" to Dallas. Debbie took over and ran the paper passionately and successfully for a couple of years. The paper changed hands a few times, and in 2017, Ben Eason bought it back, then stopped publishing the paper weekly, then laid off all but one of the remaining editorial staffers.

Today, it exists as a shadow of its former self, its old newspaper boxes scattered around Atlanta, empty, many of them adorned with stickers produced by a former writer, in the old *CL* title font, that read I MISS CREATIVE LOAFING.

In that same *Atlanta* magazine story, longtime *CL* columnist John Sugg said of the paper, "*CL* is kind of an abbreviated history of newspapers in general. They start, flourish, prosper, someone wants to become a media mogul, and they collapse and fail. There is nothing left of the alternative press."

It was late morning when my layoff happened. On my way home, I called my friend John Kessler, who was the critic at *The Atlanta Journal-Constitution* at the time and lead writer on their dining blog. "Do I have a scoop for you," I said, keeping it together only barely.

The paperwork I'd signed in order to get severance had stipulated many things, one of them being that I didn't speak publicly about my layoff until a given time that day. Kessler agreed to hold the news until that afternoon.

Then I called Ryan, who left work immediately and met me at home, and we sat and I cried. Eventually, Kessler's blog post about my termination went live, and that's when Atlanta came through.

My god. These days, media layoffs happen constantly, and the "today was my last day at . . ." Twitter post is so, sadly, common. Back then, I'm not sure I'd experienced that brand of public outcry before, fueled by Twitter in particular, and goddamn, there was an outcry. To the hundreds and hundreds of people who expressed outrage on that day, or sent me well wishes: I still remember. It was a balm. I forever love ATL.

When Felix came home, we climbed onto his trampoline in our overgrown backyard and lay there, and I told him I'd been laid off, that I wasn't a restaurant critic anymore, at least not for now. He was nine, and the proudly professional version of me was the only mother that had ever existed in his memory. I told him I didn't know what was going to happen but that we'd be okay. I had no idea if I was lying.

We were still there when my coworkers from *CL* (both the ones who had been laid off and the ones who hadn't) slowly began showing up at my house, and because of that, the trampoline became the place where we spent the evening drinking whiskey and blubbering and laughing. Ryan cooked us dinner and tried to manage the chaos of a horde of very drunken journalists who were all in some form of shock—we were a tight crew, and those who had kept their jobs were barely less distraught. I will always love those people, for this reason and many others.

The next morning, I woke up very hungover and with absolutely no idea who the fuck I was.

The GOAT

I magine a person who is universally accepted as the best in their field. The chess grand master, the Serena, the Beyoncé. Not many careers are specialized enough to have an undisputed GOAT, but a few are. Athletics is an obvious example. There's an argument to be made for music, especially in some classical circles. And in 2012, restaurant criticism had its GOAT.

Now imagine replacing that person. They have moved on to a shinier, better-paid position, and you are tasked with filling their oversize boots. You are practically unknown; they are internationally famous. They are still doing what they do, what you both do, in the same town as you. And every single move you make will be compared to theirs. Forever. Or at least until you piss off to another country.

In 2012, Jonathan Gold was only five years out from having won the Pulitzer Prize for criticism in *LA Weekly*—the first and thus far only restaurant critic to ever have been given the accolade that usually goes to arts or music writers. His writing was lyrical, intimate, full of turns of phrase that left you swooning. When he won the Pulitzer, his wife, Laurie Ochoa, was the newspaper's editor, but she left in 2009, "under pressure" from Village Voice Media, which owned the newspaper at the time.

I've spent a lot of time thinking about what those last few years at *LA*

Weekly must have been like for Jonathan: his wife and editor and closest collaborator gone; a new, young editor in her place, at a newspaper where he probably no longer felt at home, despite the fact that he'd worked there, on and off, for thirty years.

In 2012, he jumped ship, taking a job at the *Los Angeles Times*. (Later, Ochoa would also get hired at the daily.) And Village Voice Media began a national search for his replacement.

Who wants to replace the GOAT? Well, I did. Along with every other food writer in the country.

In the weeks after the *CL* layoff, I swam. I'd been running for years, combating the calorific excesses of my profession with sprints and periods where I'd see a personal trainer a couple of times a week. But a few months earlier, my hips had begun to protest, and in the weeks before *CL* cut me loose, I'd switched to swimming.

There used to be a pool at the King Center in Atlanta, and it was the place I went in those weeks afterward. In the Atlanta spring, walking up that grand, wide walkway to that pool among the blossoms and the people who had made the pilgrimage to see the place that honored Dr. Martin Luther King—I felt like it saved me. I was so angry and so lost. But my city, that place, the calmness of the water, the counting of strokes, it rescued me.

I've never stopped swimming. It's still what saves me when I'm at a loss.

At first, I took the reprieve from eating as a blessing. I reveled in the ability to cook, to be there for Felix every night, to take a break from the richness and the calories, to have some control over my diet. It felt good.

And then, about two weeks in, I freaked out. Felix was spending the night with my mom, who was living in Georgia at the time. (In the years since my mother left North Carolina for West Virginia, she had taken a six-month teaching gig in Tasmania, moved to Connecticut to go to law school, moved back to North Carolina, moved in with us for a few months in Georgia, and was, at this point, living on a horse farm outside of Atlanta. And you thought my life was complicated.) I declared to Ryan, "I need a fancy dinner! I need a steak! And a martini!"

It was so unlike me, the want for steak house stupidity, nothing like the kind of dining I'd usually choose if I wasn't working. But I'd lived so long in a world in which I might not be able to pay my gas bill (did I tell you about the summer in Atlanta where we went without hot water for three weeks, putting a hose over the open back door of the basement with a shower curtain draped around it, so we could shower in the cold hose water, only partially exposed to the backyard?), but fancy restaurant meals were always a part of my life, a professional necessity, no matter how broke we were. Living without was suddenly unbearable. I wanted the stupidest, most obvious form of that.

We went to Kevin Rathbun Steak, one of the city's ridiculously expensive steak houses. My severance was mediocre but more money than anyone had given me in a lump sum in my life before, and I justified the expense as a step on the road to fancy restaurant detox. We sat in the bar and shared a big steak and drank martinis, and I felt almost like myself again.

For better and worse, this is the life that I have: the one in which a lady who can't pay her utility bills can nonetheless go eat a big steak and drink martinis and pretend the shit end of the stick won't always be the one pointed at her. This is part of why I think my writing hit differently from all the dapper dudes who came before me—dining out was never something I took for granted; every meal felt like a pilgrimage to a temple belonging to a religion not my own but to which I aspired. If that came across in my reviews, it made them more welcoming for more readers. But I no longer had readers. I just had my hunger, that old friend who told me I should have steak and martinis even when I was unemployed.

Eventually, I started to think about what might be next. I'd applied for the job at *LA Weekly* without much expectation and with no sense of whether a move to Los Angeles was feasible for me and my family, but the timing seemed fortuitous.

I was approached by one of the other publications in Atlanta that was willing to create a position for me alongside their lead critic. It wasn't ideal, but the money was livable, and I could stay in my comfortable Atlanta life, in our big old house, with the friends and the community we'd created there. I could hold on to at least part of my identity. But before I accepted that offer, I decided to do due diligence with *LA Weekly*.

I shot off a quick email to Village Voice Media's editorial director, basically saying, *Hi, I assume you aren't considering me for Gold's position, but I have another job offer and I'd like to rule out the LA scenario before I accept.* I got an immediate response: Let's talk.

Within days, I'd had two phone interviews, one with the editorial director as I sat in the backyard of the Atlanta house watching the fireflies, and another with the food editor and editor in chief of *LA Weekly* from a rental house on Cape San Blas in Florida, where I'd absconded with friends to lick my layoff wounds and get extremely sunburned.

At the end of my second phone interview, with Sarah, the *Weekly's* EIC, she asked, "Do you feel as though you need to come out here to decide if you want the job?"

My only experience of LA at that point was LAX, a place I flew through every time I went to Australia, the smell of which is burned into my memory as the first sensory experience I had of the USA. In all those trips, since childhood, I'd never left the airport. "Yes," I told Sarah, "I think I need to come out there."

The following week, I was on a flight.

I was picked up from LAX by the food editor, Amy. She drove me downtown to meet with a couple of freelancers, and I stared out the windows of her car at the endless strip malls, the bright sunlight hiding nothing, missing the softness and overwhelming green of Atlanta, of the South. We talked, and ate amazing tacos, and went and sat at the bar at Mozza, where I had a salad with walnuts that tasted more walnutty than any walnut I'd ever had in my life.

"These walnuts are incredible," I said.

"Welcome to California," she told me.

Nancy Silverton stopped by to chat with Amy, and I gawked at this living legend who just casually came by to say hello. Another chef, who Amy later told me was Walter Manzke, came and spoke to her about Jonathan Gold's recent decision to do away with the star ratings at the *LA Times*. "The stars are something we all aspire to," he said. "They let us know if we're living up to the aspirations we set for ourselves. I don't love them, and I get it, but I'm sad to see them go."

In the afternoon, the managing editor, Jill, drove me around town on all those endless highways, showing me potential neighborhoods I might live in. "Where are the trees?" I asked her.

"This is the desert," she said, then drove me to Silver Lake, which wasn't as flat and stark as the rest of the city.

She dropped me back at my hotel near the airport, and I called Ryan and cried. "I can't imagine living here," I said. "I can't imagine sending Felix to school here. The schools all look like prison camps. There are no trees."

"It's just an interview," he told me. "Just get through it and come home to me. We'll figure it out."

The editor in chief, Sarah, picked me up, and we went to dinner at Lukshon, Sang Yoon's fantastic Southeast Asian restaurant in Culver City. The food was so good, though I barely remember what I ate, I was such a ball of nerves.

Sarah was younger than I was, blond, blue-eyed, thin, and impossibly tall in her high heels. She laughed easily but could turn serious in a heartbeat. She admitted to me that they'd had another candidate, that they'd made an offer, but that person had decided to take another job "outside of journalism." (I never figured out who that person was.)

She told me that most of the applications she'd gotten—and there were hundreds—had promised that they could be the next Jonathan Gold.

I thought about that, what it meant to be "the next Jonathan Gold." What exactly were these people trying to live up to? And the main things I could think of were things that I absolutely could not claim.

One: he was a lifelong Angeleno, someone who loved and breathed this city, a city that felt entirely foreign to me.

Two: he was known for his sense of exploration, his need to discover things, and his unending appetite. As much as I'd loved exploring when we lived in New York, something changed when it became a professional urge rather than a personal one. There was a competitiveness to it in the food world, a barely disguised sense of conquest: who can reveal the next best taco; who can put the most notches of "discovery" on their belt; who can eat the most? I'm not suggesting that Jonathan was guilty of seeing food and restaurants this way—he practically invented the genre of eating as an act of obsessive discovery, and I believe it was love that drove him, not competition—but those who wished to be like him? They were often bros who might as well have been talking about video games or women or whatever else it is that bros compete over.

I, in turn, was no longer a discoverer. I was a classic restaurant critic with a slightly filthier vocabulary and an audience in mind that was less wealthy gourmand and more ratbag line cook. Other people could do the discovering; I would then go eat there and write a thing that tells you whether you might want to eat there, too. As much as Jonathan was famous for writing in the second person ("Have you ever been frightened by a dumpling? Truly, genuinely scared?"), I don't know that he cared much about telling people whether they should eat somewhere or not, particularly when it came to buzzy new restaurants. In fact, in many of his reviews it was impossible to tell whether he recommended the place or not. It didn't matter; the point was the pleasure he took in eating and the pleasure you took in reading. (If you have managed to get this far in life without experiencing the pleasure of his writing, his book *Counter Intelligence* is a good place to start: yes, it is a book that simply collects his *LA Weekly* restaurant reviews; yes, it is as bracing as a novel.)

Third, and most obvious: I have never been particularly good at describing food in the way that Jonathan and other great food writers could. While he was apt to describe a mole negro as "so dark that it seems to suck the light out of the airspace around it, spicy as a *novela* and bitter as tears," I was just trying to find a fucking synonym for *crunchy* and struggling to refrain from using the word *delicious* more than once in a single review. Reading Jonathan was like listening to a symphony; reading me was like, well, reading a restaurant review. I cared about the culture of the restaurant, and the way the food made me feel, far more than I aimed to make poetry that did the cooking any justice. I tried to riff on bigger themes, to avoid the boring trope of simply explaining a meal in detail. I enjoyed a clever turn of phrase, I liked flouting reader expectations, I wanted my reviews to be like talking to a friend with whom you have that particular magic, the gift of banter. I was a friendly chat. I was not a symphony.

"I'm not the next Jonathan Gold," I told Sarah across the table at Lukshon. "I have no interest in being Jonathan Gold. He already exists— another one of him would be redundant. I'm happy to be me."

She offered me the job.

The next morning, Amy took me to the Santa Monica farmers market, where she again ran into chef after chef. I hung back awkwardly, avoiding introductions but eavesdropping nonetheless. We walked out to the pier, and I took in the wild majesty of the Pacific, the weirdness of this huge, flat city that runs up against that ocean. I felt better, looking at the water.

"Whenever I get bummed out or overwhelmed by LA, I come here," Amy told me.

Then I flew home.

Three weeks later, Felix and Ryan and I were on a plane, our Atlanta house packed up and abandoned, our lives hurtling toward the West Coast. Ryan had left a job he loved, helping to run the food services at a large performing arts center, in service of my career. He had no leads in LA, and Sarah, unlike Ken, was adamant he not take a job in a restaurant.

When we arrived in LA, picked up the rental car, and drove toward the apartment in Santa Monica that the *Weekly* rented for us while we looked for a more permanent home, Felix stared out the window at Lincoln Boulevard and whispered, "*This* is LA? It's so . . . ugly."

Look, man, I love Los Angeles. With a fierceness that surprises me. But the movies? All those scenes of people arriving in the city and jumping in convertibles and cruising up and down palm tree–lined streets? That is not what it's like, certainly not most of it, or any of it near the dusty wasteland of LAX. Remember the movie *Falling Down*? The one where Michael Douglas loses his shit after getting fired from his job and being stuck in traffic? That's the movie you ought to see before you move to LA.

We had three weeks to find a place to live, and we spent most of our time house hunting during the day and trying to eat our way around the city at night. The scale of the place was like nothing I'd ever known before. Yes, New York City is huge . . . but no one critic has ever been expected to properly cover the whole of New York City. You could get an apartment in Manhattan or Brooklyn and be confident you're within an hour of almost anything you'd need to write about. In LA, if you live on the Westside, dinner in Pasadena could easily take you over two hours to get to. (Assuming you leave for dinner sometime between 3:30 in the afternoon and 7:30 at night, when the highways are a complete shit show and the surface roads are worse.)

We looked at houses everywhere. Well, everywhere with a public school that didn't resemble a prison camp. Neighborhoods that now, as someone who actually knows the city, I can't believe we contemplated. Not because they were so bad but because they were so . . . not us.

Felix, who was nine, reacted to the massive change in part by adding truly fantastical imaginary details to the things he was seeing. He and Ryan took a walk down the beach in Santa Monica, gawking at the skaters and bodybuilders and tightrope walkers, and he came back claiming to have seen a creature in the water that was half man and half fish, and rainbow-colored. We went to see a house in the woods of Topanga Canyon, down a rutty dirt road, and he went exploring while Ryan and I waited on the rustic porch for the landlady to show up. Felix came running back to us, eyes wide, proclaiming, "There's a cage full of beasts! With a giant lion! I think it has no eyes!"

I sighed and knelt down, saying, "Sweetie, I know this is all so strange for you, but you've got to stop making things up. It's getting weird."

Before he could protest, the landlady arrived, all hippie jingling jewelry and flowing skirts. As she showed us around the property, she said, "There are three houses on the land. The closest one to this one is just over that crest: Marnie, who has lived here for more than twenty years. She has a DIY wildlife sanctuary, I hope you won't mind. She keeps the animals very secured. There's a mountain lion, but she's blind."

Ryan and I looked at each other, and then, once we were done looking at the dusty, overpriced house, we walked over the ridge. Sure enough, in cages that looked like they were made from chicken wire were all kinds of coyotes and foxes and bobcats and, in her own run, a massive mountain lion with eyes that had the glossy opal vacancy of blindness.

California is wild.

The three of us were in Venice, heading toward Gjelina for lunch, when my phone rang. It was Bill.

"Have you seen it?" he asked, breathless.

"Seen what?"

"Oh, fuck. Are you sitting down? You ought to sit down."

"Bill, *what*?"

"*Eater* has published a photo of you. And it's . . . not a great one."

God bless Bill. The only person in the universe, probably, who understood me well enough to know how precious my anonymity was as a critic, but also knew me personally well enough to recognize that vanity would be an issue, too. I hung up and pulled up the *Eater* LA website on my phone, bracing for the worst.

In the weeks after I left *CL* and before I'd moved to California, I agreed to host a panel for the Atlanta Food & Wine Festival, reasoning that I was no longer a critic in Atlanta so appearing in public wasn't such a big deal. It was stupid, in retrospect, but I also wanted to connect to the community I'd spent six years covering before I left town.

In those days, *Eater*'s city sites had an occasional feature called To Catch a Critic, in which they aimed to publish photos of critics who were trying to remain anonymous. Why? For the clicks. Clicks ruled everything. Clicks would soon rule my life, in this way and others.

Someone from the Atlanta event, a food blogger I knew casually, had taken a photo of the panel and posted it to his Flickr account. Someone had alerted *Eater* LA, and they had reposted the photo, along with a gleeful few paragraphs celebrating the fact that I wouldn't have the chance at even one solitary review with my precious anonymity in place. The photo was . . . blobby. As in, it was a bit fuzzy, and I looked like a fleshy blob with stringy hair. The reader comments were the best part, with many of them comparing my appearance to Jonathan's in ways that were less than flattering, to put it mildly.

The blogger who took the photo was mortified—he knew how stupid it had been to put the photo up (it was . . . not a good photo in any way, and I'll never understand quite why he did it). He removed it from his Flickr account and contacted *Eater*, asking that they take it down. Because it was his intellectual property, they didn't have much choice.

The next chapter in the *Eater*-outs-Besha saga requires a little history:

Back when I'd been living in North Carolina, writing for the little newspaper there, I had a short-lived column for a few months called Prized Possessions. The idea was I'd interview someone about their most valued physical possession and write an as-told-to story about why the object meant so much to them. I also took a portrait of the person and their possession, using my mother's old Nikon F and black-and-white film. My aim was to reveal what different people in the community valued, though, unsurprisingly, most people chose something sentimental that had belonged to someone they loved.

One of the people I interviewed was a friend of my mother-in-law's, a woman named Brenda Pollard. She lived in the old money part of Durham in a giant house that was basically a mansion but was crumbling a bit. (Her husband, Larry Pollard, gained some manner of fame because their home was next door to the Petersons', as in Michael and Kathleen Peterson, the couple who inspired *The Staircase*. Larry is the neighbor who came up with "the owl theory," the idea that Kathleen was killed by an owl and not Michael. I was blissfully unaware of this aspect of Brenda's life at the time, though I have no idea how I managed that— Kathleen Peterson died in 2001 next door to Brenda's mansion, and my profile of Brenda and her prized possession was in 2005.)

Brenda's most distinctive feature was (and probably still is) her haircut. Part bob, part mullet, her bangs extend way past where bangs usually would, past her ears, like a half bowl cut, before her thick dark hair falls to her shoulders. In my 2005 portrait of her, clutching a needlepoint-embroidered pillow that her mother gave her (reading: *Daughters are forever—I'm so glad you're mine*), she wears pearls and a blazer and a flowery brooch, looking very much like the fiftysomething Southern society woman she was. At the bottom of the photo on the *Independent Weekly*'s website, my name appears as a photo credit.

A few days after the original blobby photo was taken down, a new post appeared on the *Eater* LA site, the headline reading "Besha Rodell Circa 2005?" with that amazing photo of Brenda Pollard in all her glory.

The hilarity of the prospect of the chefs of Los Angeles posting photos of Brenda Pollard in their kitchens was matched only by the relief in how little damage that original blobby photo must have done. If someone who saw that photo could still believe I looked like Brenda, well, they could think I looked like just about any white lady under the age of sixty-five.

Along with all of this, the *Weekly*'s food editor, Amy, was becoming more and more agitated because I hadn't begun blogging. Nestled into my contract was a stipulation that along with a weekly review, one spring food issue, and compiling the annual "99 Essential Restaurants in Los Angeles" list, I was to write three blog posts *per day*. Unlike reviews, blog posts were this amorphous thing—what was I supposed to write about? That was up to me to figure out. And while I'd had a bit of a reprieve, arguing that it was impossible for me to jump right in while also trying to find a house and simply get my bearings in this town I'd spent less than two days in, total, before moving, Amy was getting antsy. "You have to start blogging," she'd growled at me when I went into the office to meet my new colleagues.

And so, my first blog post, my introduction to the fine people of Los Angeles, was titled:

WELCOME TO LOS ANGELES: YOU'RE SO UGLY!!!

Published on *Squid Ink*, *LA Weekly*'s food blog, on May 23, 2012

It would have been stupid to think I could take this job and avoid being compared to Jonathan Gold. I have to admit, though, I did not think the first comparison would have to do with our looks. And yet, that's exactly what happened when Eater L.A. posted a blurry photo taken at a panel I moderated at the Atlanta Food and Wine Festival (the photo has since been removed at the request of the photographer). "She's uglier than J. Gold . . . holly [*sic*] shit!!!!!" one commenter wrote. "Its [*sic*] Jonathan Gold in drag," another quipped.

Sigh. I don't know if I can rightfully blame Eater for trying to unmask me. The unmasking of critics seems counterproductive and dumb, but we (restaurant critics) kind of brought this on ourselves, being all self-important and wearing wigs and pretending we're spies. I certainly can't blame the commenters for being outrageous dicks—that's what the Internet was built for, right? Porn, food porn and acting out our worst selves from the vantage of . . . what would you call that? Oh yeah, anonymity.

And I've blathered on about anonymity a fair amount in the past myself. My basic point has always been that, yes, anonymity helps. Yes, it's important to try. Yes, it's impossible. I was never unmasked in Atlanta in the way Eater has been attempting here in L.A., but by the time I left there was hardly a chef in town who couldn't have picked me out. Word gets around. Atlanta is a small town in many ways. But that doesn't mean I didn't try to keep my photo out of the public eye, and to keep a low profile when reviewing restaurants. In most cases, I was able to get in a visit or two where no one noticed me.

In L.A., I have a chance to start fresh. I don't know any chefs or restaurant people here, and I hope to keep it that way. Will total anonymity be possible? Almost certainly not, although I'm fairly confident that the photos out there won't help people much in identifying me.

Which brings me to this past Monday, when Eater published another photo, claiming it is me circa 2005. Thus far, the photographer responsible for that photo has not demanded it be removed. Probably because the photographer in question may have a vested interest in people thinking that the photo is an accurate representation of my current appearance. You'd think Eater, with all its smarty-pants Internet savvy, would know the difference between a photo credit and a photo caption. But whatever. Chefs of L.A.—I look just like that! I haven't aged a day!

We landed in Silver Lake, because of course we did. It has trees! And a good elementary school. And the one and only house we went to see there was downright charming.

Shadowlawn Avenue is a very short street that ends in a cul-de-sac. It's best known as the home of the chandelier tree, a century-old camphor strung with dozens of vintage chandeliers that lit up, as if by magic, as the sun went down. The house we rented was a tidy California bungalow that had a bricked backyard with a gurgling fountain and a front garden full of flowers that attracted hummingbirds.

It didn't feel like home in the way the hulking old Atlanta house had; it felt like a sunny fantasy. Isn't that what Los Angeles is supposed to be? Everything smelled like orange blossoms, the lawns on the street were all neatly maintained by gardeners; it was beautiful and strange and disorienting.

After we moved in, Ryan and Felix had to return to the South for a few weeks, Ryan to get his truck to drive across the country, Felix to go to a summer camp in North Carolina near his grandparents that we'd already planned and paid for. Without my strange boys, I got a bit stuck.

The pressure of the newspaper's food blog, *Squid Ink*, was overwhelming. Three posts a day is a lot of posts, especially in a city you don't know. Amy had extremely high standards—she wanted it to look and feel like *Saveur*, but *Saveur* came out once a month and had a dozen articles and a six-figure budget to make that work. We—me, Amy, the interns, the freelancers—were collectively supposed to be publishing a dozen articles a day, punctuated by never-ending top-ten lists in order to meet page view goals in the millions.

Photos were a constant issue. Even if I could find three things to write about, the photos were never good enough. I am not and was not a photographer, I had no fancy SLR (Amy did, which she bought for herself, as the paper had no budget for these things that benefited them directly), and my just-okay iPhone photos were never up to snuff. Her standards are what made the blog so beloved (and it was beloved), but for those of us who were responsible for populating it, it was a sheer misery.

I have seen some of the greatest talents of my generation felled by the expectations of blogging in that era. People who went back to desk jobs after forays into writing. People who burned themselves out so thoroughly they're never, ever coming back.

I woke up every morning in a panic, with perhaps one post in mind, which I'd bang out quickly, then wait for Amy to pick it apart—the photo sucked, the tone wasn't right, she hated first person—while furiously scouring the internet for news or gossip or *something* to write about. In the afternoon, I'd get in my car and drive somewhere, often getting lost on the way, to find some dish, some cocktail, some cup of rare Japanese coffee, to populate the blog the next day. And then I'd go to dinner. In between all this, I was supposed to write a weekly review, one that would be picked apart by everyone online, because—shocker!—I was not Jonathan Gold. (As I heard it, Jonathan had been pressured for years to contribute to the blog, but never had.)

The ironic thing about the blogs was that they were supposed to change everything, but they were actually pretty short-lived. They required huge resources, they very rarely actually generated any profits, and they made us all miserable. Some, like *Eater*, morphed into something more closely resembling a traditional editorial website. Most—like the *New York Times*'s *Diner's Journal*—just eventually went away. And professional restaurant reviewing doesn't look that different today from how it did pre-blogs. Sure, there are TikTok and Instagram and influencers, and because of those things and the decimation of alt weeklies and small newspapers, there are far fewer critics now than there were a decade ago. But the day-to-day work of a traditional critic isn't that different from how it was in the days of Craig Claiborne.

During those first weekends in LA, when Felix and Ryan were gone and I was alone, I shut down. I sat in my new sunny living room and drank negronis and watched *Mad Men*. And read through Twitter to see all the snarky things people were saying about me. And missed Atlanta. And wondered how my life had changed so much so quickly.

When the boys got back (Ryan driving across the country in under three days in order to make it home in time for our anniversary), Felix took to California immediately. He wanted to learn to skateboard. He made friends fast; for once, he didn't feel like a weirdo. His school was amazingly diverse, with the kids of movie producers and the kids of domestic workers all shoved in together. Some of the parents had their snobberies, their cliques, but the kids didn't seem to adhere to those prejudices. Which was good for Felix: I, as always, was terrible at ingratiating myself with other parents, even the ones who tried hard to befriend me.

I was extremely lonely, which was partially of my own doing and partially because I left a whole community in Atlanta and didn't particularly want, or have the energy, to fit into a new one. I'd go walking through the hills above the Silver Lake reservoir, surrounded by jacaranda and bougainvillea, marveling at the houses tucked into the hillsides and think,

This is one of the most beautiful neighborhoods in the world. How can I possibly be unhappy living here?

That, plus the extreme weirdness of the city, slowly seduced me. And of course, there was the food.

It's hard to imagine now, but in 2012, LA had not been recognized as one of the world's great food cities by almost anyone who didn't live there. Even Anthony Bourdain, the intrepid explorer, admitted to not getting LA, struggling to love it.

It's not always easy to love! Unlike Paris and New York and London, it hides its charms. You have to know its secrets or you'll wind up on Hollywood Boulevard avoiding the syringes on the sidewalk while looking for something, anything worth eating. When I arrived, the more famous the neighborhood, the worse the food.

But, fuck, when you found it? The tacos, obviously, and the abundance of any type of regional Mexican or Chinese food you could desire were revelatory. But more surprising to me: the strip mall sushi, of which even the least lauded would have been the best sushi restaurant in most American cities. The ramen! Good god, I'd not had anything like it before, and then to realize it was only the beginning, that the varieties and options were unending. The Thai food, the Lebanese food, the Armenian food. The understanding that no matter how hard you tried, no matter how long you looked, there would always be something else to uncover, something else to surprise you. No wonder the obsessive cataloging of this world became Jonathan's lifelong obsession. LA is like an edible puzzle you'll never solve, but the trying is pure pleasure.

I was amazed by the number of restaurants that hadn't changed a bit since 1940 or 1950, not the décor, not the food, nothing. My vintage-loving heart swelled at the lounges where my maternal grandfather (the sometimes LA screenwriter) probably drank, and where the food and the cocktails and the whole feel had never changed.

And even in terms of modern restaurants, there were things for me to say, things that, as far as I could tell, other people were not saying. I instituted a star rating system at the *Weekly*, which annoyed the Jonathan acolytes even more. But since he'd done away with stars at the daily paper, I felt as though the city needed some kind of restaurant ranking system. I'd always worked with stars, so it felt natural.

Was I also trying to figure out how to make myself important in a town that already had its GOAT? Absolutely.

There was a status quo in LA restaurants, a flashiness and a defensiveness and an understanding that when it came to "serious" food, San Francisco was going to dominate. But what a weird world in which to try to succeed as a chef, what a fascinating place to ride that razor-thin line between appealing to the people with the money and the people with taste. I have a very well-developed theory that there are two types of chefs: the devotional chef (the one who is trying to make the perfect nonna pasta; the one who's a scholar of a particular genre and is aiming to channel perfection in that genre) and the ego-driven chef (the one who is following his own brilliance and nothing more), and I don't think I'd have made that clear distinction if Los Angeles hadn't served it to me on a dry-ice-smoking platter.

Even at home, we marveled: How are these avocados so good? How is it that the fruit trees in our neighborhood produce citrus more citrusy than any citrus that ever citrussed? The South has better tomatoes, better seasonal fruit in general (although my favorite peaches of all time—tiny, pointy, sweet/sour things—came from a gnarly old tree wedged between a duplex and a medical facility on Rowena Avenue in Silver Lake; I made Felix crazy by driving our truck into the medical building's driveway and making him climb on the roof to pick them). But California had sea urchin that tasted like floral sex perfume, tortillas that made me want to cry, fresh-kill halal butchers where you could walk in and ask for a rabbit and they'd say, "You want a white or brown one?" And when they gave it to you, after slaughtering it out back, you could take it home to fry up the liver and it would still be warm from the body heat of the animal.

I still miss everything about that side of LA. In my bones.

• • •

The stupid stuff was fun, too.

At the first restaurant I reviewed for *LA Weekly*, Govind Armstrong's Post & Beam in Crenshaw, Denzel Washington sat in a corner booth, his arms stretched out along the banquette like he owned the place. There was Natalie Portman, pregnant, hiking up the Griffith Park trail. There were Drew Barrymore and Marisa Tomei, both at the newly imported from New York Rao's in Hollywood on the same night, saying gushing hellos to each other.

There was the time I went to Rock & Brews, the KISS restaurant, with Paul Stanley. His publicist offered the meeting, and I couldn't refuse. I mainly wanted to figure out why rock stars opened restaurants. We talked for over an hour while delighted patrons approached, uber-fans who couldn't believe he was actually there. He was charming, and so gracious, and insisted that he really only did it because he wanted to offer his fans a place to go where they could rock out, and drink beer (even though he doesn't drink), and also bring their kids; there was a large playground in one corner of the restaurant and endless television screens all around playing KISS concert footage. I never wrote anything about it, but I do have a photo of Paul and me somewhere on my phone, me looking constipated, Paul looking like "the most attractive sixty-year-old lady I've ever seen," according to my friend Gwynedd.

There was the time *Food & Wine* magazine got me to go up to a mansion on Mulholland Drive and watch as Harrison Ford and his son Ben (a chef) barbecued chicken together, after which I had to sit with Indiana Jones and try to get him to talk to me about said barbecued chicken. He was having none of it until I said, "Lots of actors actually like talking about food. But we don't have to. I can ask you about *Star Wars* if you want." That worked; he laughed and then talked. I didn't ask him for a picture because it would have ruined my tough guy act, and I'm still pissed I didn't.

There are two LAs: the one people think about that's full of Kardashians and glam nightclubs and Rodeo Drives, and then there's the LA that everyone actually lives in. You can pretty much ignore the Hollywood part, and

I pretty much did—I rarely reviewed the stupid celebrity restaurants that opened there (other than Rao's), and I figured out quickly that the food was almost universally bad in places like Beverly Hills and Malibu (and also at Rao's). But living on the periphery, having those chance encounters, occasionally walking into that world could be a blast.

We lived in our sunny little house, and I tried hard to do well at my job, and we had as much fun as we possibly could. Ryan found work, first as a chef at the in-house restaurant at William Morris, the talent agency in Beverly Hills, and then at a nonprofit where he taught ex-prisoners cooking skills for the workplace. Slowly, I made a place for myself in the ecosystem of the LA food world. Slowly, *Eater* stopped mentioning Jonathan every time they mentioned me. (They did give me my own nickname, B-Rod, which I treasure to this day for its glorious, snarky, clever stupidity.) Did I ever feel at home in LA? Not really; the light was too white, the hills too brown, the ocean too cold. But as a magical fantasy, I loved it all the same.

The guy who was responsible for creating and maintaining the chandelier tree, a dude named Adam who looked and acted a lot like Perry Farrell, lived in the house with the yard that the tree sprang from, and he had an open-gate policy. There was a trampoline in his yard under the tree, and all the kids on the street jumped there. Felix's trampoline had been sold when we left Atlanta—I had no expectation we'd have space for it in LA, and maybe there was too much sadness in it after all the tears spilled on it during the *Creative Loafing* pity party. Adam's trampoline was Felix's consolation prize. We went up to his house and jumped on it all the time.

One evening, as the sun started to set, Felix and I lay on the trampoline in exhaustion after jumping for over an hour. Felix started to talk about metaphysics, as eleven-year-olds will, and the afterlife, and the way of the world.

"I hope reincarnation isn't real," he said, holding my hand, his tousled blond hair making him look as much a California boy as if he'd been born in this sunshine, us looking up into the branches of the tree and the sky beyond.

"Why?"

"Because my life is so good. I don't really want another one."

At that instant, the sun got low enough that all thirty-six chandeliers in the tree illuminated, making us gasp in delight. The breeze was warm; the birds flitted around; it smelled like flowers.

It was the best moment of my life. Nothing else will ever come close. There's no melancholy in that statement. I'm just lucky it happened.

I only met Jonathan once. We were often at the same events, but he was always surrounded by fans and other food journalists, and the thought of introducing myself to him in public, in front of the very people who were actually invested in the Besha-versus-Jonathan myth, was unthinkable.

I also saw him a couple of times dining with his family in restaurants where my family and I were also eating. There, too, it felt too exposed and awkward to approach his table and too likely to draw attention to myself during review meals. The thing I remember the most about those moments was Felix's fascination with Jonathan's kids. "They're like me," he said, in awe that there were other people in the world who had grown up being dragged to restaurants, whose whole family life revolved around eating and drinking and talking about the eating and drinking, who had childhoods disrupted by the work of criticism.

I heard through the grapevine that Jonathan liked to be mildly snarky about me, though the gossip mill is cruel and often not based in reality. People he was close with were pointedly snarky about me, on social media and in blog posts. (Including some truly bizarre missives from chef Nancy Silverton's partner—Nancy and Jonathan were close friends—who ran a website that was part satire, part news, part performance art.) I sometimes felt bad about being the first to review a talented up-and-coming chef, because if I covered that chef, then Jonathan would often ignore them—and they certainly needed his endorsement more than my own.

Jonathan never followed me on social media, never acknowledged me in any way. It was odd, particularly given the warm welcome I'd had in Atlanta from fellow critics and food writers, but I can't say I blame him. After I left *CL*, they hired my intern to be the food editor, a young woman whom I mentored and believed in. But I couldn't bear to read her work, couldn't bear to root for her success, even though she absolutely had to take the job—anyone would. Supporting her, even in my head, let alone in public, was too much to ask. It was too painful to think that someone else might benefit from gaining a position that I'd helped to make important, to see someone with the title that had formed me and then been taken from me. I don't like the part of me that felt that way, but I couldn't help feeling it.

Even though he quit and was not fired, even though he had a goddamned Pulitzer, I assume that Jonathan felt somewhat similarly about me. I assume a lot of things.

Eventually, years into my tenure at *LA Weekly*, I was on the campus of Santa Monica College, having just recorded a segment for KCRW's show *Good Food*. Jonathan was a regular on the show, and as I left the studio, I saw him ambling across campus toward the radio station, long, wavy red hair flowing, iconic suspenders in place. I stopped him, told him who I was, and said it was funny we'd never met. He agreed, made some small talk and was completely pleasant, and then went on his way. And that was it.

In some parts of my brain, I lump Jonathan in with the older men in the industry who dismissed me and mocked me: the ones who guffawed at me during the James Beard Awards after-party, the ones who talked down to me on social media and at conferences.

And in some parts of my brain, I think of him as wholly benevolent: a person who created a path for me at an extremely vulnerable time in my life, a person who made the position I held that much more important than it would have been otherwise because he made it important.

Most of the time, I wish I could see him the way the rest of the world sees him: with unabashed reverence; as the patron saint of food, and Los Angeles, and a certain brand of symphonic writing to which none of us will ever, ever live up.

Interlude

The Celebrity Shepherd

First published in *Modern Farmer*, 2013, immediately following our move to LA

My flight from Atlanta to Los Angeles is boarding in 15 minutes, but I answer the call. "Besha!" Craig Rogers' voice comes through the line, loud and smiling. "How are you, dear? It's your own personal shepherd!"

"Your own personal shepherd" is a term Craig Rogers uses a lot, and he has become the personal shepherd to enough chefs up and down the East Coast, and particularly throughout the South, that he's now one of the best-known farmers in the country. It's a distinction that's at once impressive and inconsequential—the farmer-as-celebrity pool is awfully small.

He asks how I'm doing and I tell him I'm anxious. "I'm on my way to L.A. for a job interview," I say.

"Well . . ." he says, searching for an appropriate response. "We'd sure miss you in the South."

Then he launches into the reason he's called. He's looking for an Atlanta location for his "Lambs and Clams" party, an impromptu-feeling gathering he held with Travis Croxton of Rappahannock River Oysters after the Charleston Food & Wine Festival. In Charleston, a party at midnight off the back of a truck down near the water was charming, and many of the chefs and food personalities associated with the festival showed up to eat lamb and clams and drink from the mason jar Rogers passed around. I can't see a similar party working quite so well in downtown Atlanta, but Rogers is undeterred.

He also wants to tell me about some farmers he knows who were selling milk to a large cheese producer, but were never paid. Legal action has begun. "But I'm thinking the best way for this to come to a resolution," Rogers says to me as the boarding process begins, "is for there to be some media attention." I tell him I think he's right, although I don't know who exactly would want to print a story about a legal dispute among sheep farmers.

"I just think that with all the love and feel-good stuff people are always talking about when it comes to small farmers," he says, getting worked up, "people also ought to know the flip side. It's hard to be out here on your own. People think of farmers and they think of sunshine and planting seeds and all that, but this is a business, and we get ripped off. I just think people ought to hear about that as well."

Three months later, I'm riding on the back of a golf cart that Rogers is driving. I'm holding a PBR and we're careening through the pasture of his stunningly beautiful southern Virginia farm. "Look down," he says. "Now say something nice about my grass."

"Nice grass," I say, and I mean it. It's been a good year, weather-wise, here in Patrick Springs, Virginia. In the foothills of the mountains the grass underneath us is thick and, to me, the color of heaven. This is my first trip back to the South since moving to L.A., and what I don't say to Rogers is that all this green, all that vivid life-giving grass, is making me feel as though my heart might burst.

L.A. is nice. But it is not very green.

The softly tumbling hills of the pasture are dotted with tents. In the distance, the Blue Ridge mountains rise, living up to their name in a blue-gray haze. Rogers owns 100 acres, but he farms close to 1,000. Unlike many other meat farmers who have become semi-celebrities in the food world (Will Harris, Bill Niman), Rogers does not sell meat produced on farms outside his own.

This is no ordinary day at the farm. It's the first day of Lambstock, Rogers' annual party for chefs and "friends of the farm," a three-day bacchanal that's achieved legendary status in the restaurant industry. Those tents in the field belong mainly to chefs and cooks, some of whom have traveled thousands of miles to spend a few days camped in Rogers' sheep pasture.

I first heard about Lambstock from Mike Lata, the James Beard Award–winning chef from Charleston. "It's this party in a field," he said, swirling whisky in his glass on the back landing of an Atlanta restaurant. "For chefs and cooks. We just get together and drink and cook and get to be ourselves. There's no media there, just a bunch of guys hanging out. It's so awesome."

Rogers conceived of Lambstock as a thank you to the industry that supports him, and 2012 was the third year of what Rogers calls "a party in my backyard."

"These guys work so hard," he says, speaking of the chefs and cooks he supplies. "I wanted to give them a few days where they could just relax and be themselves." That theme "be yourself" comes up a lot when people talk about Lambstock. These days, well-known chefs see a lot of each other at events and food festivals around the country, but there's a sense that because of the public and media, chefs have to constantly be "on," the face of their restaurants, salesmen for their cookbooks. Lambstock is a place where they can just come and hang out and have fun, drink, build fires, swear, and cook for each other.

In previous years, Rogers has been protective of Lambstock. In 2011, a large sign was posted at the welcoming table in his driveway declaring that no tweets or articles were allowed without Rogers' express permission. In 2012, he gave all that up, and as a result there was much more media attention given to Lambstock, including a fawning blog post on the *New York Times* dining blog. "I was trying to protect Lambstock in the past," Rogers says. "I wanted the chefs to feel that they could come here and not be scrutinized. But they themselves were telling everyone what was happening here, so I thought 'why bother?'" But still, Lambstock remains a party for the chefs, not an event for the public. It isn't about promotion. Except, of course, for Craig Rogers.

At festivals, Rogers is a striking figure, six foot one, rotund in overalls, wearing a wide-brimmed hat, carrying a shepherd's crook, and usually standing beside one of his lambs roasting on a spit. He would be almost comical if he weren't so endearing and passionate. Rogers is fond of saying "I'm just a simple shepherd," but of course this is a lie. He's as complex as they come.

Rogers was born in Vermont and had a great aunt who was a dairy farmer, but that was the extent of his agrarian background. His original career was in academics. He has a Ph.D. in Chemical Engineering from Virginia Tech, and was the Dean of the College of Engineering at the University of South Carolina. Google Rogers with the right search terms and you'll come across reports of research he championed to reduce helicopter noise and how, in the 80's, he established something called the "Smart Materials and Structures Laboratory." He says he and his wife were looking for a retirement farm when they saw a sheepdog trial on campus. "I thought it was the most amazing thing."

They bought the farm in 2002 and got into competitive sheepdog trials. "I noticed early on that the guy with the most sheep usually won. So I became a bit of a sheep herder. It got to the point where eventually I had to find something to do with them."

Having traveled and dined quite a bit in his academic life, Rogers had always loved lamb. The first lamb he slaughtered, he says, "was the most horrific piece of meat I had ever had." So he started researching breeds, trying to find out which lamb would taste the best. "I set out to find something I would enjoy. It didn't have much to do with chefs."

Once he finally got his lamb tasting the way he wanted it to, he tried to find a chef who might appreciate it. "I got it in my head that Bryan Voltaggio was the guy," he says. It turns out he was right. Voltaggio introduced him to some other chefs, who introduced him to chefs in Charleston, who introduced him to Sean Brock, the chef at Charleston's McCrady's and one of the most feverishly adored young chefs in the country in recent years. "And for me, Sean Brock was like the parting of the Red Sea."

Rogers has figured out what many farmers have yet to turn to their advantage: that America is preoccupied not just with food but with chef culture. Also unlike many other farmers, Rogers has learned to sell his own product. That sense of salesmanship has him befriending and selling directly to chefs, as well as working hard to get his name out there and promote his sheep farm, Border Springs, as a brand. He attends festivals, makes connections with journalists and food celebrities, throws parties, and is generally everywhere all the time. He stands as a symbol of the changing nature of farming, where farmers come out of the field and smack into the middle of our food-obsessed culture.

And he has no signs of slowing: he was recently part of a dinner at the James Beard house, an honor usually only bestowed on chefs or restaurateurs, not producers. He has hired executive chefs to help him build "lamb shops" in historic markets in D.C. and Philadelphia, next-generation butcher counters where meat from his farm is for sale alongside chef-driven to-go items. "People don't know what to do with lamb," he says. "You have to show them." (He's long been part of local farmers markets all over the South, usually traveling thousands of miles in a week to get from market to market—my mother has run across him on Saturday morning in Winston-Salem N.C. on the same weekend he's been spotted by friends in D.C. and Baltimore.)

Besides being everywhere and knowing everyone, he is now contemplating jumping into the restaurant business itself. A possible concept, location and business partners for a small restaurant in the D.C. area have arisen, and Rogers says he's "considering the possibilities."

People's reactions in the food community to Rogers' name vary from extreme affection to weary eye-rolls. "Why does he have to be at every damn thing?" one chef said to me recently. "It's just too much." There's an irony here, that the people I've come across who distrust Rogers' affection for attention are chefs—folks who have only very recently begun to enjoy the spoils of fame from what has traditionally been a blue collar profession. The problem with Rogers' approach, as I see it, is that he's too straightforward about his quest for notoriety. In the too-cool-for-school world of chef-dom, this is off-putting.

Rogers bristles at the notion that he's "everywhere," as more than one person has put it to me, or that he's too much of a self-promoter. Sitting in a field surrounded by sheep, it's hard to see him as anything but a guy trying to build a successful business. "Once people come out here to the farm, I stop getting calls from their restaurants asking for the shipping department," he says, alluding to the fact that *he's* the shipping, marketing, sales and lamb-birthing department. "I want these guys to see where their food comes from. I'm asking people to come enjoy my hospitality. I'm inviting you to a party in my back yard. Lambstock is about community, not self-promotion."

On my last night in Atlanta before moving to Los Angeles, I attended a dinner that was part of the Atlanta Food & Wine Festival. It was held at a mansion in one of the city's wealthiest neighborhoods, and as I pulled up the circular driveway I saw an odd sight. On the perfect green lawn in front of the castle-like house, a makeshift pen with six or seven sheep was set up. Rogers was standing beside them in full Scottish shepherd regalia: kilt, jacket, hat and shepherd's crook.

Like so many culinary extravaganzas these days, the dinner was supposed to honor the farmers and producers who make all our fancy eating possible, or so goes the farm-to-table mantra. At the end of the multi-course, boozy meal, which took place under twinkling lights in the mansion's manicured jewel box of a garden, Rogers was invited to say a few words. He stood tall in his kilt, and in front of 200 or so of Atlanta's (very tipsy) one percent, he launched into a 20-minute lecture on the history and misunderstanding of the shepherd.

He's talking about Thomas Jefferson (who brought the first Merino sheep to the United States). He's talking about slaves (who looked after Jefferson's sheep and moved out West during emancipation). He's talking about the birth of Christ. "And when the angels came to the shepherds in the pastures to announce the coming of Christ to indicate that this was the good news for everyone, they were referred to as *mere* sheep herders!" Rogers is fired up. I don't think many of us know what the hell he's talking about.

At Lambstock, I ask him why he thought it was important to stand up in front of all those people and try to explain to them the struggle of the shepherd. He sighs. "Look, here's the thing with the shepherd shtick," he says. "Even today, shepherds out west do not wish to be called shepherds, it's such a derogatory term. It's always been the disenfranchised who end up doing the shepherding work. We've never had the romance of cowboys. If anyone were to actually take a look at the history of shepherding, and how horrible humankind has been to a single profession, and it's generally because it's been a profession of the displaced. So if you could learn somehow to create respect for shepherds then you could create respect for anyone. Cowboys have a voice. I don't know who's the voice for the shepherd. And I just think it's an incredibly honorable profession. So if a bunch of rich people are going to eat my lamb and then offer me the stage? That's what they're going to hear."

When you arrive at Lambstock and drive down the long shady driveway of Border Springs Farm, one of Rogers' "volunteers" meets you with a golf cart to help transport your tent and belongings out to the field. Apparently word has gotten out that I'm a journalist working on a story, and one of his volunteers approaches me on a golf cart as I sit and watch the Lambstock guests arrive.

"That Craig. He sure likes to talk, don't he?" the guy, whose name is Steve Godfrey, says ominously. Godfrey's farmer's mustache conveys none of the irony of the 'staches and mutton chops of the arriving chefs. "Come talk to me later and I'll tell you about the *real* Craig Rogers." Before I can answer, he's driven off.

The juxtaposition of Godfrey and the chefs, some arriving with extra swagger on motorcycles, reminds me of something Rogers said to me once. "A lot of people in the food community talk a really good game. But it makes zero difference to the people living and farming in Patrick County, Virginia. I'd like to see *those* people's lives changed for the better by this food movement."

Later, I track Godfrey down and ask him to make good on his promise of an explanation of the *real* Craig Rogers.

"Four years ago today, the doctors decided they had to take my heart out and put it back together," Godfrey says, at first quietly but then with a fierce edge. "Craig come down while I was in the hospital and looked after my livestock and tended to my wife and kids. When I came home, he came and stayed with me for a week. Cooked my lunch, helped me get dressed." He pauses, to steady his voice. "That's what kind of guy he really is," Godfrey says.

He looks down and walks off. As he goes he calls out over his shoulder, "He still talks too damn much, though."

The Part of the Meal Where I Take Notes in the Bathroom

A THREE-PART HISTORY LESSON:
FOOD, DRINK, SERVICE

The best meals, the best restaurant reviews, the best memoirs do more: more than simply feed you; more than simply assign a thumbs-up or thumbs-down; more than just tell the story of one person's life. The best of all these things teaches you something bigger, about pleasure, about culture, about why we are who we are. In this way, I've tried to structure this book like a good meal, a good review, and—obviously and hopefully—a good memoir. If the amuse-bouche was my weird beginnings, the appetizer my early career, the entrée the part where I consider the world of criticism and where I fit into it, then this is the part of the meal where I scurry into the bathroom to take notes—the geeky part. The part where I try to give you more than a review or meal or life story and delve into the history that underpins the ways in which all of us eat, drink, and dine out.

We Are What We Eat

Delmonico's. James Beard. The Four Seasons. Julia Child. The Rainbow Room. Alice Waters. To hear most food writers tell it, these are the names that have shaped American gastronomy: people and places catering to a very specific type of diner.

Understanding these names is essential to understanding the way we see ourselves as a dining public, but they aren't particularly helpful in understanding how the majority of Americans actually eat, or how they dine out, or what's important to them when they do.

What prompts people to leave their homes and go to a restaurant? When considering fancy restaurants, the answer has historically been uninteresting—"Because I'm rich, so I can" is not a very insightful way to think about the culture of dining out. What about everyone else?

My writing career coincided with a massive change in dining culture, a shift that turned caring about food and restaurants into a populist sport when for so long it had been considered the frippery of the wealthy. But so much happened before that pivot took place; things that set the stage for it: chain restaurants, fast food, and more. How did it happen? Why? Who was responsible?

It was in Atlanta that I began to develop an obsession with the way normal people eat, as opposed to the way the food media at the time pretended people ate. I was working on our food issue, which was themed "Around the World in Atlanta," the premise of which was that you could eat your way around the globe without leaving the city. We profiled restaurants that transported diners to another place, another country. But for the centerpiece, I wanted to profile a restaurant that was wholly Atlantan, that captured the culture of dining in that particular city.

I suppose I could have picked one of the historic soul food joints, or somewhere like the Colonnade, a place that had been serving Sunday suppers to a cross section of the city—from church ladies to drag queens—since 1927. But even those places catered to a certain clientele, even if it was a beautifully diverse sampling. Where does everyone eat? What has Atlanta given the world?

I decided to profile Waffle House, which was founded in Avondale Estates, a suburb of Atlanta, in 1955. And in an effort to mirror the "around the world" theme, I decided to title the issue's central story "Around the Clock at Waffle House." The gimmick being, I would spend twenty-four hours at a Waffle House.

The story wove together my experience of sitting in the restaurant, one of the busiest in town, especially overnight since it was close to a lot of nightclubs, with the history of the business and my overall theory about the culture of Waffle House. An excerpt:

> As a hometown brand, Waffle House is far more regional than Coca-Cola. Driving south from the Northeast, or east from the West, signs for Waffle House along the interstate let you know you're home. There's something about the interior of a Waffle House that's comfortingly bland, like the vibe of a crappy motel room. You could be anywhere. Those round light fixtures, the yellow and white tiles, the counter with its plastic-backed stools. Waffle House excels at making each location feel almost exactly like all the others. The food is what it is: Cheap. (Did you know you can add a second waffle to your order for 99 cents? Did you know that a grilled cheese costs $1.90?) But I don't think many people come to Waffle House for the food. I think they come for the comfort of sameness.

This was in 2010, at a time before *Eater* ran loving odes to fast food, before *New York Times* critics might review Señor Frog's. It was pretty much unheard of for food writers to take middle- and lowbrow American food seriously. To read about the history of American gastronomy at the time, you'd think that the names I mentioned at the beginning of this chapter were responsible for the most important developments in the way we as a nation ate. In writing and thinking about Waffle House, I realized that there was this whole other history that was mostly being ignored outside of certain academic circles and that food writers were overlooking the true history of American restaurants for reasons that came down to not much more than snobbery. Because that alternative history? Was (and is) fascinating.

Waffle House was the beginning, for me, of an obsession with where we came from. If I was going to make my life's work be about the ways that we eat out, shouldn't I be considering the ways that everyone eats, not just the privileged few who eat in fancy or trendy restaurants? And shouldn't I know how those ways of eating out came to be?

I never stopped loving fancy restaurants, but my interest grew to encompass so much more. I became fixated on fair food, traveling with Felix to the Iowa State Fair in order to see if I could connect the curiosities of the fair concession stands to trends in chain restaurants (I could). I traced many of America's best-known indulgences (soda, ketchup, ice cream cones) back to the world's fairs of the 1800s. I deduced that the very idea of snacking was popularized at those fairs. And from fairs, I was led to cafeterias and the origins of the American restaurant—the origins of *fancy* American restaurants are fairly easy to trace and have been written about extensively. But again, I was far more interested in the ways in which regular people, working- and middle-class people, started eating outside their homes. And the cafeteria—introduced, like so much, via the fair—is a huge piece of that puzzle.

Cafeteria is a Spanish word meaning "coffee shop." It was commandeered for American purposes by a guy named John Kruger, who ran an exhibition at the 1893 Chicago World's Fair modeled on the smorgasbords he'd experienced in Europe. Kruger's exhibit didn't resemble what the cafeteria would become in many meaningful ways. But the word entered the American lexicon, just one more piece of our edible identity for which we have a world's fair to thank.

While the word came to America via Kruger, the YWCA of Kansas City, Missouri, established what many food historians believe to be the first example of the type of dining that became the American cafeteria in 1891, providing low-cost meals for workingwomen. Even earlier, in 1885, the Exchange Buffet opened in New York City, serving an exclusively male population. It was perhaps the first self-service restaurant. There were no plastic trays or steam tables at any of these early examples, but the idea of serving oneself in any capacity was new.

The trays and tray line were added in 1898 by a chain in New York City called Childs Restaurants. This combination of sit-down dining with a tray you loaded up at a tray line caught on all over the country and especially in California, which many people claim is the real birthplace of the cafeteria. In May 1905, a woman named Helen Mosher opened a restaurant in downtown Los Angeles that she called the Cafeteria, where customers chose their own food at a long counter and carried it on trays to their tables. This was not the first restaurant with that name—the New York Public Library's menu collection contains many menus from 1900 belonging to a New York City restaurant called the Cafeteria, but there is no evidence to suggest it actually served food in the cafeteria style. A restaurant in Boston opened in 1903 calling itself a "cafeteria" and operated without waiters, with guests serving themselves from steam tables. Despite these other earlier examples, it is Mosher who usually gets credit for the name *cafeteria* sticking to this style of dining, and her wildly successful restaurant spawned many imitators in LA and around California. Though the origins of the cafeteria are Eastern and Midwestern, even New Yorkers—who got plenty of cafeterias of their own over the next few years—thought of the genre as a California invention.

It's impossible to think about the cafeteria and what it means in

American life without thinking about the whole idea of lunch as a meal and how it's had to evolve over the last 150 years. Until the early twentieth century, lunch—like breakfast and dinner—was generally a meal eaten at the table with family. The rise of factories and the massive changes in working life saw many people going farther to their places of employment and needing lunch options that were quick and easy. Oftentimes lunch was packed at home and brought to work, but cafeterias and lunch counters began to crop up on city streets as an alternative to the bagged lunch. Before that, working-class Americans rarely ate in restaurants at all.

The big cities had saloons and oyster houses, and travelers ate at inns as part of the fee they paid for boarding. But the vast majority of Americans never ate anywhere but in their homes or at community gatherings, such as fairs, barbecues, and church potlucks. Cheap, efficient, and unpretentious, the cafeteria provided a dining out experience that could be enjoyed by all Americans, not just the elite.

Look, I don't know about you, but I find this shit *way* more interesting than whatever epiphany Julia Child had in France. That's cool, too, if that's your jam. It was certainly my father's jam, a man who cooked his way through Julia's books religiously and even befriended her in Cambridge when they were both living there. But my father's *main* jam was history (he was, among many other things, one of the world's foremost scholars on Martin Luther and spent much of his free time translating the writings of Luther from Latin to English). I never quite cottoned on to that history-obsessed side of my brain until I started wondering why there was so little curiosity around the way normal people eat out.

I wove this line of inquiry into my work as often as I could. In Los Angeles, I convinced my editors to allow me to review Outback Steakhouse, to grapple with my own Australian identity as seen through the lens of its best-known avatar in America, and to ask, not just "Is it good?" but "Why do people eat here?" (Read on to learn the answers to those pressing questions.) That question has formed the underpinning of much of the restaurant writing I've done since.

When *Punch* launched, in 2012, a new website dedicated to all things booze, it launched with stories about wine, stories about cocktails, and a story by me about the history and culture of the forty-ounce—its history and my own malt liquor–soaked adolescence. In 2013, I was asked to give a talk at the Southern Foodways Alliance annual fall symposium, the topic of that year's conference being pop culture. I wrote a talk about Cracker Barrel, interweaving the story of the chain with my own uneasy relationship with the South and becoming part of a Southern family (Ryan's). In researching Cracker Barrel, I stumbled into a whole other line of inquiry, about the rise of chain restaurants.

There are two men that Cracker Barrel—as well as every chain restaurant in America and beyond—have to thank for inventing the genre, and those are Fred Harvey and Howard Johnson. These pioneers understood changes in the ways Americans would travel and provided for those travelers' needs earlier and better than anyone else. America's chain restaurants sprouted from the country's dependence on rail lines, then turnpikes, and finally on interstates.

Credit for the concept of chain restaurants should probably go to Fred Harvey, who established his Harvey Houses beginning in 1876. Prior to Harvey, there had been multiple restaurants owned by one entity, and sometimes with a shared name, in large cities. But Harvey started the first national chain along the railways that ran from the West Coast through the Southwest and into the Midwest. Harvey himself had been an aspiring restaurateur as a young man and then worked for the railroads during the time when Americans were venturing west in great numbers. Having ridden the trains extensively himself, he set out to fix the well-known problem of terrible food at the depots along the way. A deal was struck with the Atchison, Topeka and Santa Fe Railway, in which they gave Harvey space at their depots for him to set up restaurants and would transport goods for those restaurants on their train cars free of charge. Any profits made would be kept by Harvey. The deal's underlying premise—that travelers would be grateful enough for decent food along the way to boost the railway's ticket sales significantly—proved correct.

The resulting Harvey Houses were the first restaurants to adopt many of the attributes we now associate with chains: they all adhered to a uniform architectural style, so they were easily identifiable before patrons even saw the signs; waitresses and other employees dressed identically; and the restaurants were placed strategically along travel routes. Harvey also came up with one of the first methods of consolidated distribution. He had a refrigerated boxcar that traveled twice a week between LA and Kansas City, bringing fresh California produce east and Midwestern meats on the return trip. By 1883, there were seventeen Harvey House restaurants stretching across the country, and they remained one of the most recognizable brands in America until their decline in the 1940s and '50s, when cars and then airlines became the country's preferred modes of transport.

But for most of the twentieth century, there was no more recognizable and pervasive chain restaurant than Howard Johnson's. Started as an ice cream stand in Massachusetts in 1926, Howard Johnson's pioneered the magic ingredient in chains, the component I lauded in that Waffle House story: the comfort of sameness. Harvey may have dabbled in providing similar experiences across his restaurants, but Johnson was the first to standardize everything, from the iconic orange roof, to the twenty-eight flavors of ice cream, to the look and behavior of his waitstaff.

Johnson was also the original wildly successful restaurant franchiser. He sold his first franchise in 1935, and by 1939, there were 150 Howard Johnson's stretching the entire length of the East Coast. A key strategy of Howard Johnson's was understanding new developments in automobile travel and placing restaurants along roadways, including the new turnpikes being built in the first half of the twentieth century. Howard Johnson's signs along highways alerted travelers when there was a Howard Johnson's coming up two miles ahead—a strategy that was very successfully adopted by Cracker Barrel in later decades.

Many restaurant companies did not survive the Depression and World War II, but Johnson kept the company afloat by securing government contracts. And when the war usurped most of the young men who would have been cooks, Johnson figured out ways to centralize the preparation of the food, leaving only basic assembly necessary on location. While the obvious descendants of Howard Johnson's are the sit-down chains—the Cracker Barrels and Outback Steakhouses and Red Lobsters and Applebee's of the world—fast food also owes a huge debt to the company's legacy, thanks to its production and franchise models.

In the '50s, the first Howard Johnson's motor inns opened, adding another important category to the comfort of sameness America so admires: the budget motel room. There was a time when Howard Johnson's was basically the only place where many middle-class American families would eat or stay during road trips. My mother, the kind of ex-hippie parent who never let me drink soda or chew gum or eat fast food, nonetheless has a powerful longing for Howard Johnson's, remembering stops there during her childhood with the kind of golden glow only childhood nostalgia can bestow. When we arrived in America in the early '90s, eating clam strips at a roadside Howard Johnson's was one of the first experiences she was eager to share. I was excited mainly because as a teenager I was a predictably enthusiastic Kurt Vonnegut fan, and I knew the brand through his short story "Welcome to the Monkey House," in which all Howard Johnson's locations had adjacent suicide parlors, meant to tempt the members of a future overpopulated society that had discovered a means to eternal life. The fact that, in 1968 when that story was published, Vonnegut imagined Howard Johnson's as the most recognizable and ubiquitous location in American life ought to give you some idea of its success.

Our early '90s meal there was just in time—the company was bought and sold and merged with other businesses over the following few years. The last Howard Johnson's, in Lake George, New York, closed in 2022. But the American appetite for the comforts of consistency across state lines and in convenient places was fully entrenched.

Today, food media is far more open to discussing and examining and even celebrating the ways that most Americans actually eat. The "I love a thing that has been traditionally looked down upon" is a bona fide genre of food essay, and James Beard Awards have been won for articles covering chicken tenders (and *cough, cough* the forty-ounce). Since my Waffle House story, twenty-four hours in a Waffle House has become a bit of a trope, with *Bon Appétit* magazine doing a version of that same story in 2015 (albeit with the cooperation of the restaurant—my twenty-four hours was fully gonzo) and some dude going viral in 2021 after losing his fantasy football league; the full day at Waffle House was his penance. But I'm still fascinated with these histories, and I think the comfort of sameness explains a lot more than just familiar dining rooms and that odd serenity that comes over many of us when we step into a motel room that looks like every other motel room. Molten chocolate cake? Tuna tartare? Restaurant critics love to bemoan these ubiquities because we eat out too much and get bored of the repetition, but restaurants serve them because people *buy* them. Over and over and over.

And to state the obvious: knowing our history helps us to understand our present. If restaurants, how they evolved and became part of wider American culture, came first in my line of inquiry, other facets of the food world followed. And perhaps, for the first time, my decades-old proclamation to my mother—that my interest in food, in booze, in waitressing was just as noble as her interest in politics or art—became properly intellectually justifiable.

OUTBACK STEAKHOUSE REVIEW: PLEASE DON'T CALL THIS FOOD AUSTRALIAN

Published in *LA Weekly*, June 2013

Consider the Bloomin Onion.

Two thousand calories.

One hundred sixty-one grams of fat.

Crispy, oily, sweet, crunchy. A big slick of salt and grease. Slightly disgusting. Completely addictive.

The Bloomin Onion is an almost perfect example of the gluttony and fun inherent in the tradition of American fair food. The Bloomin Onion is a triumph of Americana.

You'll notice that I said "American fair food" and not "Australian." That's because, despite its marketing, nothing about Outback Steakhouse, home of the Bloomin Onion, is Australian. Don't be fooled by the guy on the ads with the thick Australian accent. Don't be fooled by the "Aussie cheese fries" or the "walkabout soup" on the menu. Outback Steakhouse is 100 percent American.

Lest anyone think me an unbiased observer, let me dissuade you of that notion. The whole concept of Outback Steakhouse is an affront to me. Australia is my country of birth, and I'll admit I'm touchier than most—many Australians are quite cheerful about their status as the funny drunk uncle of the world.

But that reputation was no fun for me when I arrived at an American high school with purple hair and a bad attitude right on the heels of *Crocodile Dundee*, the 1986 movie that depicted a brawny, endearingly clueless Australian crocodile wrestler. I wanted to talk about The Cure; people wanted to ask me about kangaroos. "Are you from the Outback?" kids at school would ask, snickering, and I'd think of my hometown, Melbourne, with its Victorian houses and old Italian cafés and leafy avenues, and sneer to keep from crying.

Just the name "Outback" makes me angry—in the cynical hands of public relations professionals, it's lost all meaning. The dry center of Australia is many things: an inhospitable desert, a wonder of nature, sacred land to our indigenous population. In America it's just a word attached to all things Australian to conjure a dumb guy in a funny hat who says "bloke." Given that I blame *Crocodile Dundee* and its Outback-flavored aftermath for ruining my adolescence, it's no wonder I'd never set foot in an Outback Steakhouse before.

And yes, Outback Steakhouse is in some ways a direct result of *Crocodile Dundee*. It was the film's huge popularity that inspired the four American founders to brand the restaurant, founded in Tampa in 1988, as Australian. None of those founders—Chris Sullivan, Robert Basham, Tim Gannon and Trudy Cooper—had ever been to Australia. Restaurant-industry veterans of chains like Bennigan's, Steak & Ale and Chili's, the quartet had one big idea: Contrary to popular belief, Americans were not looking for healthier options. Quite the opposite. They wanted steak. And fat. And, apparently, battered and deep-fried onions specifically engineered to pack as much fat and grease into every molecule of their being as is allowable by the laws of physics.

As a matter of fact, the owners of Outback specifically *didn't* visit Australia because they didn't even want to take the chance that they'd be influenced by its culture or cuisine. They just wanted to think of it as cute and fun and full of fuzzy animals and people who talk funny. If there's a better symbol for the way that most Americans have approached me over the years about my Australianness, I can't think of it.

I decided to take on Outback for all these reasons. Like any good nemesis, it had to be faced. I also was intrigued because people love it. Here's the thing about these successful chain restaurants that most food obsessives don't want to admit: There's a reason people love them. And it's not just price and familiarity and convenience, although those things play a big part in their popularity. There is also something about the food that humans with taste buds very much appreciate.

On my first visit, to the Glendale location, we slid into a booth adjacent to the bar, and I eyed the almost-Aboriginal art adorning the walls. As our waitress arrived to introduce herself (she didn't say "G'day," thank sweet baby Jesus, though I'm sure she probably was supposed to), the Men at Work song "Land Down Under" started to play on the stereo system. "Oh my God, this is awesome," my American husband beamed as he watched me try not to wriggle out of my skin with 23 years of pent-up disgust.

Asking someone for "shrimp on the barbie" was maybe one of the hardest things I've ever done. I've spent years railing against the very concept, declaring that I've never had a barbecued shrimp because it's basically made-up—people don't even call them "shrimp" in Australia, they call them "prawns."

"We'll have the shrimp on the barbie. And the Toowoomba pasta. And the Bloomin Burger." My soul cracked at the edges with each word.

Yet it was hard to deny, when those shrimp arrived, that they were pretty good: well-seasoned, fat, cooked pretty much perfectly. The puce-colored dipping sauce accompanying them was salty and slutty and gross—or drunk-food delicious, depending upon your mood. You can say that about almost anything at Outback Steakhouse.

The Toowoomba pasta is famous for being one of the most calorific entrees on the planet. (During my visits, just eating a few bites here and there of each dish still made it practically impossible to leave before consuming 1,000-plus calories.) They somehow manage to cram 1,344 calories into one bowl of fettuccine with shrimp, crawfish, mushrooms and Parmesan cream sauce.

It's a regular-sized bowl, but eating it is like eating cream-and-seafood-flavored buttercream icing—big, steaming, gloppy mouthfuls of savory icing. It's disconcerting, and I felt like death for hours afterward (and I ate a total of perhaps three or four mouthfuls). And yet: The seafood tastes fresh and sweet; it was harder to stop shoveling into my mouth than I'd like to admit.

And the steaks? The steaks aren't very good. But they're big as hell and cooked right and incredibly cheap for something as inherently decadent as steak. They aren't thin and gray; they're big and meaty. They just have no tang or depth. And maybe it's just me, but sometimes I feel as though I can taste the barely perceptible flavor of misery in a piece of meat. The cow's misery? The cook's misery? I've declared more than once that you can taste love in food, so why not misery?

Still, it's hard to argue with a $20 filet that's as big as your head and comes with a wedge salad covered in glop and a substantial side. If I were a kid with $60 in my pocket and a girl who needed impressing on a Saturday night, I could see the appeal. Baby, I love you so much, Imma take you to Outback and you can get the big steak.

And then, of course, there's the Bloomin Onion, Outback's signature dish, its crowning glory. Over a number of meals at Outback and a number of weeks of thinking about Outback, I had a lot of conversations with people about the Bloomin Onion.

At first, people would hesitate, waiting to see if they'd be shunned for proclaiming their Bloomin love to me, a grumpy Australian, and a food critic no less. But once prompted a little, the floodgates opened.

"Why is a Bloomin Onion so much more delicious than any onion ring?!?" one friend demanded passionately late one night, a few drinks in. Another admitted that said onion was the one reason she secretly looked forward to her annual visit to her small hometown, where a visit to Outback with the folks was the blowout meal of the trip, and the Bloomin Onion the highlight.

After ordering this juggernaut twice, America, I say embrace the Bloomin Onion in all its disgusting glory. Just know that it's yours, not mine. And definitely not Australia's.

We Are What We Drink

Our TGI Friday's server looks concerned. While there are many reasons he might give pause—the fact that my party of three is drinking so very many cocktails, or that our boneless chicken wings have gone mostly uneaten, or that my friend Greg has turned a disquieting shade of pink—the server is balking at my drink order. "It's very sweet, that one," he cautions. "We put the cotton candy on the top and then pour the vodka over."

It should be alarming to be told by a TGI Friday's server that the drink you've just ordered is "sweet," because sweet is really the only flavor profile available on this cocktail menu. I've already had the Barbados Rum Punch, the Ultimate Long Island Iced Tea, the Strawberry Henny—none of those came with a warning when ordered. But apparently the Pink Punk Martini is caution-worthy.

I press ahead. "Let's do it," I say.

I'm about an hour into an experiment at the TGI Friday's in Union Square, New York City, in which I've endeavored to bring together my smartest booze-obsessed friends and collectively drink our way through the TGI Friday's cocktail menu. My dear friend Greg Best, who has been an integral part of Atlanta's cocktail evolution, happened to be in the Northeast for a family vacation and agreed to take the train down for the day and join me. And Dave Wondrich, who is basically a demigod in the drinks world, also signed on to help. There aren't many people who are referred to as "cocktail historians," but that's a title regularly applied to Dave. He's also one of my favorite humans, which is an important attribute if you're going to be spending hours and hours with someone trying to force down Ultimate Long Island Iced Teas and Pink Punk Martinis. I had a lot of questions and a lot of drinks to try, and God bless him, Dave was willing to be subjected to both.

Sometimes my food history obsession unfurled in libraries, poring over old menus, digging through scholarly texts. And sometimes, when I was very lucky, it found its purpose while drinking with people I love.

Why TGI Friday's? Because that chain in particular plays an important role in the era of American drinking I was hoping to understand.

A decade or so ago, Dave began referring to this era as the "dark ages": that period in drinking after tiki died and before the booze revolution, when sexual innuendo and massive amounts of sugar were the most important ingredients in American cocktails. The Sex on the Beach, the Harvey Wallbanger, the Fuzzy Navel—for decades, these drinks and their brethren reigned supreme on the cocktail menus of bars all over America. Interestingly, the actual Dark Ages were not called the Dark Ages until they were over; in retrospect, humanity recognized the bleakness of the past. To call America's fondness for sickly sweet drinks the "dark ages" presupposes that we've moved on. Yes, there are craft cocktail bars even in small-town America these days. Yes, a whole industry and profession have arisen out of the movement toward better drinking. But like in many other instances, we're ignoring the way the majority of people still behave. In the chain restaurants of America, the dark age of cocktails roars on. And so I set out to pickle myself in darkness, one drink at a time, while simultaneously learning about why America has spent most of the last sixty years mired in boozy concoctions that taste more like the candy aisle and less like anything that might put the word *adult* in the phrase *adult beverage*.

TGI Friday's did not invent this type of drink. But its founder, Alan

Stillman, did invent the type of bar that would go on to become the main purveyor of mid-late-twentieth-century cocktail culture. Because before TGI Friday's opened in 1965, young men and women rarely drank together in bars at all.

Understanding TGI Friday's, and understanding who was drinking what prior to the 1960s (and why), might seem like pure nerdery. But when I started reviewing restaurants, cocktails were barely part of the conversation. Greg is one of the people who changed that, certainly in Atlanta and the South, and all of a sudden, the "cocktail revolution" was upon us. Bartenders like Greg were thinking about drinks as thoroughly as chefs were thinking about food. It was a massive change, and, like the history of American restaurants, I felt as though I needed to understand where we came from, culturally, to have a decent handle on where we are and where we're headed. The ways in which culture and history affect what we eat and drink are the parts of my job that I find most thrilling— otherwise, it's all just: Is it good? Which is a necessary question, but it isn't the most interesting question. Good restaurant criticism is always about so much more than that.

"What's interesting to me is not that everything got so crappy," Dave is telling me as I wait for my Pink Punk Martini. "It's that the crappiness was a rational response to what people were handed in the '60s. Booze had gotten worse and worse. Old people were so cranky by then. All they wanted was straight gin."

If you spend a lot of time thinking about cocktail culture, you hear plenty about Prohibition and what it did to gut the great tradition of American drinking that sprang up in the previous century. The history of the cocktail is long and fascinating, and if you want the full story, I recommend Dave's book *Imbibe!*, which gives as good an accounting as any. But the short version is this: the Brits invented punch, but the cocktail as we know it was an American innovation. From the mid-1800s up until the beginning of Prohibition, bartending was a thriving and respected profession in the United States. When alcohol was outlawed in 1920, most of those great bartenders left the country, heading to Europe or Cuba or other places where their craft might still be legally practiced. When the Eighteenth Amendment was repealed in 1933, ending our status as a dry country, very few of those bartenders returned. So that was the first, most obvious blow to American drinking.

What happened in the rest of the century had as much to do with who was drinking as who was (or wasn't) making the drinks. The generation that came of age just as Prohibition ended was also the generation that would soon be decimated by World War II.

"If you think about the World War II generation, that was a traumatized generation," Dave says. "By the '50s, they were all like, 'Fuck it.' You either went into tropical escapism or insane alcoholic minimalism."

That alcoholic minimalism became what Dave calls the "cult of the dry martini." The tropical escapism was tiki. "People were so asshole-ish that they thought a Manhattan was weak, it was gross because it was sweet," Dave says. "All they wanted was a dry martini. And by 'dry,' they meant no vermouth at all. That was the only acceptable drink. Or scotch."

If the war had psychological repercussions that led to straight gin as the drink of choice, there were also social and economic side effects that dealt new blows to the American cocktail. Who would have thought the GI Bill—the 1944 law that provided college tuition and living expenses to returning veterans—would influence what we drank for the next fifty years? Dave explains, "The GI Bill pulled the business apart, because all the working-class people who would have gone into bartending got college degrees. The perception was then that they were too good to be bartenders."

By the time the '60s came around, there weren't any bartenders left who even knew how to make classic cocktails. The tiki era came and went quickly, and while it was ubiquitous for a while, it was built on a very strange revisionist nostalgia for a part of the world familiar only through wartime. "Which is ironic because everyone who had been in the South Pacific had been there in army fatigues," Dave says, "and a great many of them never came back. It became this weird tropical escapism, but it couldn't last very long." Tiki, gin, and scotch—which were what was left—were seen by a new generation as stuff for old people; that was what your grandparents drank, or worse, your parents. The boomers and then the disco generation wanted nothing to do with mai tais *or* dry martinis.

My Pink Punk Martini arrives, and it is anything but dry. The waiter puts a martini glass in front of me that has a large hunk of lurid pink cotton candy in it. He then pours a pink mixture—vodka, cranberry, and pineapple juice—over the top as we ooh and aah and I take video footage on my phone. The cotton candy dissolves into the liquid, forming a hot-pink sugar sludge that is alarming in both taste and texture.

I take a sip. "How that is, girl?" Greg asks me. "'Cause you just dropped two teeth."

Teeth, years, dignity. This drink is taking a lot from me.

Greg tries his newly delivered Peach Honey Smash, made with honey-flavored bourbon, peach, citrus juice, and a wilting mint sprig as garnish. He recoils in horror, then sighs. "It tastes like a praline."

I try the smash and exclaim, "It tastes like a peach Cisco!"

Dave tastes and says, "There is a hefty dose of nail polish remover in that drink." Which only proves my point: peach Cisco tasted exactly like peach soda and nail polish remover. Greg is too young to have had peach Cisco, and Dave is too classy. I explain that Cisco was a fizzy fruit-flavored fortified wine popular in the early '90s that came in a 12.7-ounce bottle and looked like a wine cooler. Terrible teenagers such as myself used to lovingly refer to it as "liquid crack." It was made by the same people who made Wild Irish Rose. I was under the impression it had gone out of business, in part because so many kids were giving themselves alcohol poisoning from drinking it, neglecting to heed the tiny writing on the label that said, "Serves four." But a few years back, I found a bottle of strawberry Cisco at a gas station in Florida, so I suppose it's still around. Anyway, if you're nostalgic for peach-flavored Cisco, go get yourself a Peach Honey Smash at your nearest TGI Friday's.

Greg has no such nostalgia, poor guy. He's struggling and has been since his first sip of the nuclear-strength Ultimate Long Island Iced Tea he ordered upon arrival. "My body really doesn't know what to do," he says, shaking his head in defeat, his ears glowing a shade redder. "I literally feel high right now. I am using all of the Force, everything I have."

Greg Best taught me, along with the entire city of Atlanta, the philosophy of pleasure and craft and hospitality that characterizes the best of the modern bar movement. When he and his partners opened Holeman and Finch Public House in early 2008, the dark ages were very much still upon the South, even in the good restaurants, and those bars that were serious were also terribly pretentious, a posture Greg has always vehemently rejected. His entire career, as a bartender and bar owner (these days he is co-proprietor of the Ticonderoga Club), has been about railing against everything that I'm currently forcing him to imbibe.

For a short while during my *Creative Loafing* days in Atlanta, Greg wrote a column for me, with the express aim of getting people to drink better booze. If Dave and I are giddily plowing through these drinks, I can see Greg is having a harder time, a torment that feels existential in nature. When he talks about using the Force, he's doing it because he's a HUGE NERD but also because consuming these drinks feels to him like giving into the dark side after a lifetime of fighting for the resistance.

And yet, there's an argument to be made that Greg, along with the rest of us, should be thankful for TGI Friday's and its influence on American drinking. In 1965—the year the birth control pill became available to the public and the year TGI Friday's launched—there was no culture of men and women hanging out together in bars. There were dive bars, which were almost exclusively patronized by men, and swankier bars where businessmen drank, and where women might go but not that often. Again, those were the bars of the previous generation; no fun-loving young person would hang out in the dark-wood lounges of the *Mad Men* era. Where could you go to meet people of the opposite sex, now that dating was a whole new game?

And that's where TGI Friday's comes in. Founder Alan Stillman set out to create a place where men and women could get together and drink, a place that felt familiar and safe and not grotty or stodgy like the bars that came before it. In a 2010 interview with the website Edible Geography, he says that he was "looking to meet girls," plain and simple. And so, for his new Upper East Side bar, he borrowed from the dating rituals of the past. Where would a boy and a girl have gone prior to the sexual revolution for a slightly chaster kind of date? The ice cream parlor. Hence the décor of TGI Friday's, the red-and-white stripes, the soda-fountain interiors.

If this type of bar grew out of ice cream parlor culture, no wonder the drinks turned out to be so sweet. And if they were spawned by the sexual revolution, no wonder the names became so smutty.

TGI Friday's was a massive, instant success, and many other similar bars popped up immediately, many of them on the same block. Stillman claims that not only did he invent the singles bar but that TGI Friday's was the first establishment ever to have lines or a waiting list to get in. On weekend nights, the New York City police had to close off the block because the crowds flocking to Friday's and the other bars that had opened were so massive, the street became one huge party. Singles bars—many of them known as "fern bars" for their leafy, inviting interiors—were soon popular all over the country.

With a whole new market for cocktails and a whole new type of bar to sell to, many of the popular cocktails of the '60s, '70s, and '80s were corporate inventions, thought up by liquor companies and then heavily marketed. In the novel *Cocktail*, on which the Tom Cruise movie is based, author Heywood Gould describes the situation:

> It was the era of the fancy cocktail. The saloon culture was expanding to include people who had very little experience with alcohol, and would have been much happier in an ice cream parlor. The liquor companies responded to this new market by creating recipes for its childish palate,

improbable, dyspeptic combinations of liquors, fruit juices, and heavy cream.²

Dave tells the story of the ultimate corporate creation, the Harvey Wallbanger, which was put together by the distributors of Galliano—the garishly yellow vanilla liqueur—who hired a marketer and the head of a bartending school to create a recipe and an advertising campaign to go along with it. The cartoon surfer they came up with promoted the drink of vodka, Galliano, and orange juice with his slogan of: "Harvey Wallbanger is the name. And I can be made!"

"It was a whole culture and movement, based on drinks that are objectively terrible," Dave says. "But it was also the first instance of creative thought in seventy years. There was a new canon of drinks for the first time ever."

Our palates are shot, overloaded with so much sugar, and Dave has tried to cheat the system by ordering a rum and Coke with lime. He's rewarded with what is undoubtedly the worst drink we've tried all afternoon, Pink Punk Martini included. I think he kind of deserves it for his avoidance of the mission and also because he called it a Cuba Libre—which is some seriously pompous shit to be saying in a TGI Friday's—before catching himself and switching to "rum and Coke with lime." Still, we are flabbergasted as to how they made such a simple concoction taste so much like carpet cleaner. Greg theorizes that it has something to do with this location using Pepsi instead of Coke, though the acrid flavor of the drink can't possibly be thanks to Pepsi alone. But (I'm going to let my own pomposity speak for a second here) this TGI Friday's is winning lots of awards for crappiness. The corn chips that came with our spinach artichoke dip were crisped in obviously rancid oil. The boneless chicken wings, something we ordered because it seemed fitting and none of us had ever had a boneless wing before, were too salty to eat and came with

2 Heywood Gould, *Cocktail* (New York: St. Martin's Press, 1984).

blue cheese dressing that tasted like sugared mayonnaise. Not all TGI Friday's are quite as dismal as the one in Union Square, which seems to operate most of the day mainly as a convenient restroom for the area's many NYPD officers. The flow of cops is endless.

Dave is actually surprised at how bad the drinks are and how little the company has seemed to "make the leap" toward better cocktails, especially because he credits TGI Friday's for taking one of the first major steps in the journey back toward decent drinking. "Once they became a huge chain, things started to get out of hand," he says. "So they created this bar training program that standardized all the drinks, all the pours. And the folks that came out of that program were really some of the first truly professional bartenders at the time."

Another unlikely thing he gives credit to, in terms of moving us toward a better drinking culture? The cosmo, which emerged in the late '80s. "The cosmo was one of the first turns back toward real cocktails," he says. "It was a bridge. It brought people back to the cocktail glass, it brought people back to the idea of standing around and drinking a cocktail."

Like almost every cocktail, the cosmo has origins that are very much up for debate. Bartenders in Miami; Provincetown, Massachusetts; and New York City all claim the drink as their own creations. But wherever it came from, it emerged right around the same time that Dale DeGroff was reviving classic cocktail culture at the Rainbow Room in New York. DeGroff is seen as the father of the modern cocktail movement, and the last thirty years have been a slow crawl toward the moment in time where we are now, where cocktails are seen as a vital part of the food revolution and where bartenders are rock stars and where the most popular drink in America might be the Moscow mule.

Wait, what's that you say? The Moscow mule is an okay but fairly boring vodka drink, one that's hardly emblematic of the great leap forward that's happened in American bars over the past couple of decades?

Well, yeah, exactly. It's far harder to wrench Americans out of our sugary predilections than to simply offer up quality alternatives. Some important drinking rituals, too, have never resurfaced.

We talk about the fact that Americans still haven't found a way back to the cocktail party, something that was prevalent in the '50s and early '60s. It's ironic, I say, that Alan Stillman may have inadvertently killed the cocktail party, because he claims that what he was trying to do was mimic the cocktail parties he went to in the apartments of the many airline stewardesses who lived on the Upper East Side in the '60s (due to its proximity to the Fifty-Ninth Street bridge). He wanted to take that energy and put it into a bar. Ever since, cocktails have been drunk almost exclusively in bars. I remember Greg writing a column for me years ago about how people needed to bring cocktail culture back into their homes if we want it to stick as a part of American life. An excerpt:

> There was a time in which the cocktail was a critical part of our nation's daily ritual—a tool to cast off the burdens of the workplace, the flame that sparked the move toward relaxed togetherness at the end of the day. The cocktail disconnected us from the daily grind and returned us to home life. Cocktails also fueled social gatherings, stimulated free thought and brought us closer through very real sensory experiences. Let us return to this most civilized ceremony.[3]

Greg went on to open a specialty liquor store in Atlanta in the hopes of encouraging the home bartender. When I ask him about it, he shakes his head. "I was foolish to be hopeful when I opened the bottle shop because I saw these enthusiasts who were hoping to get their hands on these products," he says. "But all they ended up doing was [turning] into collectors. No one has cocktail parties. They all just brag about what they have, but no one fucking uses any of it."

---

3 Greg Best, "Cheers: Returning to Cocktail Civility," *Creative Loafing*, June 29, 2020. https://creativeloafing.com/content-231621-cheers-returning-to-cocktail-civility.

He sees this as a failure, but I'm quick to remind him of the very real and positive influence he has had on Atlanta and that others like him have had on dining culture in general. Cocktail lists in restaurants are just as important to me as a critic—sometimes more so—as wine lists. They show whether the place is serious about creativity, about customer pleasure, about investing in staff who might add a whole other level of fun to a venue.

Greg also had a massive influence on my own family. My brother, Fred, when visiting us in Atlanta, spent an evening shadowing Greg at Holeman and Finch. The experience was so inspiring to him—the way Greg thought about drinks, and the history of them, and the idea of hospitality—that he turned around and moved back to Australia and opened an American whiskey bar. He still works in the booze industry to this day, with one of his main hustles being whiskey tastings that focus on the history and culture that inspired the different styles of whiskies worldwide. Nerdery for the win!

We allow ourselves a beer break, sucking down Dos Equis as if it is the water of God. Greg's girlfriend has joined us at the table after a much more cultured afternoon at the Met. We celebrate by ordering the nine-hundred-calorie mudslide with four straws. "Who invented the mudslide anyway?" I ask Dave.

"I have no idea," he says. "People are obsessed with who invented what drink and where. I'm constantly being asked about this or that drink. I know many of the answers, but also, sometimes it doesn't matter. Sometimes it does. But sometimes it's just some guy in some bar, and it caught on." These days, it seems, Dave is much more interested in the cultural forces that drove us to drink what we drink than the moment of genesis, unless one part of that equation reveals the other.

The mudslide is pretty delicious, in the same way anything with enough chocolate syrup and ice cream would be delicious. The four of us lean in and suck it down, as giddy as teenagers on a double date at the soda fountain circa 1954.

40 OUNCES TO FREEDOM

Published on *Punch*, October 2013

In the summer of 1992, exactly one year after I moved to Hartford, Connecticut, with my American mother, I returned to my hometown of Melbourne, Australia, to visit my father and friends. In the year I'd been gone I had changed immeasurably—or so I imagined. I scoffed at my Australian friends as they danced in exaggerated sexual gyrations to Prince. None of them had even had sex yet! I rolled my eyes as they sang along to Public Enemy. They didn't even know any Black people! I was so much more worldly, so much badder/bolder/better. I was 16 and insufferable. Is there any other way to be 16?

But the complaint I made the loudest, to anyone who would listen—even my poor father who had brought me up to recognize a classical composer by a few bars of music and wine grape varietal by scent—was that Australia had no 40-ounce bottles of malt liquor. What a bore, to have to drink beer after beer to achieve intoxication. How irksome to not have your own personal vehicle to that intoxication, in one convenient receptacle. "A 40 is, like, the perfect amount of drunk," I'd blather, as if anyone cared.

After two painful 40-less weeks I returned to Hartford with a mission. In those days I refused to eat or sleep on planes, and by the time I landed, in the early afternoon, I'd been up for around 38 hours and hadn't eaten in just as long. After a bleary hello to my America-residing family, I took a bus to the North End, went to the liquor store that would sell to me, and bought a 40 of Olde English. I threw in a strawberry Cisco for good measure. Then I parked myself on the soft green slope of Keney Park's eastern border, and consumed both.

Later, after a car ride with a boyfriend who had resumed relations with his ex during my Australian sojourn, I threw up in the shoe department of a Bob's Store.

That year, 1992, was just about the apex of the 40's strange cultural impact and appeal. Malt liquor had been around since the 1930s, born of the Depression and the rationing during World War II, when brewers didn't have enough malt to make beer. By the mid 1960s, malt liquor companies had begun to advertise specifically to an African-American clientele, and over the next two decades, that advertising grew more and more raunchy. In the mid 1980s Colt 45 brought on Billy Dee Williams as a spokesperson. His famous tag line was "The power of Colt 45, it works every time," with ads showing Williams holding a can of Colt 45 with a randy-looking woman touching him suggestively. In 1986, the first poster for a new malt liquor called Midnight Dragon featured a Black woman dressed in red, garters showing, straddling a chair and sipping a 40 through a straw. The caption read: "I could SUCK! on this all night."

According to Pete "Bruz" Brusyo, the proud New Jersey owner of the world's largest collection of 40s, the first beer to be sold in that specific bottle was called A-1, and the oldest known bottle is from 1961. But it wasn't until the '80s that the 40 became common. It's not clear why malt liquor started being sold in that particular quantity. A *New York Times* story from 1993 quoted a spokesman from the Miller Brewing Company as saying it was a matter of "retailer and consumer convenience," and cited the fact that store owners loved 40s because they took up so much less space on the shelves. After the mass introduction of 40s, malt liquor consumption in America increased by tens of millions of cases over only a few years.

Many things have been blamed for the rise of the 40 in the late '80s and early '90s, but the usual culprit cited is rap music. By the late '80s, 40s were showing up in many rap songs—Eazy-E had an entire song dedicated to Olde English, called "8 Ball," on N.W.A.'s first album.

Then came Minott Wessinger. Wessinger was a descendant of an established brewing family in Portland, Oregon. In 1987, he began brewing a new malt liquor—St. Ides. After hearing rappers praise 40s and malt liquor brands without prompting, Wessinger correctly assumed that some of

them might be open to a commercial relationship. The resulting adver-
tisements are practically a hip-hop genre unto themselves, with everyone
from Eric B. and Rakim to Snoop Dogg to Notorious B.I.G. to WuTang
Clan appearing in St. Ides commercials. And who can forget the classic
words of Ice Cube: "Get your girl in the mood quicker, get your jimmy
thicker with St. Ides malt liquor"?

St. Ides sales went through the roof.

That same *New York Times* article from 1993 also talks about the
dangers of the 40 craze, particularly for underage minorities. There was
a huge public backlash, particularly from within the Black community.
Many African-American scholars saw malt liquor as specifically targeting
Black youth, or as being used to control and keep down people of color.

In 1992 I lived in a depressed American city, and there's no doubt
we escaped our shitty school and home lives (many of them fraught with
issues of poverty) by saying, "fuck it, let's go drink 40s in the park."

When, in 1993, I moved to a far wealthier community in New York,
the kids drank 40s there as well. It's undeniable that the long-term cost
and impact of malt liquor was far greater for poor, urban America than
it was for the suburban baby hipsters who drank 40s on the weekends
outside of punk shows. But still, for a few years, it was as if the 40 was
a universal language amongst disaffected American teenagers from all
walks of life.

But the astronomical success of the 40 was short-lived. Rappers
moved on to cognac and Cristal, Ice Cube moved on to Hollywood,
Snoop Dogg moved on to . . . Hot Pockets. Many cities actually banned
the sale of 40s. You can still buy them, of course, but the 40's share of
the market, compared to the 1990s, is negligible.

Occasionally there are signs of a resurgence. In 2004, Dogfish Head
announced it would put out a high-class 40 called Liquor de Malt, capi-
talizing on the nostalgia many of us feel for the 40 while also appealing
to the fact that many ex-40 drinkers are now into craft beer. (Currently,
Liquor de Malt is on hiatus.) And the 40 never really lost its cachet as

a provider of good binge drinking opportunities for people looking for that type of thing. "Edward 40-hands" is a more recent frat-house phenomenon, where two 40s are duct taped to someone's hands and not removed until both have been finished.

My last 40 was consumed not that long ago, I'm somewhat ashamed to say. After quite a few drinks in proper bars, my friend Wyatt and I decided it would be a good idea to get 40s and play bocce on a Midtown Atlanta restaurant's bocce court, hours after the restaurant closed one night. It was and wasn't a good idea, as is usually the case with these types of things. In other words, nothing bad happened and I felt like shit the next day.

But the great part about it, the best part about it, was that feeling of freedom that accompanied drinking in the middle of the night in the open summer air, wandering a city as if it were ours, all of it, not just a collection of points and buildings we travel to in order to get things done. We stumbled down to the gas station on 10th Street and then back to the dark lawn of the bocce court, brown paper bags in hand.

That's the thing about 40s, the reason almost everyone close to my age has an intense nostalgic reaction when I bring up the subject. As stupid 16-year-olds, we sat in parks and on train tracks drinking sweet malt liquor, and dreamed of the day we'd be old enough to go to bars. That's when life would really start, we imagined. Now that we're adults, we long for the days when we roamed our cities in the dead of night, or when the plan for a summer day stretching out ahead of us could be as simple as "wanna get 40s?"

It's not lost on me that some people's lives are still like that, and that those lives aren't enviable. Or that many of the friends I had who spent the afternoons skipping school with me to drink malt liquor went on to serious drug abuse, beyond our teenage dalliances. That's what makes the idea of drinking 40s on train tracks so sweet, because that kind of drinking happened before everything went to hell. That period between childhood and adulthood, when you taste debauchery but it hasn't yet ruined anyone's life, is so fleeting.

For me, that sweet debauchery tasted of malt liquor. The 40 taught a generation how to drink, and how not to drink. I drink esoteric wines now, and mix cocktails at home, and enjoy the fruits of the craft beer revolution. These things bring me great pleasure, but none of them hold nearly the same allure as that disgusting, sweet, half-warm bottle of Olde English on a summer day in 1992.

To Serve and Be Served

The most expensive meal I've ever had in my life was at Tour d'Argent in Paris in the summer of 2015. It was a meal for which Ryan and I had been saving since we met. At some point during our first year together, we bought a bottle of champagne that came in a metal tin, and we began collecting change in that tin to pay for one blowout meal when we finally made it to Paris. Fifteen years later, we cashed in all of that change and made the reservation. Our fifteen years of savings covered about a quarter of the bill.

As a food writer, I know I'm supposed to spend my vacations tearing through the best restaurants of whatever city I'm visiting, educating myself but also racking up points on the foodie scoreboard of most places visited, most food eaten. I can't help but resent this expectation. I hate the competitive nature of the food world, I hate thinking about eating as a game. I'd like my personal relationship with food to be based on pleasure rather than status. When I cook at home, I make comforting family recipes rather than elaborate meals, and when I'm on vacation, I like to be on vacation—eating in restaurants is my job. It's a job I love, but it's still a job. Going places because I feel I *have* to go to them, because they're important/hot/whatever, feels too much like work. Wandering into some café because it's there and looks like fun is vacation. Dragging my family around a city looking to tick boxes is not.

All of this is to say, I know Tour d'Argent is not the place on which a modern-day food obsessive ought to blow her budget. The five-hundred-year-old dinosaur (they claim that age anyway), which is the inspiration for the silly French restaurant at EPCOT Center and also the restaurant in *Ratatouille*, is well past its prime, and there are plenty of Michelin stars and exciting young chefs in Paris far worthier of attention. But Tour d'Argent's old-fashioned appeal is exactly why we chose it. Ryan came up in kitchens in the '90s when places like this were legendary, the utter apex of dining. He'd never been to Europe before. He wanted that classic haute cuisine experience, one you simply cannot get in the United States.

And man, was it fun. Being taken up in the little elevator into the grand dining room with its sweeping view of Notre Dame. The multitudes of waiters, the obvious insane wealth of the other patrons, both gaudy (the Brazilian tourists at the table next to us) and elegant (the many Parisian elderly couples who are regulars). Felix, who was eleven at the time and had grown up eating out with me, had never been somewhere so fancy in his life—outside of eating with royalty, I'm not sure there *is* anywhere fancier—and his awed expression was worth the price of admission. It was the first place in years that gave me the feeling of being out of my element in a restaurant, out of place, outclassed. That feeling was part of what drew me to restaurant obsession in the first place—I loved crashing a party to which I obviously wasn't invited.

At Tour d'Argent, a tomato salad cost 80 euros, the deep-blue carpet screamed old-school wealth, and the wine list was encyclopedia thick. We marveled at the number of old white Burgundies on the list, wondering what was up with that. Don't even the best white Burgundies usually lose their beauty after fifteen years or so? There were bottles on this list approaching forty years of age. Granted, it was one of those lists that had every single available vintage of chosen wines, but still. We were intrigued.

A large Hitchcock-esque man approached the table and asked if we needed "direction" on the list. This was David Ridgway, the longtime sommelier at the restaurant, a Brit who has adopted all the attitude of the French. We asked enthusiastically about his older Burgundies, wanting to learn what he had to offer and why. He sniffed at us that you really shouldn't drink these wines when they're old, but then flipped through the pages of the list and pointed to bottles that we might buy. "You could try this," he said, his finger pointing emphatically at the price of the wine rather than the name, "or this," flipping a few pages over. No explanations of the wines were given, no information was relayed at all. And then he looked at us, both bored and expectant.

The snooty French waiter is an icon of Parisian culture. And yet, as an American, it's almost impossible not to be shocked by barefaced insolence.

I've learned almost everything I know about wine from similar interactions in American restaurants, asking the question and engaging, soaking up the knowledge of the professionals. That night at Tour d'Argent, we chose a bottle that was far less expensive than what we were willing to pay (most of his selections had obviously been made with the preconception that we had no money to spend, which is hilarious when you take into account that this would be a meal that cost well over $1,000) and that was disappointing because it was past its prime. We were stupid tourists, and it was a smart sale for him. Unload the plonk on the rubes.

Is it ridiculous for me to say that this interaction was part of the fun of dining at Tour d'Argent? It was all so silly. We had the famous pressed duck, which was delicious, and ordered the theatrical crêpes suzette for dessert, which were pretty crap and got my kid drunk thanks to the uncooked alcohol in the sauce. We walked home giddy with the very Parisian-ness of it all. I wouldn't have exchanged it for any meal in the world.

But it brought something to the forefront of my consciousness that I guess I'd always known but never had reason to feel so viscerally before: it gave me a burning appreciation for American-style service. I realized that, had I been born in Europe, I almost certainly never would have become a food writer or critic. My social class would prevent it. I'd never be let into that world.

In New York in the early 2000s, when Ryan and I used to go to restaurants way out of our league, servers and sommeliers viewed us with suspicion, but as soon as we ordered or asked the kinds of questions we posed to Mr. Ridgway, we were embraced. Often, *because* they knew we didn't really have the money to be there, we were treated better than the wealthy customers at the other tables. It was understood that this was truly special for us, and we were taken care of as a result. This notion, of taking care of someone, is not something I believe Mr. Ridgway adheres to. But it *is* inherent to the ethos of American hospitality, as I learned it when I was waiting tables and as I've experienced it as a customer.

And I started to wonder: Who is responsible for that brand of graciousness? Where did it come from? Who put the hospitality into our hospitality industry?

For almost the entire history of upscale American restaurants, we have looked to France as a model. We cooked French food, we fashioned our fancy establishments after places like Tour d'Argent. The first restaurants in America were mainly in hotels, and employing a French chef quickly became the way for a restaurant to distinguish itself. In the two hundred years since, French food and a mimicry of French service has dominated. Sometime in the last thirty years, we began to break with that model, to create our own high-end culture and also to covet other cuisines, but before that, fine dining was done in the French style.

Snooty waiters continue to exist in America at the very high end, but in the last twenty years, Danny Meyer and other restaurateurs have led the charge to move away from snobbishness even at the most expensive restaurants. Not so in France, where even at the lower end, servers are predictably mean and arrogant.

There's a type of American service that you see—particularly in midrange chain restaurants—that has its roots firmly planted in American culture. Where did it come from? Is it just that we are such a polite, gracious nation we wouldn't have it any other way? (LOL) Is it because servers in America rely on tips and so must ingratiate themselves with customers? Or is it that our idea of servitude was established during slavery, requiring a submissive, deferential tone (as opposed to Europe's history of formality and haughty professionalism in its servant class)?

This last, ugly likelihood is more probable than our overwhelming graciousness. America's long-standing reliance on tipping, which is often credited with creating a more customer-focused service culture than that in Europe, also happens to be a relic of the aftermath of slavery, when many companies avoided paying Black workers in the service sector by having those workers rely on tips rather than wages.

But I also think that, particularly as it relates to chain restaurants and America's most popular kind of high-end dining—steak houses—there are two entities that can be given a lot of credit. One is Harvey House, America's first true restaurant chain. The other is Lawry's the Prime Rib in Beverly Hills, California.

Of course, it's difficult to give credit for an entire part of our culture to one or two people or institutions. The concept of hospitality is not a product for which I can look up a patent. But there were developments at a couple of eateries early on in the life of American restaurants that, at the time, were seen as revolutionary and now are commonplace. And like many of the great changes in American dining, these developments started to take place around the beginning of the twentieth century.

In some of America's earliest restaurants, which were mainly in hotels, waiters were trained in military style complete with a chain of command, dressed in military garb, and entered the dining room in military formation. In the nineteenth century, Black waiters were prized for their evocation of slavery. In his book *Turning the Tables: Restaurants and the Rise of the American Middle Class, 1880–1920*, Andrew P. Haley writes, "No group was viewed as more fit for restaurant service in the nineteenth century than African Americans. Evoking images of slavery, the black waiter became part of a restaurant's aesthetic, a physical reminder of servitude." By the turn of the century, though, Haley notes, a different form of racism had taken root in many parts of the country, and white waiters—particularly those who had trained in Europe—were the most sought-after.

There are dining rooms in America today with echoes of those same ideas about service. The most formal restaurants still value European-style hauteur and military-style precision. The snooty waiter in American fine-dining restaurants is a dying breed, but thirty years ago, he was a fixture of high-end hospitality. You'll notice I say *he*—that's no mistake. If strict formality was a priority for a restaurant, men dominated service positions in those types of establishments.

And gender played a huge role in the move toward an American style of service. The first restaurateurs who made congeniality a priority did so primarily by hiring female servers.

Fred Harvey, founder of Harvey House and originator of the multi-city chain restaurant, began employing an all-female service staff in 1883, a time when the only employment available to women was as teachers or domestic helpers. Harvey believed these women would be more gracious and welcoming to customers than male servers, especially in the West, where the men tended to live up to the "wild" cliché. According to an interview conducted by travel writer Erna Fergusson in the 1930s with a former Harvey House manager named Tom Gable, the original switch from men to women happened at the Raton, New Mexico, branch when a group of waiters got into a brawl after hours. Many of them were too beat-up to work, and Harvey was incensed. He fired the entire staff and hired Gable, who had no restaurant experience, to be the manager. According to Gable, it was he who suggested to Harvey that women who were used to working in homes in the East would be less likely "to get likkered up and go on tears." He goes on to say, "And that is how I brought civilization to New Mexico. Those waitresses were the first respectable women the cowboys and miners had ever seen, that is, outside of their own wives and mothers. Those roughnecks learned manners."

Harvey placed ads in newspapers in Denver and Kansas City and then later along the East Coast. To qualify, women had to be white, have completed an eighth-grade education, be of "good moral character, attractive and intelligent." The Harvey Girls, as they came to be known, signed six-, nine- or twelve-month agreements, agreed to go wherever they were assigned, and also to abstain from marriage for the duration of their contract. They lived in boardinghouse-style accommodations run by the company. They dressed modestly and were not to wear makeup or chew gum. Despite these strict rules, the idea of leaving home and traveling alone for work—to the Wild West!—was an unheard-of amount of independence for young, white, educated women in the 1880s and '90s. The Harvey Girls became iconic symbols of the civilization of the West. In 1946, Judy Garland starred in a movie called *The Harvey Girls*, about a woman who escapes a bad mail-order bride situation by becoming a Harvey Girl.

The reputation of the Harvey Girls gives some indication of why, when early cafeterias opened, they often advertised having an "all-female staff." The idea that women were more likely to treat customers the way they might treat their own families in the home became pervasive, but it was still limited to more casual restaurants—roadside eateries (such as Harvey Houses), cafeterias, and diners.

If there was one pioneer on the higher end of the restaurant spectrum, it was Lawrence Frank, the founder of Lawry's the Prime Rib in Beverly Hills, which opened in 1938. Inspired by the Harvey Girls, Frank also decided to hire an all-female waitstaff for his restaurant, which served only one meal, inspired by the hearty dinners he had as a child in Wisconsin: prime rib, carved tableside from a large rolling cart. Waitresses dressed in maids' uniforms, complete with pointy maids' caps. Along with a grand dining room and a sense of drama surrounding the meal, one of Lawry's key ingredients was making customers feel welcome.

Richard R. Frank, Lawrence Frank's grandson and former CEO of Lawry's, met with me in his Beverly Hills office a few years ago. "My grandfather used to say, 'I want everyone to feel welcome, from the hod carrier to the bank president.'" (A *hod carrier* was a bricklayer's assistant.)

"He did that in a number of ways, but he did feel that women as servers had a softer touch, were maybe friendlier," Frank said. "They set a different tone."

Frank recognized the feat that his grandfather pulled off: convincing customers that the basic American meal was something to aspire to.

"It's really just meat and potatoes," he said.

But this was the genius of the elder Frank—take a meal everyone is familiar with and put it in a setting that feels special, then treat the people who come in to eat that familiar meal very, very well. It's a formula that's still working eighty years later, and it's one that's used by countless chains today, from Houston's to Olive Garden to the Cheesecake Factory: make something familiar feel fancy, and treat the people well.

Lawry's originated many, many other small touches of American service that we now take for granted. The company believes it was the first restaurant to offer valet parking and also the first to introduce the doggie bag so that customers could take leftovers home. (This practice is still not common in most other parts of the world.) Frank was insistent that salads be served on cold, refrigerated plates and warm food be served on hot plates. The spun salad that is a part of every Lawry's meal, which the server spins tableside as she tells you the history of the salad and its dressing, was an anomaly at the time Lawry's opened. Up until then, most salads served in America were of the fruit or potato or meat variety, and they were mainly served after or alongside the main course. The *Los Angeles Times* had a column in the early 1900s called Salad Symposium that printed salad recipes from home cooks, and most of them had ingredients like bananas, celery, mustard, and a half cup of sugar. A savory green salad served at the onset of the meal was a total departure from the norm. Other Lawry's staples—creamed spinach and baked potatoes in particular—were not standard fare at steak houses, and company lore theorizes that it was Lawry's that popularized these things as must-haves on meat-centric menus.

Of course, the name *Lawry* is best known for the seasoning salt Lawrence Frank created right around the time the restaurant was opened.

Customers started stealing it off the tables, and Frank wondered if people might buy it as a retail item. He sold ten cases to a Ralphs supermarket grocery buyer, and a seasoned salt empire was born. These days, McCormick & Company owns the seasoned salt and spice branch of the Lawry's brand, but the restaurants remain family owned.

My first visit to Lawry's in Beverly Hills wasn't long after I returned from that trip to Paris. There's so much about the restaurant that screams hospitality, and most of those things have not changed since Lawrence Frank established them, despite the fact that it is now a small chain with locations around the country and internationally. Guests always enter the grand dining room via three steps down, to give an air of majesty. There are free meatballs and thick-cut potato chips in the bar while you wait for a table. Waiters are as performative as they are obsequious. This all might have seemed hokey to me in my regular role as a restaurant critic, but post-Paris, I was simply grateful. Especially when I looked around the room at the other customers, who were far more diverse than any other set of diners at any other dining room in Beverly Hills. Lawry's is still the place where people come who just want to be treated well, who may not feel comfortable at the trendy restaurants LA has to offer, and who certainly don't want to deal with the pretension of true fine dining.

Equal opportunity laws forced the company to allow male servers in the early 2000s. But the waitresses still dress in the maid's uniform, spin salads, and serve them on cold plates, and the prime rib is still carved tableside from custom-built carts. (The company boasts that the carts cost as much as a new Cadillac.) At some point, Lawry's started decorating their carvers with large gold medals after six months of service, worn around their necks on thick red velvet ribbons to signify a certain level of experience. There's a sense of ceremony to the place that has never been modified and a sense of hospitality for which I was—and remain—incredibly grateful.

I'd like to say that if I were able to locate the originator of today's preferred style of service in America—that is, the overly familiar "Hello my name is blah blah and I'll be taking care of you this evening, have you dined with us before?" shtick—I would hunt that person down and throttle him or her. And yet this urge to complain about the minutiae of modern American dining has grown tiresome. Critics especially are guilty of picking apart every little thing that happens in restaurants and whining about those things. I don't mean specific things in specific restaurants— that's our job, after all—but trends and oddities we can generalize about. I blame the grind of the newspaper food blog, the constant need for clicks, which drove us to stupidities such as: "Brunch Sucks"; "Brunch Is the Best Meal, Actually"; and "Why I'm Sick of Small Plates." But there's also a bubble you find yourself in as a critic, and a sense of self-importance that festers inside that bubble, which makes you think every minor annoyance that crosses your mind is worthy of a headline.

Despite my own admonition, I'll admit to being frustrated with this current style of service—especially the tendency for servers to explain what a menu is, as if you've never seen one before in your life. I believe that people on both sides of the equation know that the waiter speech is unnecessary, but no one knows how to avoid it anymore. It's become so rote we just play our roles automatically: I tell you whether or not I've dined here before, you tell me what a small plate is, we both pretend that "we try to use local and sustainable produce wherever possible" actually means something.

But I managed to find the beauty in this silly interaction on that same 2015 trip to Paris. As I said, I spend most vacations avoiding trendy of-the-moment restaurants because to do otherwise is too much like work. But during the last two days of our France trip, my brother, Fred, and his then girlfriend came over to Paris from London, where they were attending a friend's wedding. My brother's girlfriend was the restaurant critic at the daily paper in Melbourne (I know that having a critic sister and a critic girlfriend is a little weird and coincidental, but so it goes), and she fit the profile of the modern-day food obsessive much better than I did. In other words, she ate voraciously like it was a blood sport wherever she went. (These days, our roles are perhaps reversed—I am still a critic and food obsessive; she lives blissfully on a farm and raises chickens.)

And so I found myself for a couple of days being dragged, quite happily, to various restaurants around Paris that were the new hotness that summer. The research had been done for me, I wasn't required to have an opinion, and it seemed like the best of both worlds.

At one restaurant we went to, the cheekily named Clamato, the floppy-haired waiter crouched beside our table and asked if we wanted flat or sparkling water in a manner that was instantly recognizable. When he popped up to get the water, he pointed to the menu and said (in French), "The wine list is on the back of the menu, food on the front. I'll be back in a second to walk you through it."

"Oh my god," I said when he walked away. "Are we about to get the small-plates-meant-for-sharing speech *in French?*"

And we did. Almost word for word. And then I asked him about one of the weird white wines on the list, and he excitedly explained it to me in rapturous detail, adding that it would go particularly well with the oysters we'd ordered. And I felt stupidly, unabashedly grateful that America's silliest service tropes had crept across the Atlantic and landed in Paris on that sunny afternoon.

Palate Cleanser

In 2016, Eater *gave me the opportunity to visit my home-town of Melbourne and write a big, thinky story about why it haunted me and how it had shaped me as an eater and person. I'm including that story here because my life was about to change drastically, and I think it does a good job of setting the stage for where my head and heart were—which led to that change. It also is just one huge love letter to Melbourne, a city that deserves everyone's love, and I'll shove Melbourne propaganda into every-thing wherever I can. Melbourne! Is the best!*

The City That Knows How to Eat

First published on *Eater*, December 2016

In 1976, Australia birthed three things: The AC/DC album High Voltage, the bratwurst stand at Melbourne's Queen Victoria Market, and me. When I was a kid, my AC/DC-loving stepfather and I would brave the throngs in front of the bratwurst stand to claim our breakfast: Two regular brats, please, with mild mustard on half white rolls, along with a flat white for my stepfather made on the old espresso machine that grunted and whirred a few feet from the smoking grill.

After breakfast, we would embark upon our Saturday food-shopping ritual, a serious undertaking that circled outwards through the Vic Market's 17 sprawling acres of indoor and outdoor stalls. In the fruit sheds I could smell the edge of rot; in the chilly meat building whole carcasses hung, dead eyes staring. In the deli section, a vintage paradise of chrome and marble booths built in 1929, gold-painted lettering spelled out the businesses' names and specialties: French pastries, tea, confections, cheese, olives, butter, bratwurst. I marveled at stalls festooned with hanging kielbasa, and stalls where they scooped thick Greek yogurt from tubs, and stalls with delicate European chocolates displayed like jewels.

Shopping was a skill and a joy and a competitive sport. My stepfather haggled with the meat guy and selected the best vegetables hawked by old Greek men who shouted:

"Bananabananabanana!!! Onedollaronedollaronedollar!!!"

At the time, if you had asked me what I might miss most about my Melbourne life, the Markets wouldn't have even crossed my mind. Boys, friends, record stores—these were the things I considered most meaningful.

In 1990, my American mother decided it was time for her to return home, and for the rest of us—four kids, one husband—to go with her. I arrived in Denver, Colorado, as a pissed-off 14-year-old with purple hair and a funny accent, separated from my father and my friends. My new home seemed to lack any discernible street life, only cars and tidy neighborhoods and malls. The most visceral culture shock came in the aisles of American supermarkets, which were sterile and bright and exciting in a morally ambiguous kind of way. The yogurt was different (sweeter), the candy was different (better), the cookies were called cookies, not biscuits. Rather than the vibrant, stinky thrill of Vic Market's maze of stalls, in Denver, shopping for food was an act of sanitary consumerism. For my stepfather especially, the pleasure of shopping, and therefore of cooking and eating, was blunted. What had been a raucous joy became a cold chore.

My first true American friendship came once we left Denver and moved to Hartford, Connecticut. Toby was a crazy goth gay kid who wore black-and-white-striped tights with jean shorts and Doc Martens and only ate fluffernutter sandwiches. Like the rest of my new peers, he seemed to revel in his general dislike of food. The first time I went to his house, we stood in his gleaming, stark kitchen while he piled marshmallow fluff onto peanut butter toast and listed everything he wouldn't eat: "Meat, vegetables, rice, soup. I used to eat pizza but it's bad for my skin."

By the time I left Melbourne, my friends and I had already started throwing elaborate dinner parties together. We scoured the city for the best fish and chips, obsessed over new restaurants and declared our allegiance to old ones. Stuck in abstemious America, I poured most of my petulant, goth-kid energy into yearning for Melbourne like a lost love-of-my-life, a mythical home that no one in this myopic, poorly nourished country would understand.

"Australia," Toby said as we stood in his kitchen, his mouth sticky with peanut butter. "That's in Europe, right?"

Do we not know how to eat in America? I felt that way when I arrived and I feel that way now, though we're doing much better these days. (After all this time, I count myself as part of that "we." I hold dual U.S./Australian citizenship, and embrace all the tricky and proud self-examination that comes with identifying, even partially, as American.)

For the past decade, in my work as a food critic, I've witnessed America's food revolution firsthand, and seen how a combination of changing tastes and rising culinary ambition has reshaped entire cities. I lived in Atlanta as the New South's food identity blossomed, and I'm now in Los Angeles, right as the world has finally stopped turning up its collective nose at the city's culinary riches. I have massive amounts of admiration and respect for the chefs, farmers, writers, and cooks who have pushed America to this point. But something profound is still missing, something that feels like it's at the very root of my homesickness.

Why am I still not over Melbourne? I've lived in Colorado, Connecticut, New York, North Carolina, Georgia, and California, and all of them still, in some way, feel like home (except Colorado—sorry Denver). I spent 11 years in Melbourne (we moved there when I was three) and have now spent 26 in the U.S. And especially now, when avocado toast is taking America by storm (avocado toast is a 100 percent Australian invention, insofar as any one ingredient on a piece of bread can be), what is it exactly that I miss so deeply?

Traditionally, American chefs and food writers have looked to Europe to learn about cultivated eating. The story of the American ingenue taking her first bite of French baguette (with real butter!) or her first taste of a small, scarlet, perfect strawberry in a Provence marketplace—it's so ubiquitous that it's an utter cliché. America, we are told to believe, was settled too recently, was too influenced by industrialization, is made up of too many disparate cultures, and is burdened with too much shame to have a through-line of shared history that might allow a pure and pleasurable relationship with food. We fetishize Asia; we romanticize Europe. We reserve our most rapturous food epiphanies for travel.

But there is another young nation colonized by Anglos and defined by waves of immigrants that has incredible bread and strawberries and joie de vivre—America has just been too distracted by the kangaroos to see it. Beyond the cultural commonalities (including different brands of the same kind of shame), some of contemporary America's biggest food trends are right out of my hometown's playbook. Being from Melbourne and working in the American food world is like constantly being told—with great gusto—that the sky is blue. In the quarter-century I've lived here, I've seen America discover the joys of decent coffee, farmers markets become ubiquitous, and avocado toast spread like a plague. Food halls! Super creative breakfast using fresh ingredients and international flavors! Next-gen delis! All of these things have been happening in Melbourne since the 1980s, or in some cases, the 1890s. And not just as passing trends; they infuse the entire culture. The frumpily dressed grannies of Melbourne drink cappuccino and roast their legs of lamb with lemon and white wine and rosemary.

This isn't just teenaged nostalgia talking: I returned to Melbourne this summer and discovered that the magic very much persists.

Melbourne is a port city, built around the seashell-shaped curve of Port Phillip Bay. For 40,000 years or so, it was inhabited by tribes of the Kulin Nation, hunter-gatherers who took advantage of its lush, temperate climate. French and British explorers began showing up around 200 years ago, and the area was colonized by the British in 1835. The Victorian gold rush in the mid-nineteenth century sparked an explosion of both population and wealth. The city's grand, Victorian architecture is the kind of extravagance only gold could buy.

If the gold rush gave the city refined taste—during those years Melbourne consumed more Champagne than any other city on Earth—

successive waves of immigration expanded its palate. The city's famous cafe culture springs from a well-timed Italian influx: After World War I, the U.S. put policies in place that effectively halted the flow of Italians to America, and Australia became the favored alternative. Through a trick of timing and history, that switch from America to Australia coincided with the invention of the espresso machine. The Italian coffee culture that never quite made it to America blossomed in Melbourne. I know, I know—New York had an espresso machine in 1904 or whatever, but I'm not talking about one or two or ten cafes. I'm talking about hundreds of thousands of people who brought their taste for espresso with them.

Even before the rise of Italian cultural influence, the dominant Anglo culture built much of Australia's social life around old, hulking pubs on practically every corner. Pubs have always been much more welcoming (and family-friendly) than any bars I can think of in America. That familiarity with a communal space primed Melbourne for the European-style cafe, another place in which to lead life publicly and socially.

Though the boom of Italian immigration to Melbourne began in the 1920s, it wasn't until 1954 that the first real Italian cafe opened. Pellegrini's, located on Bourke Street in the middle of Melbourne's Central Business District, brought to fruition 30 years of espresso-loving immigrants making Melbourne their home. My father, who was 20 at the time, remembers that opening distinctly. "There was nothing like it, there had been nothing like it before," he says. "It was the beginning of Melbourne becoming what it is."

Pellegrini's is still open, with its red mid-century signage, checkered floor, and a menu and atmosphere that have remained unchanged for more than 60 years. If it established Melbourne's cafe culture, its longevity reflects another key facet of the city's dining persona: The persistence of old-school family-run places that cater to the same people decade after decade. These restaurants used to be everywhere in the U.S., but we've lost many of them over the past half-century. It's not just a loss of history; these restaurants are surrogate family who know your tastes and the names of your kids.

I've always been a sucker for the kinds of fantasy novels wherein a hidden world is revealed, just beneath the surface. Melbourne has a lot of that. Many of the most interesting places to eat and drink are down alleyways, which wind through the guts of the city's center and grow odd little businesses like weeds.

Over the 60 years since Pellegrini's opened, its influence—and the influence of the many immigrant restaurants that opened after 1954—has meant great coffee, and it's meant something much more. From early morning until late night, Melbourne's sidewalks are clogged with tables and chairs and people eating and drinking and sipping lattes as trams clang down the streets. Out in front of the Vic Markets, people carry their bratwursts and croissants and share happy conversation before they do the week's shopping. The cafes of Melbourne are not just places where great coffee happens. They're places where breakfast happens, where lunch happens, where mid-afternoon drinks and people-watching happen. Woven into the fabric of the city as surely as the tram tracks that criss-cross its streets and the wrought iron that spindles across the facades of its Victorian row houses, the cafes of Melbourne are where life happens.

If Pellegrini's is Melbourne's original cafe, Mario's, located on Fitzroy's main drag, was the next great leap forward. Opened in 1986, Mario's was (and is) an Italian cafe with the bearing of a classy restaurant. They had all-day breakfast and really good coffee and carefully made bowls of pasta. Owner Mario Maccarone told Gourmet Traveller earlier this year: "We elevated the idea of what a cafe could be.... We looked a bit like a restaurant, but you could still come in and get Vegemite on toast." Take away the Vegemite and Maccarone sounds like a lot of American restaurateurs circa 2012, but he's talking about 1986. Mario's turned Melbourne cafes into places where serious food happened, and where breakfast was as important as dinner.

It also primed Fitzroy's Brunswick Street to become the cafe capital of the universe. There are a few neighborhoods in Australia that might try to claim that title, but my money's on Fitzroy, which also puts Williamsburg and Silver Lake to shame on the hipster scale. You can't walk two feet in Fitzroy without stumbling over another cafe serving pumpkin, pomegranate, crispy kale, and goat cheese on toast, another craft cocktail bar with a more exclusive cocktail bar upstairs that you have to buzz into, another shop selling gorgeous clothes you can't afford. My brother lives above a disgustingly trendy barber shop that might as well be called "Bespoke," and a women's clothing store called "Who Invited Her," which simultaneously makes me want to applaud and claw my own eyes out.

Mario's and its neon cursive sign are still an iconic part of the neighborhood, 30 years after its opening. And all around it are evolutions, cafe menus which reflect an ever-broader array of cultures. There are more Greeks in Melbourne than any city in the world outside of Greece. Refugees from the Lebanese civil war flowed into the city during the '70s and '80s. In the 45 years since the repeal of the "White Australia" policy (yes, it was really called that), the city's Thai, Vietnamese, Chinese and Indian populations have swelled. Somehow, despite the very real racism faced by each of these groups as they arrived, their food has become integrated into the life of Melbourne in a way I'm only just beginning to see in big American cities.

Those Greek and Middle Eastern and Asian influences have been folded into Melbourne's cultural identity, and they reverberate through the kaleidoscopic flavors found on its best cafe and restaurant menus. From Thai-style omelettes and creative congees to chicken and makrut lime scotch eggs, breakfast in this city alone could kick the asses of America's best seasonal small plates.

While eating and drinking at Gerald's, a cluttered storefront wine bar in Carlton North, the owner Gerald Diffey plonked down beside me and my brother and shared his fiercely held, basically proletariat beliefs about wine. "I don't really care how preciously you fondled the grapes, or where it was aged—who gives a fuck?" Diffey said amicably. "People forget that a lot of the pleasure and magic of wine is that it tastes good and gets you pissed." Sitting with a rowdy, foul-mouthed wine evangelist while drinking a casually poured, mind-bending riesling, I felt as though

I had slipped into the life I might have led, had it not been taken from me (or me from it).

It would be foolish to suggest that I've never had a meal in America that felt spiritually similar to what Melbourne offers so effortlessly. Portland sometimes comes close to finding that groove. Grand Central Market here in L.A. has some commonality with the Vic Markets, though the Vic Markets aren't burdened with the same strains of gentrification that plague GCM. Bacchanal in New Orleans, the wine shop with a sprawling, cluttered backyard where you can sit for hours drinking wine, eating cheese, and listening to music, feels more like home to me than almost anywhere else in the country, even though I have no personal connection to New Orleans.

Most of the literal interpretations of Melbourne I've come across here—the meat pie shops, the Australian cafes—are a little sad, though one or two in Brooklyn come close to the real thing. Sqirl in Los Angeles, a relaxed cafe celebrated for its creative rice bowls and lovely baked goods, is basically a very good Melbourne cafe on a corner in East Hollywood. Unsurprisingly, chef and owner Jessica Koslow spent time working at a bakery in Melbourne.

I'm sure that a food-obsessed American reading this might be able to come up with a plethora of other examples, places, and things that sound similar to the things I'm claiming as unique to my hometown. It's true that the differences are subtle—food as a way of life, a birthright, a source of pleasure, and a shared culture rather than a means of constructing identity or differentiating status. But to me they feel profound.

Don't get me wrong: Melbourne has plenty of crap, artifice, and hyped-up places that may or may not deserve the hype. There's a casino full of restaurants with international superstar chef names above the doors. Ben Shrewy forages his way through every big-name food magazine, and his restaurant, Attica, is currently at number 33 on the World's 50 Best list, serving dishes made with wallaby blood, as well as a fine-dining take on . . . avocado toast. I'm sure Attica is great; I'd love to eat there one day. But my hometown's greatest culinary gift, the thing I miss the most, the thing I've been looking for ever since I left, is the city's underlying attitude: That food is just a part of everyday life and, damn, isn't everyday life wonderful?

Am I overthinking this? Maybe I should write an essay instead about how sick I am of tasting menus. About all the things servers do that mildly annoy me. Maybe I should just move back.

My brother has moved back to Melbourne, as has my sister, and my stepfather. My stepfather tells a story about something someone said to him in the leadup to our move to America. He was 30 at the time, and our move would be his first trip outside of Australia. This friend of his, who had spent some time in the U.S., said: You'll go there and everything will seem familiar. You'll understand the language. The food will taste somewhat similar. The way people deliver the news on TV, the way people sing at rock shows, the way people drink at bars: It will all feel comfortably recognizable. And then after you've been there for a while, you'll begin to understand the real difference between America and Australia, and that difference is vastly more profound than anything you might point to on the surface. And then you'll realize you are as alien to that place as you might be on Mars.

I'm not sure on which planet I belong. Otherness is such a part of my identity that if I were to return to Australia now, I don't know who I'd be. The dominant narrative when it comes to immigrant stories is the struggles faced upon arriving in a new land, and the confusion of trying to survive while looking and speaking and thinking differently. In those regards my experience can't begin to compare to people leaving their homes in China or South America or Africa or even Europe. I'm white. I speak the language; I look the part. But the thing I share with immigrants and expats of all stripes is the intense feeling of otherness that comes with missing home, the belonging to different earth, different air, a different ocean. Leaving is the key event of your life—you spend all the time after trying to reconcile the person you were when you belonged somewhere with the displaced person you've become. It's this very condition that pushes people to recreate a taste of home in their new lives. It's the exact dynamic that created so much of the food culture I've spent my life longing for.

I've continued to displace myself, over and over again, moving away from cities once they become comfortable and familiar. My last move, from Atlanta to L.A., was the most wrenching since leaving Melbourne. I came to a city I'd never visited, where I knew no one, to take a high-profile job as a complete unknown. "I'm not from here" is at the core of who I am.

When I got back to L.A. after my summer trip to Melbourne, I had a conversation with my mother, another installment in the long line of conversations we've been having for 25 years, the one that goes: Why did we leave? Should we go back? What is it that we're missing so very much? What is the difference?

And my mother told me something I'd never heard her say before: "America was settled mainly before the Industrial Revolution, and it was all about pioneering, all about rugged individualism. Australia has this reputation of being settled by convicts, but the truth is that most of the country is built on immigration that came later, after the Industrial Revolution. These were working people, and they were familiar with the mindset that came along with that. Unions! Solidarity! America was built on going out and conquering the West, all by your fucking self. Australia was built on the idea that you look out for your mates."

That's what I miss. The comfort of living in a place where the underlying principle is that we look out for one another. If that ethos leads to good coffee and grilled lamb chops, all the better.

In America we read the blogs, we obsess about which chef is leaving what job and what storefront will become the next hot restaurant. We stand in line for rainbow-glazed ramen burger bagels. But in the end, our newfound food obsessions founder on that with which America has always been concerned: Commerce and status. I see—especially in the food world—an urge to connect, to put more stock in pleasure, to find some sort of fellowship in our dining rituals. Our seating is increasingly communal. Practically all of our semi-upscale eating is now done off of shared plates, in an attempt to force togetherness. These gestures are genuine, and yet they're received as fashion.

Culture is so interconnected. Maybe Australians can have their carefree, joyful attitude around food and life because they get so much paid vacation, because childcare is affordable, because there's no gun violence, because there's not so much pressure, because the great Australian dream is to have a house and some kids and a few good friends. Because ambition is undervalued. Because life isn't as scary.

In Melbourne, the look-after-your-mates ethos, the pubs and cafes, have created a food culture as charming as Europe's, as exciting as America's, as varied as Asia's. A place where the past and the future are often friends, where community feels tangible, where it's okay to relax. No wonder it haunts me.

And yet—I love living in L.A. I love my work, and the people and places I write about. One of my greatest joys and achievements has been conquering the West, all by my fucking self. So maybe I am American after all. And maybe it's too much to ask America to learn how to blend its rugged individualism with a sense of community. In the wake of the most divisive presidential election in modern history (and its proconsumerist, anti-multiculturalist results), this seems like a particularly ludicrous thing to hope for. Maybe I'll just have to make do with avocado toast.

On this trip, as with every Melbourne trip, I went and stood in the throng at the Vic Markets and bought myself a bratwurst and a flat white. I ate standing at the counter that runs along the inside wall of the grand stone entrance. I felt embraced by those walls, by the spirit of the immigrants who have passed through over the last century, by the otherness and longing for home that has inspired so much good food and good living. I gave thanks for that longing, for the German guy in 1976 whose desire for a taste of home made the bratwurst in my hand possible. I gave thanks to Melbourne and also to America, for making me who I am.

(Bittersweet) Dessert

LAX-MEL

I t began with my mother leaving Australia in the first place.

It continued when my brother, Fred, finished college, then bummed around India, and then slept on my couch for a while in Atlanta, and then moved home. Once he got back to Australia, there was no question he was staying.

My sister Grace followed, two years later.

It started to solidify in December 2012, when a gunman entered Sandy Hook Elementary, the school that my uncle had attended (my mother grew up partly in Sandy Hook), and killed twenty-six people, including twenty six- and seven-year-olds. I was supposed to interview Eddie Huang on the phone that day from my house in Silver Lake and only just got my sobbing under control enough to make the call at the allotted time. I'd met Eddie before, was okay at playing his cool-kid game, but could not muster it that day. "I'm sorry if I'm a bit shaky," I said. "This country is fucking me up."

When the interview was over, I walked the two blocks from our house, past the chandelier tree, to Felix's elementary school, needing with a desperate pull to touch my child, to take him out of this place that seemed so safe but that no longer was. I wasn't the only parent there, looking wild-eyed, asking to sign their kids out early, looking at one another with desperate fear, like: *How do we bear this? This is not bearable.*

Eventually, we lost that house in Silver Lake, our magical oasis. The woman who owned it decided to move back in. At that point, with half of Brooklyn having decided to abscond to Los Angeles and most of them wanting to live in Silver Lake, we were priced out of the neighborhood.

(Ironic, I thought, that I'd been priced out of Brooklyn a decade earlier by these same people.)

We moved to a house on a busy corner in Eagle Rock, where the only thing within walking distance was a Vons supermarket and the sound of traffic rattled the windows all night. Early one morning, our cat slipped out the top of a window that she'd never managed to reach before and was carried off by coyotes. On the eve of the 2016 election, I panicked and spent the night filling out paperwork online to secure Felix's Australian citizenship.

The night of the election, Ryan and I went to eat at a new sushi joint in a strip mall in East Hollywood, one of those places that's fantastic but also so common in LA that people barely stop to understand how good they've got it. I turned off my phone when we entered the restaurant, well before the election results started coming in. We blissfully ate house-made silken tofu topped with dashi gelée and sweet crabmeat, and aoyagi clams on perfectly vinegared rice, avoiding the inherent anxiety of Election Night. When I stepped back out into the cool LA evening after the meal and turned on my phone, it felt as though I'd stepped into a different universe from the one I'd left a few hours earlier.

My review of the sushi restaurant, which came out the following week, began: "The sky is blue, we're all going to die, and Los Angeles has the best sushi in America." A decent snapshot of my frame of mind at the time.

And then: news came down that *LA Weekly* was for sale. At first, there were rumors that someone amazing was planning to buy it, someone with deep connections to the city and a genuine love for the newspaper. But those rumors started to fade. Anxiety settled in. I'd been through this before; I had a pretty good idea of what was likely coming down the pike.

I don't remember how I first heard that *The New York Times* was opening a new bureau in Australia, with a bold plan to try to capture the local market as well as function like a normal bureau, covering things of international import. I do know that I used old family connections, people my mother knew from her college and *NYT* days, to figure out the right person to contact to express my interest. I pitched a couple of stories about Melbourne, newsy stories that I thought fit the bill of what they might be looking for. I told them I was going to Melbourne anyway, would cover the bills.

At the same time, Fred was going through a rough breakup with the restaurant critic, and I felt desperate that I was so far away from him when he was hurting so badly. Everything lined up, everything was pushing me in one direction: home.

We leaped before we knew where or how we'd be landing. I published those couple of stories in *The Times* (a thrill to see my byline in those pages that I still feel to this day) and had a vague promise of more work when and if I got to Australia, but nothing solid.

We bought plane tickets, moved out of our house when the lease was up, moved into a series of sublets.

And then, a phone call (it's always a phone call): The *Times* bureau chief in Australia. "We're thinking that we might like to bring on a restaurant critic here, as part of our launch into the Australian market." It felt like all my dreams, every professional aspiration and every personal need, coming good at once.

My last night in Los Angeles, I went to Vespertine, for the final meal of what would be my final review in LA. Vespertine was (and is) one of the most bizarre restaurant experiences in the world, and I doubt it could exist anywhere other than in Los Angeles. Inspired by the undulating glass box of a building in which it resides, it is as much art project as restaurant, as interesting and infuriating and pretentious and kinda amazing as all of that sounds. You start on the rooftop as the sun sets around you, birds swooping in huge formations in the fading white California light, sipping a drink that's topped with an alien-looking passionfruit flower. Much of the food does not resemble food: a bowl lacquered with a black, grainy, skinlike layer that feels like a membrane against your knife and your teeth, which gives way to a layer of raw halibut with green strawberries; a bizarre and ingenious take on chips and dip that involves a crackly swoop of dried kelp (served inside a stone circle that looks like a gothic giant's wedding ring) along with a creamy emulsion of yuzu and sea lettuce, dotted with wild fennel flowers.

A soundtrack follows you from the garden and into the building and throughout your evening, and in my review, I said that it "sounds less like music and more like the universe shifting its astral gears."

What a way to say goodbye.

The next night at LAX, we stood in the departures hall of Tom Bradley with Ruby and my mother. Somehow, the weight of all the history of that place and what it had meant in my life overwhelmed me. I knew what these kinds of goodbyes meant. The other side of the world is very far away. "It's going to be okay, Besh," my mother whispered in my ear as I sobbed into her shoulder.

She didn't know it would be okay, obviously. For her or for me. And my tears were partially fueled by guilt, that I was leaving her—the last time I'd left a parent, it had been the end of who we were.

We went up the escalators toward security, but before we went through, I fished two bottles from my bag: the last of the Pappy Van Winkle from a bottle someone had given me as a departing gift when I left Atlanta and an airplane bottle of special reserve Pappy that had been part of the departure lunch box at a conference I'd attended. I gave one to Ryan, and we clinked bottles next to the huge windows that looked out over the airfield. "To America," I said.

I wrote my last review for *LA Weekly*, of Vespertine, on the plane.

We arrived in a cold, angry Melbourne: to this day, I'm not sure if those first September days in 2017 were particularly awful or if my years in LA had ruined me for any kind of winter. But my memory is that it was freezing and raining sideways for weeks on end.

Fred and Grace met us at the airport with hugs and yelps, and we piled into a minivan taxi to take us to Fred's apartment in Fitzroy, where we'd spend the first few days before heading to Queensland to visit my father. "You did it!" Grace said jubilantly as we sped along the highway in the taxi.

"We did it," I said. "I can't believe we did it."

I think it really was only in that moment that the enormity of what we'd done began to hit me, which sounds insane, I know. I'd been think-ing about this move for a decade and actively planning it for a year. But the logistical intensity of that kind of planning can serve as an imped-iment to comprehension: I was so caught up with figuring out where we'd live, how we'd arrange visas and tickets and passports, how and where our things would be stored—hell, we'd lived in three houses in the previous four months—that I'd spared very little time thinking about the actual thing we were doing, beyond the job I was walking into (even that I had very few specifics on, only that it would be freelance and cover the whole country).

For the first few weeks, I was in a dazed kind of fog that was quite pleasant. What a shock, to have history in a place—not just recent his-tory, not even just my own history. A few blocks from the sublet where we landed in Melbourne was the giant terrace house, the one where my family had lived with Sarah and her mother and various other house-mates, the one in which my parents broke up, the one I'd come home to from that fateful meal at Stephanie's.

But also: on the same street as our sublet, a three-minute walk up Bruns-wick Road toward Lygon Street, was the building that had been the breakfast cereal factory owned by my father's father. I walked past these structures with wonder—I had a tangible past!—a feeling I'd not had since I was a teenager (and that I'd so thoroughly taken for granted back then, it barely registered). Everywhere I went, memories came rushing at me: my elementary school grounds; the train station where I'd made a fool of myself at fourteen trying to talk to a boy I liked; the church where I'd taken ballet lessons that I hated with vehemence. Things I might have lost, things I *had* lost but had now regained. I basked in the clear purple and yellow light, wondered at the shining streets after the rain, in the way the clouds looked like benevolent anger. My blood thrummed with the word: *home!*

That deep sense of belonging was given an equal and opposite foil in the form of alienation felt by Ryan and especially Felix. In my reconnection with my hometown, I understood, maybe for the first time, just how much Ryan had given up by leaving North Carolina, by betraying the history of the seven generations that came before him. Neither he nor Felix had much experience feeling like an alien, like they were in the wrong place, like their cells did not belong. I'd made a whole personality from that feeling.

It took Ryan far longer to find a job than we'd imagined it would. He wasn't allowed to work for the first three months while his visa was being processed, and even then, he struggled to find his place. In LA, he'd fallen into the nonprofit world, working with an organization that trained people coming out of prison and the foster care system how to be cooks, while also repurposing food waste and making meals for unhoused and elderly people. He loved it; he understood the students, he felt good about his work, the hours were better than restaurants', and his livelihood held no potential for conflict of interest with my own. But the culture of Australia was so different, and people were unlikely to hire someone with no local experience.

Felix became . . . the only word I know to describe it is *terrified*. Constantly, achingly terrified. My once buoyant and confident boy, who turned fourteen the week after we arrived, struggled to talk; at times, it seemed as though he struggled to breathe. At school, he was mute, baffled by the teenage customs and prejudices of his Australian classmates. "They tease people here for being poor," he told me. "In LA, my rich friends insisted they weren't rich." Racism and homophobia were thrown about casually, as banter, in a way that would never have flown in the Los Angeles public schools he'd attended.

I'd made so many excuses as to why this would be different for him, why an international move at this age wouldn't wound him the way it did me. He was not leaving his father behind. He was not going from a good school in a nice city to a huge, terrible, urban school in a crap city. (Sorry, Hartford.) He would have his aunt and uncle. He would have me.

You can't project your own experiences onto your kids. The worst thing to ever happen to you is still the worst thing to ever happen to you.

Not long after we arrived, the news came down that *LA Weekly* had been sold to a sketchy group of investors that had connection to the weed industry and a group of right-wing businessmen from Orange County. Almost the entire staff was fired. I probably gave up a decent severance package by leaving before the downfall, but I'm not sad to have avoided the worst of the trauma of having another newspaper that I loved be decimated, of seeing my coworkers endure that, of enduring another layoff myself.

Around that same time, during the Melbourne Food & Wine Festival, an American writer and minor food celebrity I'd never met before invited me to a late-night party in a laneway in Melbourne's central business district, ostensibly because he wanted me to find him weed. He was drunk when I arrived, and we didn't get much of a chance to talk, but he did mention that he was sad to hear about the breakup between my brother and his restaurant critic girlfriend. The writer was traveling with a small posse, including a young woman who was also fairly drunk, and I commented to the young woman that it was startling to find my brother's personal life the topic of international conversation. "It's crazy to me," I said, "that the world is so small now."

"It doesn't mean anything," she said.

"Excuse me?"

"I just think, you know, that we travel to all these food festivals all over the world, and people are kind of the same everywhere, and the fact that we're all so interconnected now . . . it just doesn't mean anything. Here is the same as there and everywhere else. The world is tiny. So what?"

Tell that to my kid, I wanted to say, who had finally realized that his life in LA was over, that his friends would move on and grow up without him, who was experiencing crippling grief and anxiety over just how big the world is and how far away in it he was from everything he knew. Tell that to fourteen-year-old me. When I left Australia, it was as if my entire life, everything I'd ever known, was just gone. And now, some dude I've never met before is in an alleyway telling me he knows about the intimate details of my family's love life, even though he doesn't live here or have any meaningful relationship with anyone I actually know? It *is* crazy.

There are so many breezy narratives about moving somewhere with your family for the adventure, to give your kids a global viewpoint, whatever, and they're lies. Or maybe they aren't. Some people might be able to live that way, move that way, and think of it as flippantly as this drunk chick in the alleyway, but not I. The world is fucking huge. Distance is real. And when we arrived in Australia, my family felt like extraterrestrials.

But did that sense of otherness give me an advantage in my work? I think so.

Writing for *The New York Times* in Australia was a tricky balance. I knew instinctively that Australians would not appreciate being told what Australia is and isn't like by interloper Americans. Australia wants to be appreciated by the outside world, but we're also so used to being reduced to simple caricatures, and we have a real chip on our shoulders when it comes to what we see as America's arrogance.

I'm not sure anyone at *The Times* anticipated that dynamic. I imagine they thought Australians would be swooningly grateful that a paper so important and serious deemed Australia worthy of their consideration. As such, *The Times* did almost no formal promotion or explanation of what the hell we were doing. The bureau was announced, and that's pretty much it. I asked if we could run something explaining that we were going to do restaurant reviews here but that they'd be very different from what *The Times* does in America (or what Australian critics typically do in Australia), which is: assign ratings to new or important restaurants. The higher-ups in New York said they wanted "the work to speak for itself." I get the sentiment, but again, I think there's an element there of: *We are* The New York Times, *therefore, everything we do is important; therefore, no explanation is necessary.*

From the beginning, I was tasked with writing about things that might be interesting to an international audience. Which meant that it had to have a larger cultural story to tell than just: *Here is a restaurant, it is good (or bad).* It had to reveal something about the nature of Australia, or a certain community or city. In that sense, it was some of the most meaningful and exciting work I've ever done.

On my very first assignment, covering a Japanese café in the hinterlands above Byron Bay in northern New South Wales, I was in awe of my luck. We drove up the winding, hilly roads through subtropical forests, pulled into a town called Federal (population: 700), and found the beaten-weatherboard building that was now home to Doma, a café serving sushi but also kaleidoscopic salads with flower petals and yuzu, and burgers with Greek halloumi cheese. We sat outside in the sunshine, surrounded by kids and dogs and hippie locals, and I said to Ryan and Felix (who were with me because we were visiting my father, who lived nearby), "Holy shit, this job is going to be *fun.*"

And it was. I got to see more of my own country than I ever had when I'd lived here as a kid, more than most Australians do in their lifetimes. I quickly relocated that lost urge to explore, to discover, and found that in this instance, I was fervent about it. (Was it because it was in my home country? I'm not sure. I do think it had to do with the fact that it was different from what any other critic was doing in Australia.) I found fantastic Thai food in the middle of Kakadu National Park in the far Northern Territory. I found beautiful Mexican food in the residential suburbs of Adelaide, a prize all the more precious because Mexican food in Australia is mostly terrible. I wrote about fancy restaurants in old mental hospitals in the wilds of Tasmania, about the things I noticed that had been here when I left but were disappearing when I returned (milk bars; salad sandwiches), about new-school versus old-school Australian Italian cooking, about meat pies, about pubs.

Readers were confused. Americans didn't know why, all of a sudden, the paper was running stories about Australia. Australians didn't know why I wasn't covering the hot new restaurants. But slowly, I built a loyal audience in both places.

Because the bureau was so small, there were things about it that reminded me of working at an alt weekly. I did some editing of younger staff writers. If there was a story outside of food that I wanted to pursue, there was often a path to getting that story published. I wrote about the rehabilitation of the tiny penguin habitat on an island just outside of Melbourne. Later, I wrote about the horrible and inhumane police-enforced lockdowns that happened without warning in the early days of COVID at a few public housing facilities, affecting mostly African refugee residents. I'm so proud of those stories.

If the work was fun, it was also entirely unsustainable from a personal perspective. I was freelance, writing two reviews a month, getting paid $1,000 for each review. That's $24,000 a year. Because most of the stories required extensive travel, to scout for subjects and then eat at each restaurant three times, it was a full-time job. I tried to flesh it out with other freelance gigs, and I often wrote the weekly newsletter that went out to Australian *Times* subscribers. But for the first time since those times in Atlanta, we were seriously, dangerously broke.

Again, my life was the strangest dichotomy: a world of travel and dining and exploration and extreme privilege; a life in which I struggled to pay rent, when sometimes we couldn't afford groceries but my budget allowed for us to go out to dinner. Ryan eventually did find work, and things were precarious but doable. But I was so, so sick of the threat of poverty, of being that close to the edge. I was too old for it. Too far along in my career.

And if I thought leaving the country would shield me from some of the horror of what living in America is like, I was wrong. Years later, I still wake up in the middle of the night to read the news coming out of the United States, because waking up to a full day's worth of chaos that's already happened is just too stressful. It turns out that the awfulness of putting kids in cages, of kids dying in classrooms, is no less distressing just because the distance between you and those kids is greater.

On one particularly awful night, I woke up at 3:00 a.m. to the news that there was a shooting and hostage situation at the Trader Joe's in Silver Lake, where we'd shopped almost every day, where many of our friends and neighbors still shopped.

And that Jonathan Gold was gone, succumbing to pancreatic cancer that had been diagnosed only days earlier.

Ryan woke up to me crying and shaking, my heart utterly broken for the city I loved, for Jonathan's wife, Laurie, and most of all for his kids.

We took our first trip back to Los Angeles not long after that, mostly to see Ryan's parents in North Carolina, and to visit my uncle in Atlanta, who had recently lost his son, my closest cousin, to cancer. But we squeezed in a few days in LA. As soon as we arrived, in the early morning, we went to find a burrito. And for the first time in a year, sitting outside in that white LA sunshine, pouring salsa from tiny plastic containers onto the best Mexican food I'd had in a year (from a totally nondescript cart on the side of the road near LAX), Felix began to look like himself again. It was like watching a painting that had been drained of all color fill in from its edges, the beautiful shades of Felix reemerging. I recognized it as the same relief I felt upon arriving in Melbourne, that deep wonderful understanding that he was home.

Did I interview for Jonathan's job at the *Los Angeles Times*? I did. Despite myself, despite never wanting to live through that dynamic again. For the money. Because Australia was harder than I'd thought it would be. Because I still and forever love Los Angeles.

But mostly for Felix. I felt, honestly, that it might save his life.

The hiring editor brought me in for a meeting on Felix's fifteenth birthday—he and Ryan went to Six Flags without me. It was a very strange interview, and I realized that most of the questions seemed to be asking my advice about how to navigate the situation I'd gone through at the *Weekly*. In other words: Can you please tell us how a critic might live through replacing Jonathan Gold? They were looking for advice, but not looking at me.

A few nights later, in Atlanta, I saw Bill Addison, who was working at the time as the national critic for *Eater*. I told him about the weirdness of the *LA Times* meeting. He sighed and told me they had already offered him the job, days before I even went in for the interview.

Two weeks later, after visiting family and friends around the country, we flew out of Los Angeles at midnight, the time that almost all flights from LAX to Australia leave. Felix was quiet beside me, and I gripped his hand as the plane gained speed, closing my eyes, wondering if he'd retain the parts of himself he'd found here, even a little bit, or if he'd go back to the mute, colorless, scared kid he'd become over the past year. Just as the plane began to lift off, I opened my eyes, and the small oval window beside me was filled with the red neon of the sign from the building along the side of the runway: *Los Angeles Times*. I knew it was close to the airport but hadn't realized it would be the last thing I'd see, glaring in the nighttime, taunting me as I left America behind, again.

When we arrived in Melbourne, it was early morning. We took an Uber home, silly with jet lag. I used to try to stick it out through the day, push through until evening, before collapsing into bed, but nowadays, I allow myself a two-hour nap when I get in, just enough to clear the worst of the fatigue from my head. I had just hit my pillow, my mind on the very edge of consciousness, when my phone rang.

It was Fred. His voice was quavering. "It's Papa," he said, using the name we'd been calling our father since we were children. "He's had a heart attack. He's in surgery in Brisbane."

I got out of bed, picked up my still-packed bag, called an Uber, and went back to the airport.

Ian

Three weeks later

"Am I alive or dead?" my father gasped, sitting straight up in his hospital bed, clutching at nothing in the darkness of the room. I was only half awake, laid out on the floor beside his bed, having only just arrived a couple of hours earlier from an assignment in Western Australia that took me away for too many precious days. At around 10:00 p.m., I relieved Georgina, my father's youngest child, who was doing the bulk of these overnight shifts.

My father often woke in the night, terrified, and none of us could bear the idea that he might be alone through any of this. That, plus the fact that the nurses woke him at 6:00 a.m., urging him out of bed and onto a scale to be weighed, and that he found these early-morning disturbances upsetting enough that more than once it seemed as though the stress was going to give him another heart attack, his monitors beeping like wild. He needed someone there as an advocate, as comfort.

"You're alive," I assured him, sitting up and taking his hands. "You're in the hospital. George went home. I'm here."

"Besha? I'm alive?"

"Yes, it's me. You're alive."

My father was the type of man who looked to be about sixty from when he was forty-five to when he was eighty, partly thanks to a beard he wore for most of his life, which had turned gray by the time I was old enough to remember it. He was never sporty, but always active, and the heart attack that began his end, while I was on the plane back from LA, happened when he was dragging the trash bins up his half-mile driveway. A few hours later, he was in surgery and I was on a plane toward him, hoping I'd get there in time.

He made it through the initial surgery, and for a while, it looked as though he might pull through. When I arrived from that flight, delirious with jet lag and fear, he'd been sitting in his hospital bed smiling serenely. But he was immediately confused and flustered by the indignities of the medical interventions he required. He didn't want to eat much of anything other than ice cream. He couldn't distinguish between books and screens, wondering why he couldn't highlight something in a novel the way he would on a computer screen, why he couldn't click out of a television show. It reminded me of the ways in which iPhones derail my own dreams: I look to get directions or call someone, and the phone doesn't work, because my brain does not possess the necessary technology; and in the dream, I can't figure out why. He was suddenly stuck in that frustrating dreamlike limbo all the time. This is a man whose greatest strength had always been his intellect, his good sense. To be frail in this way, to have his mind betray him, was an indignity he could hardly bear.

He went home for a while, to be cared for by his wife, Mel, and Georgina, and occasionally Fred and our stepbrother, Peter, and me, and then went back to the hospital. I flew between Brisbane and Melbourne and Western Australia, where I was working on a story for *The New York Times* travel section, as well as a big profile for the food section about Nigella Lawson, who was headlining a festival in Margaret River. The juxtaposition of these things: the wine country flanked by the brilliance of the Indian Ocean; the extremely famous lady who, I was realizing, was extremely misunderstood; the anxiety of another phone call saying,

"You'd better come back. He's taken a turn for the worse." Those weeks were as surreal a time as any I've ever known.

They were also a gift. If he was confused and panicked much of the time, he also had spells of extreme contentment, times when he sat for hours and held my hand and told me he loved me, said how lucky he felt that I was there, that all his children were there.

The last time I saw him conscious, it was a good day. Fred and Georgina and I decided to bust him out of the hospital room—he hadn't been outside in weeks. We procured a wheelchair, looked that the coast was clear of meddling nurses, and rushed him down the hallway and into the elevators, him whooping with laughter.

He was so happy when we got him outside, so glad to have the sun on his face. I have photos of him with Georgina that day, out in the hospital courtyard, smiling as big as I've ever seen him smile. I left them there in the courtyard to catch a plane and go back to work.

He eventually went home again but was only there for a couple of days before he lost consciousness. I made it back in time to sit with him, read to him, stroke his head, but he wasn't really there anymore. There was a bed set up just outside the room where he was, and I lay there looking at the wall of books he'd read throughout his life, wishing I could still ask him about them, having the awful realization that the long and stilted and fascinating conversation we'd been having for forty-two years was over. He died in the middle of the night with Mel by his side on my third night perching on that bed, staring at those books, unable to sleep.

Before I left Australia, my father and I had a relationship as close as any I've had in my life. But he was contained, and hard to read, and not built for intimacy that reached across oceans. When we'd see each other, it always took a few weeks for us to regain that closeness—so much of the time, we misunderstood each other, made gestures that fell flat, lacked rhythm. And then, just as we began to get that rhythm back, I'd have to leave again. I think of that last year of his life in much the same way, us just getting ourselves back, and then he had to leave. It wasn't enough time. But I'm grateful for it all the same.

It also was a helpful reminder of why I was here, in this country, with my extended family. The universe was whispering to me. Which is a good thing, because I needed something to tell me it was going to be okay after the flip-flop of arriving and adjusting and then hoping for a minute that we might get back to Los Angeles.

I was too wrapped up in grief to care about the loss of the LA dream, much, apart from the hope that it dashed in Felix. But he probably needed that hope to be dashed in order to move on. Slowly, he started making friends. Slowly, he started to become himself again. He has never quite lost the anxiety of being a strange person in a place that's not his home. But he is going to make the best of that, just like I did. I only wish he got to know his grandfather better, because they are so alike in so many ways.

In a daze, I stayed for the funeral and then went back to my work for *The New York Times*, traveling the country looking for stories.

My mother came to visit for Christmas, and we decided to make a pilgrimage to the farm where I was born and where she had first lived when my father brought her back to Australia. My father, a huge C. S. Lewis fan, had named the farm Narnia.

My earliest memories are split between the farm and Cambridge, Massachusetts, where we lived for a couple of years when I was very young. But it was Narnia where my sense of self took shape. I clambered up trees in the orchard, I saved lizards from our pet cats, I chased the cows, I picked fresh fruit from the trees and strawberries from my father's long strawberry patch behind the house. In springtime, a dip in the paddock beside the house filled with rainwater, forming a temporary grass-bottomed pond, and lily of the valley sprang up all around it. At night, I dreamed I was the queen of the fairies.

My mother and I drove the six hours from Melbourne, stopping in each small town along the way. We were retracing the journey my mother had taken more than forty years earlier. As we got closer to Club Terrace, the tiny postcode where the farm was, the land became more intimate, wetter, more verdantly claustrophobic. Tree ferns and a towering grove

of eucalyptus trees hugged the two-lane freeway. Cell service became
spottier.

My mother was excited and nostalgic, pointing out landmarks along
the way, remembering the times she had traveled this road with my father
and then with me.

I, meanwhile, was a bundle of stress and grief and shock. I pushed it
behind a stony façade just as my father often did when he was feeling
uncontrollable emotions. He could be the softest, kindest man alive. But
he also could be stoic, sometimes to a fault. I felt inhabited by his resistance to messy emotion; the tides of grief and cold suppression swelled
and struggled inside of me as we drove deeper into the forest.

The old Club Terrace post office and general store looked as though
it had been abandoned for decades, its small timber frame gutted and
infiltrated by vines. We took the narrow, winding dirt road up from there,
past the nicely kept farms of our former neighbors, my mother wondering
aloud about each family and their whereabouts.

When we got to the gate to the farm, it was open. We drove down
the long slope of the driveway, past the paddock that led down to the
river. The old house was still there, but obscured by strange, shoddy ad-
ditions, walls and structures that looked like a child's cardboard fort, like
a shantytown compound. The yard immediately surrounding the house
was strewn with old plastic toys, a broken-down car, and a bus painted
with peace signs and John Lennon quotes. Dogs barked at our arrival. I
stopped the car a good distance from the house, feeling the intense anxiety of our intrusion. This is a place where someone might move if they
never wanted visitors.

The fields were overgrown and full of blackberry brambles. We got out
of the car, and my mother walked toward the house to see if anyone was
home. I felt rooted in place, anchored to the ground. Tiny birds flitted
around the fences nearby. It was eerie and close and isolated. The dilap-
idated paddocks felt like they were calling out to me to rescue them. It
was so green—greener than any green I'd ever encountered, wonderfully,

suffocatingly green. Isn't there a C. S. Lewis book where the kids, now adults, return to Narnia and find it crumbling and overgrown?

My mother walked around the house calling, but no one answered.

I was relieved when she returned to the car. But when we reached the top of the driveway, she jumped out again. "Let's go down to the river!" In a flash, she had disappeared into the brambles, finding her way down the steep slope to the riverbank, calling back for me to follow her. At seventy, she was still tiny and nimble, and I felt large and awkward and unsure of my footing in comparison. I have always felt this way with her, and she has always pressed ahead, encouraging me to do things I'm scared of or simply don't want to do.

I tried to follow, but it was too much: the juxtaposition between us, my father's obvious presence and dreadful absence. This had been his land, his life. He loved this place fiercely. And here it lay, uncared for and overgrown, and here I stood trapped in its closeness, its magic, the land of my birth, and I couldn't even tell him about it because he was gone. I stood at the top of the ridge and cried as my mother splashed happily along the riverbank below.

We decided to stop for dinner at the Bellbird pub on the way back to our motel. My parents and I had often eaten there on weekend evenings when I was small—my first meals outside of home—and I remember the smell of the beer-stained carpet in that pub as clearly as the smell of the wet springtime in the forest and farmland that surrounds it. Once, as a three-year-old, I tried to buy a biker a drink at its bar.

Back when we lived there, the four sawmills in Club Terrace shut down early on Friday afternoons and the workers went straight to the pub. By 4:00 p.m., the place was packed. When my mother and I arrived at 5:30 p.m. on a Friday evening that December, we were the only customers. The sawmills had shut down years earlier. The barkeep seemed perplexed that anyone was there, let alone two American women looking for dinner.

"Where are you ladies from?" he asked. That question I get asked everywhere, every day. I looked at my mother, searching for an appropriate response, and she grinned at me as she saw the shock spread across my face.

"I was born in Club Terrace, Victoria," I said. And then, for the first time in my life: "I'm from here."

Early the following year, about eight weeks after my father died, I got a phone call from the editor of *Food & Wine* magazine in the United States. It was out of the blue, and I assumed he wanted me to write a story for them about something in the Southern Hemisphere. What they actually wanted was far more involved, and terrifying, and incredible.

"We're launching a project called World's Best Restaurants, in partnership with *Travel + Leisure*," the editor told me. "The idea is that we send one critic around the world to pick thirty restaurants to be on the list. We want that critic to be you."

A Day on the Road

On Sunday morning, I wake up at 5:30 a.m. My alarm is sounding, but the room is dark, and for a long moment, I have no idea where I am. Not just which bed, which room, but which time zone, which country, which continent. Which hemisphere.

The note on my alarm helps. "Flight to Munich, 11:55 a.m. Leave by 6:30!" it offers, and the situation slowly comes into focus: the hotel room in the Italian countryside, the hour drive ahead of me to get to the airport, the dinner tonight somewhere . . . in some country . . . I'll check the itinerary when I get through security.

I get up, shower quickly, and pack the few of my possessions that are scattered around the room into my suitcase. Usually, I'm already packed by now, but last night was complicated, and I got in late. I'm staying at a farmhouse/hotel in Puglia, Italy, about ten minutes from the restaurant I was sent here to cover. The restaurant, Antichi Sapori, is in a small township with no accommodation, and I had to have the woman from my hotel call the restaurant ahead of time to arrange for one of the waiters to bring me back last night—there are no cabs in this part of Puglia, a fact no one thought about when booking this part of the trip. So after my meal of fresh fava beans topped with sharp cheese, a smattering of antipasti, toast with a puree of wild herbs, baked artichoke hearts, two servings of pasta, and grilled sausage, beef, and pork, I had to wait for service at the restaurant to end before I could get back, and after trying to stay awake through writing a dump of notes about my meal, I passed out before getting organized.

Luckily, I have a system in place. The opportunities for doing laundry are scarce when you're only ever in any given country for twenty-four hours or less, but I only wear my black jumpsuit for a few hours each night to go to dinner, so it can last a week or more. Underwear are washed in the sink and dried with a hair dryer. Leggings and oversize shirts for the plane don't take up much space. Shoes and coats are the real issue: on one trip, I might be in the tropics and then three days later in the snow, and it's hard to pack footwear and outerwear for both of those things when I often have to walk from my hotel to the restaurant and back. I have a blazer and one wool coat that takes up half my suitcase when not in use, and a pair of suede ankle boots that have worked thus far, though they're getting a little beat-up—especially given that they need to suffice as appropriate garb for some very fancy restaurants.

I scoop up my toiletries, refold my jumpsuit, pull my freshly cleaned underwear from the towel racks, shut my computer and stuff it, along with my many power converters, into my backpack, and wish this lovely room goodbye. The sun is just rising as I crunch down the driveway toward a black car that's waiting to take me to the airport. I look longingly at the tables that are being set for breakfast, the open-air dining room overlooking a sweep of valley that stretches toward the sea. I've never been to Italy before, and the violet light and long stone walls and hazy magic of this place make me want to linger, to sit at one of those tables and drink strong coffee and eat fruit with the other hotel guests. But no such luck. *I'm not hungry anyway*, I tell myself. I have not been hungry in months, what with all the scheduled lavish meals on my itinerary. Besides, I have a dinner appointment tonight in ... somewhere ... Slovakia? Switzerland? I need to check.

My cell phone isn't working in the car, and anyway, I'm too terrified to look because the speedometer is inching toward 165 kilometers per hour, the driver swerving and swearing in Italian. I try to do the math to figure out how fast we're going in miles and fail. It is just one more part of my brain that's scrambled, along with the part that tries to vacillate between multiple time zones, Fahrenheit and Celsius, dozens of currencies, dozens of languages.

Once I'm at the Bari airport, I secure some Wi-Fi and look at my itinerary, housed in a Google doc that changes all the time depending on what the folks at the magazine have been able to wrangle. (For instance, tomorrow night, I may or may not be dining at Noma in Copenhagen. There's a backup reservation somewhere else if they can't get me in. They've been trying for months, and apparently as of right now, it's looking good.) The itinerary says I'm headed to Slovenia, via Munich. Once in the departure lounge, I begin the daily panic about my newest destination: How will I get from the airport to the hotel? Will I need cash? If so, what is the currency where I'm going?

These are things you'd figure out weeks or months in advance on any normal trip, but when you're in a new country every day, in transit or eating or sleeping in a mad rush, the details tend to fall by the wayside until the last second. At least in Europe, I'm not having to make sure my visa is in place for every different destination. I only rarely have to use my language translation app. But it's still head-spinning, overwhelming, and deeply exciting.

The project is a collaboration between *Food & Wine* and *Travel + Leisure* magazines, and the idea is to offer an alternative to the Michelin guide, and the more recent World's 50 Best Restaurants, a list run out of the UK by *Restaurant* magazine. Both of these entities tend to focus on fanciness, though both are trying to change that, given the changing proclivities of culinary adventurists: Michelin now gives out "Bib Gourmand" distinctions for places they recommend that do not meet the criteria needed to gain a coveted star; the World's 50 Best encourage voters to nominate any and all kinds of restaurants, mostly without success—the list is still made up almost exclusively of places that fit under the fine-dining umbrella.

Both Michelin and the 50 Best have struggled with the various pitfalls of their individual setups: Michelin has been accused of favoring European and Japanese formality over food cultures that don't value the trappings of that formality; the 50 Best is, at its heart, a popularity contest—winners are based on the number of votes each restaurant gets from a pool of global voters. That makes it a system that is somewhat possible to game—if you have a really great PR firm that invites likely voters in for lavish comped meals, for instance. It also favors popular destinations like New York and London. A tiny restaurant in the forest in Tabasco, Mexico, that's very hard to get to? It doesn't stand a chance.

My mission is to find those places, to provide an alternative to the other lists and avoid those pitfalls. These lists and awards have vast influence on where and how people eat, influence that has only grown in the last decade. These magazines understand that their readers now travel to eat as much as any other reason, and the world of dining is being shaped, in a very real way, by the power of these accolades. Could we provide an alternative that dug deeper, that at least tried to mitigate the issues that the other lists face?

I'm not seeking out the most rarefied dining experiences but instead trying to find the places you would send a friend if you found out they were visiting a certain locale. Perhaps that might be fine dining—certainly not many people would argue with the premise that when in Copenhagen, one ought to get to Noma if one is able. But fine dining is not the only kind of essential eating. There are some fantastic high-end restaurants in Bangkok, but are they more vital as a culinary experience than the crowded marketplaces that contain a dizzying array of deliciousness? Absolutely not.

I'm looking for a sense of place, experiences that could only be had in a particular country or city. I'm looking for the food that you might travel across the world to get. And I'm traveling across the world, mostly solo, and still anonymous, to make those discoveries.

When I first got the phone call and had the project described to me, I was terrified. Terrified because I knew how hard it would be. And terrified because I knew I had to do it—who could say no to a proposition like that?

The magazines have put together a panel of global experts to recommend places I should visit. I don't have the time or the budget to spend three weeks in Paris eating at every possible contender, so we've trusted others to give us good options, and often, I'm only in any one country long enough to visit one or two places. The world is huge (it really is!), and thirty is a small number. If a nominated place doesn't feel right for the list, it's not hard to cut it. The harder part is narrowing it down to thirty, making sure all parts of the world are well represented, finding the balance and diversity that will make our list stand out from the others.

No one has ever attempted a project quite like this before, and we're making up the logistical part of it as we go along. Everything is always precarious—a state of being that is not unfamiliar to me, although not usually felt while alone and untethered from anything resembling home. There are scores of people helping to book my flights and hotels and making restaurant reservations, but when things go wrong in the moment, there's no one for me to call, no contact person to help me figure out a plan B.

Which is the exact situation I find myself in when I touch down. The itinerary says that the hotel in Slovenia is a two-hour taxi ride and will cost €150 each way. But when I arrive at the Ljubljana airport and approach the first taxi driver in the taxi rank, he laughs at me. He is not going to drive me halfway to Italy. I try a few more taxis, then start to panic. My dinner is in four hours, and I have to check into a hotel two hours away before then, I'm not sure how far the restaurant is from the hotel, and I have no idea how I'm going to get to the restaurant from the hotel anyway. I'm also not convinced that, even if I could find a taxi driver to take me where I need to go, I'd find anyone to bring me back early tomorrow morning. I google "driving in Slovenia."

"Driving in Slovenia is quite easy, generally safe and on the right side of the road. The roads are in excellent condition."

I head to the car rental office.

Thirty minutes later, I'm on the road in a boxy white car, driving out of Ljubljana. At first, the landscape is flat, a blur of slightly barren suburbs that are almost charming because the architecture is so pared back in a Scandinavian way. But before long, I'm winding up a mountain, the road twisting steeply between dense trees. It's early May, springtime, and the forest is speckled with baby green and flowers. The internet was right: the roads here are fantastic, which is a blessing because the winding, steep drive is quite dramatic otherwise.

After I've come over the top of a crest, the trees part, and I let out an involuntary yelp of joy and surprise. Spread out before me is the most beautiful valley I've ever seen, like some kind of alpine fairyland. The mountains all around are steep, and vibrant green, and covered in flowers and small clusters of ancient stone buildings. I pull over and step out of the car, the cows in a nearby field eyeing me suspiciously. The mountains lining the horizon are capped in snow, but the valley is bursting with spring. I'm laughing out loud, awestruck. For the thousandth time in the last couple of months I ask myself, yet again: *How did I get here?*

It's in moments like these that I fill up with wonder, with a sense of deep, bewildered gratitude that my life looks like this. It's an important counterbalance: just a few days earlier, in a small garden in San Sebastián, Spain, I wept on the phone when speaking to Ryan. I was lonely and exhausted, and I missed my family desperately. I knew that when I got home, that would be hard, too; I get used to the travel, the solitude, the hotel rooms. Home is overwhelming, dealing with the needs of a kid and a husband and a cat and a parrot (I'd do almost anything to try to cheer up a very sad Felix, it turns out, including agreeing to live with a bird for the next few decades). And just as I start to settle back into homelife, I have to get on the road (or in my case, in the sky) again.

A month earlier, three weeks into the North American leg of the trip, I'd ended up in a hospital in Atlanta with a fever of 104, dehydrated and with a flu that was threatening to turn to pneumonia, a result of the relentless travel and the time on planes and the inability to stop and rest when the initial illness came on. In that hospital room, hooked up to IV fluids and antibiotics, a nurse had bustled in wearing a mask (uncommon back then) and proclaimed that while nursing was a decent job, her real passion was food. "How can I do what you do?" she demanded, pen poised over a notebook, hoping for step-by-step instructions.

"Does this look like fun to you?" I'd croaked.

She stared at me for a long second and then motioned to her scrubs and said, "Does this?"

Standing on that mountainside in Slovenia, giggling to myself at the magical landscape that stretched out before me, I wished I could send a message to that nurse, an apology. Of course this was the best job in the world.

And, of course, there was the food. Despite my whining about being un-hungry on an existential level, there were constantly experiences, dishes, and flavors that broke through that lack of appetite and made me gasp, made me remember all the reasons I love restaurants, made me connect with the location in ways that felt profound.

I did eat a lot of fancy food, some of it transcendent, a lot of it pretentious and tedious. Noma, for all its wonder, has spawned a thousand imitators, restaurants that forage and pickle and ferment their local ingredients to the point of ridiculousness. Sometimes it works, and sometimes it doesn't, but certainly, there's a lot of sameness in the world these days. And when it doesn't work, it *really* doesn't work. I was able to take Felix with me when I went to Korea, and we ate at an astoundingly expensive restaurant that was housed in a huge, stark space with only a few tables and some of the most preciously austere food I've ever encountered. When the waiter dropped off a plate that was, I kid you not, a twig garnished with tiny pink flowers, Felix looked at me and said, "I love how the richer you are, the more likely the restaurant you visit is gonna be like, 'Here, have a stick.'"

It tasted like stick. I ate a lot of meals that blurred together, in places that have the Michelin stars, that sit near the top of lots of lists. How was the regular traveler supposed to distinguish between the worthy and the foolish? That wa my mission.

But I also ate glorious fatteh at a breakfast bar in the streets of Beirut, slick slivers of Sicilian sashimi crammed in at the counter of Swan Oyster Depot in San Francisco, bright lime-drenched mariscos from a truck in Tijuana, psychedelically funky laab from a stall at a marketplace in Bangkok. In Oaxaca, I traveled down a backstreet in a neighborhood near the airport and found a house where a young chef was making a five-course tasting menu that included tempura-fried huauzontle, a local wild green that tasted of pure chlorophyll, while the chef's mother made fresh tortillas on a wood-fired clay comal. In the mountains of Peru, overlooking an ancient agricultural site, I ate dusty-pink lamb tartare, slightly sweetened with cabuya nectar, and silken chocolate made on-site. In Tokyo, I waited in line and sat elbow to elbow with locals, slurping the best ramen of my life.

The food made me crazy. At times, the food tortured me. But when I took that bite, the one that whispered, "Yes, this belongs on this list, yes, this is the best in the world," the food was still and forever the point.

I get back in the car and drive down into the Soča Valley, through tiny medieval towns that cling to the sides of mountains, the roadways lined with sprays of yellow and purple flowers. When the Soča River comes into view, as I drive into the town of Most na Soči in the heart of the valley, I am again overcome by giggles. The river is an unworldly color, a luminous turquoise, like someone has emptied the Caribbean Sea into this riverbed and ramped it up with blue food coloring. I feel a kinship with the first human explorers to enter this valley: Who else would come all this way, make this trip, and have no idea what awaited them?

There have been times during this project when my lack of preparation was problematic, even dangerous: the time I drove across Jamaica in torrential rain on terrible roads with mudslides whooshing all around me; the time I was dropped on the edge of the medina in Fès, Morocco, at 9:00 p.m. with no cell service and no cash and no idea how to get to my riad buried somewhere in the heart of the medina's maze. But occasionally, it makes for the kind of discovery that modern travel rarely allows for: the kind when you find yourself in a country that, until that morning, you'd never even thought about before, let alone researched.

I drive along the river and look longingly at the towns I'm passing, church steeples rising from their twisty, ancient centers, wishing I could stop and explore just a little. This kind of frustration is constant, and I tell myself that much of what I'm doing is making a list of places to which I'd like to return—the travel I'm doing right now is just a scouting trip. That meal in Peru's Sacred Valley was less than forty miles from Machu Picchu, a place my father and I had always dreamed of going to together, a place I vowed to him I'd get to eventually. To go all that way, to be so close to something so remote and hard to access, then to turn around and leave, was a special brand of head-fuck.

The road to my hotel climbs back up a mountain on the other side of the valley, above the cloud line, the steep slopes dotted with baby goats. A tall, blond man welcomes me and shows me to my chalet, the exact structure you imagine when someone says *chalet*, a triangular wooden building perched over the mountainside, its interior perfectly minimalist, the bed in a loft up a steep set of stairs. I barely have time to take a quick video from the balcony overlooking the scenery before I'm hurried into a cab with guests from another chalet who are also headed to Hiša Franko, the restaurant where I'm booked to visit that evening.

Hiša Franko is located in the nineteenth-century house where chef Ana Roš and her family live, on the floor of the valley. As soon as I step through the doors, I understand that this restaurant is going to do justice to the breathtaking setting I've spent all day gawking at. A convivial staff welcomes me, offering a glass of nutty Slovenian sparkling wine and ushering me into the warm, red-walled dining room.

Wine begins to flow, and a flurry of small bites land on my table: a tiny salad of chickweed and green pea sitting atop an airy green cracker smeared with smoked bone marrow; a taco made from kale, elder blossom, and hazelnut miso; a piping-hot savory doughnut with a filling of intensely delicious lamb brains.

I'm giggling again.

I text Bill Addison:

Besha: Slovenia is fucking me up. Not sure I've loved a place so much, so instantly.

Bill: Amaaaazing. Wine must be 100% to your taste.

Besha: It is. But also? It's like Aspen and Middle-earth and New England had a hot European baby.

Bill: Here for that very Beshaleba description.

And then I text the part that won't make it into any magazine or newspaper piece:

Besha: There's this young sommelier here, who keeps feeding me VERY good wines, but introducing them from his crotch, like all of them are his huge penis? The one that came from a magnum was especially special. He nearly nudged my cheek with it.

When the butter for my spelt-and-whey sour bread arrives, it's covered in bee pollen, which tastes of pure springtime. Cuttlefish is shaved in a pile so it resembles lardo and is served with fried bread soaked in asparagus milk. There is a playfulness to this food that doesn't detract from its elegance, a lack of ego that allows pleasure to be the defining factor. You get the feeling that Roš is interested in one thing only, and that is delight.

I scurry to the bathroom to take some notes and also to photograph the toilets—I'm taking photos of everything, including the bathrooms of every restaurant I think will wind up on the list and every hotel bed I've slept in on the trip. I won't post any of this until later, lest someone figures out what I'm up to and disrupts the anonymous aspect of the project, but I know the social media needs will be intense when we launch the list.

Roš, blond and slight but sturdy, comes by and greets every table. She leads a tour of the kitchen, the wine cellar, the cheese cave. I'm enthralled, but also barely standing upright. The travel, the wine, the intensity of the day and the days before it and the days ahead of it feel overwhelming. I've taken dozens of photos, written pages of notes on my phone, in order to combat the fatigue and tipsiness that will blur the memories of this night. But right now, I just want to lie down.

I share a cab back up the mountain with the same people I came down with, all of us now gushing about the meal we just had. I stumble into my chalet, peel off my clothes, and step into a shower, then clamber up the stairs to the loft bed. I set my alarm, making calculations in my head: two-hour drive, rental car return, two-hour cushion at the airport for an international flight: 7:00 a.m., seven hours from now; a luxury, really.

Tomorrow, after a drive and two flights, my luggage will be lost. I will be in Copenhagen. I will be eating at Noma in the baggy shirt and leggings that I wore on the plane.

I will be so, so tired and so, so lucky.

Michelle

n March 2020, Ryan opened a restaurant.

To say that my husband's career has suffered because of my own would be a gross understatement. He is a good fucking chef. And he's never been able to prove it, other than for a brief time in Atlanta when he was the chef at a bar that was supposed to be a dive and he somehow made it into a destination.

When we moved to LA, one of the stipulations of my job was that he wouldn't work in restaurants. It was the right call, for me and the paper, and in some ways for our family; restaurant hours suck when you have a kid. But it made those long-ago dreams of Ryan and Matt feel even further away. He worked as a chef at the studios, and as a chef at the talent agency William Morris, and eventually at a nonprofit, which he loved.

But in March 2020, after two and a half years of struggling to find meaningful work in Australia, he finally realized the dream of his own restaurant. On a trendy stretch of Smith Street in Collingwood, he was given access to a little storefront with a beer garden out back for a rent that seemed reasonable. Grace took a few weeks off work to help him, procuring North Carolina paraphernalia and helping him set up the admin side of things. The place was called John Henry, the nickname of his maternal grandfather, the Durham dentist. His aim was to introduce Australia to real North Carolina barbecue, hush puppies and all.

In March 2020, I was in Brazil. And then Colombia. And then Mexico City. And then Tabasco, Mexico, where I took an hour-long taxi ride to the middle of the forest and ate the most incredible tlayudas of my life with a goat and a three-legged dog looking at me from the doorway. And then Miami, and Jamaica, and Houston, and Austin, and Saint Lucia, then New York City. Between Sunday, March 8, and Friday, March 13, I entered the United States three separate times, each time standing in long security and customs and immigration lines. On the last of those flights, people were wiping everything down with bleach wipes. No one was wearing masks yet. No one but me. (My brush with severe illness the year before, when I'd wound up in a hospital in Atlanta, had put me in the habit of wearing masks on planes—at first to protect other passengers from my own sick self and then to protect myself from ever getting that sick again.)

In New York, I spent a strange few days staying with my friend Osayi in Brooklyn. I'm amazed she let me come, given all that plane travel, all those airports. But no one knew what to do in those early days of COVID, and we missed each other, and she welcomed me in. We wandered my old Brooklyn stomping grounds as the city shut down around us. We made it to Wildair, but my Le Bernardin reservation was canceled the morning I was supposed to dine there. Other reservations in other cities were also disappearing, one by one. The editor of *Travel + Leisure* called me—we'd been in contact multiple times over those couple of weeks, the folks from the magazines wondering if I was okay, if I was uncomfortable with the idea of staying on the road. I was too naive to be scared. But things changed so rapidly, and this time she said, "I think it's time to send you home. Go eat wherever you want tonight, on us. And tomorrow, we've got you on a plane back to Melbourne."

Osayi and I went to Al Di La, an old favorite of mine and Ryan's from back in our Brooklyn days. We ate tripe and malfatti made with bitter greens, and braised rabbit, the last restaurant meal I would have for six months, and I said to Osayi, "Hopefully, I'll be back in a few weeks when this thing blows over."

I got one of the last flights out of LAX to Melbourne before they closed the borders.

In March 2020, Michelle Polzine went into the hospital for a procedure to remove an ovarian cyst. It was supposed to be routine; Michelle planned to reopen the charming San Francisco restaurant she owned, 20th Century Cafe, within a few weeks.

Remember Michelle? My original restaurant terrorizer? She of the long, red hair and the punk T-shirts? She of "what are your intentions"? That Michelle.

When Michelle woke up from surgery, the medical intervention had been far more drastic than originally planned. Doctors had removed all her reproductive organs, diagnosing her with clear cell carcinoma, a rare and aggressive form of soft tissue cancer. Four days later, San Francisco issued a shelter-in-place order, shutting down every restaurant in the city.

This is not a COVID chapter. This is a chapter about the kitchen culture that Michelle and Ryan and I were slowly poached in, and about one person's attempts to reverse or correct that culture, and the ways in which that has been impossible.

I, as much as anyone, want to see a kinder, gentler restaurant world in the aftermath of COVID. I, as much as anyone, want to see the kinds of shit that went down at Goldie's—the place that taught all three of us what we loved and hated about this business—banished from the lives of the cooks and owners and journalists of tomorrow. And Michelle's story, to me, is one that proves just how difficult that transition is likely to be.

Michelle was blindsided by her cancer and also somehow not surprised. She felt as if in some way, she had manifested the illness.

"I gotta change the way I am with myself and people," she told me at the time. "Not sure how, but I can't go on as Miss Anthropy anymore."

When Michelle's restaurant opened on the corner of Gough and Oak in Hayes Valley in 2013, it appeared to me as though she had conjured it from her very being. She is a dedicated lover of vintage, and the café was not her first project in re-creating something from another era. Her wardrobe is the most obvious and visible proof of this—when she's not working (and sometimes when she is) she dresses almost exclusively in clothes from the 1920s to the '40s—but her apartment in the Mission is still that magical time capsule, and the café was another re-creation, of the historic cafés she had encountered in Prague. If I loved 20th Century Cafe from the get-go, that's perhaps because I know and love Michelle, and it seemed like such a perfect embodiment of her obsessions and talents.

When it opened, I couldn't understand why it wasn't receiving more attention. But the food world back then was a very different place from the food world of today. Specificity, oddness, daytime restaurants, women, pastry chefs—none of these things got the attention and adoration that's more commonplace now.

Michelle heard through the grapevine that the critic at the *San Francisco Chronicle* at the time, Michael Bauer, declined to consider the café for a review because it did not serve dinner. Meanwhile, in Los Angeles in 2013, both Jonathan Gold and I were flipping our lids over daytime café Sqirl, along with the rest of the city. (I gave Sqirl a four-star review when it opened, though it was not open for dinner and you had to stand in line forever to eat there—it was one of my most controversial takes.)

There were few other places like 20th Century Cafe: it was a pastry-focused neighborhood restaurant before food media celebrated such endeavors as ambition. It was casual, yet held an air of sophistication and formality that other cafés did not. Michelle being a woman mattered, too. After years in the business and all that came with it—sexual harassment, lack of respect for pastry skills, normalized cruelty—she opened it in part to operate a different kind of workplace, one with a majority-female team, and one that she could be proud of. She tried to address the pay disparity between front and back of house—and the animosity it creates—by sharing all tips among all staff. "Unfortunately, that means we didn't have good service," she says. "But the dishwashers made more than I did." She wrote profit sharing into her business plan, but the business never made enough money to pay out anything. She tried to build a system in which employees could have some ownership stake in the business, "but when it came down to it, employees didn't want the pay cut and all the responsibility and hard work for the future payoff that ownership entails, and I don't blame them."

From the beginning, she had tremendous difficulty being a manager. "I always thought that everyone was like me, that they didn't want or need a boss. I did for my employees what I did for myself: set the bar almost completely out of reach, then tried like hell to reach it." She went to therapy for years to try to be a better boss, to have empathy for what her employees were going through.

But for all kinds of reasons, some of them personal and some of them structural, it never really worked. "The more time marched on, the needier employees became," she says. "And as the female warrior rather than nurturer archetype, I was woefully ill equipped for this task. I became terrified of my employees and in constant fear of offending them. Nobody understood or cared how overwhelmed I was." She was occasionally suicidal. People would quit and she didn't have the energy to hire anyone new, so she took on the extra tasks herself.

Michelle objects to the word *toxic* as it is often used in relation to the restaurant industry. "Every place and every person has good and bad qualities," she says. "Yelling at me from across the room when I'm going too slow is not toxic to me; sitting me down for a talk about how I can be more efficient with an 'I have so much respect for you' thrown in is toxic to me. One woman's energy vampire is another woman's guru." But she admits, and I observed, that the energy and camaraderie at 20th Century Cafe that Michelle was trying to create had soured. It was not that different from the culture she aimed to escape.

Michelle's story, as I see it, is one of what it's been like to be a woman in restaurants over the last twenty years, of the changing nature of what's considered important in the food world, and of the impossibility of change in an industry that's dying for it.

I have not had many dessert epiphanies in my life, especially since leaving the sugar cravings of childhood behind. But most of my adult dessert revelations were thanks to Michelle. There was the coconut layer cake she made at Goldie's, a dream of fluffy cake and creamy icing, years before Sean Brock and Ashley Christensen made New Southern cooking the hot new thing. The only coconut cake I'd had prior to that was saccharine, almost slimy, nothing like the pillowy wonder Michelle created. There was the panna cotta she made while working at Delfina, and which I ate on that long-ago trip to San Francisco to attend my first AFJ awards, which stayed solid only long enough to make it to your mouth before collapsing into milky silk on the tongue.

And, of course, there was the honey cake, the multilayered, widely copied dessert that became her signature. It was based on something Michelle tasted in Prague. "I didn't really think about it for a couple of years," she says. And then she came across something similar in San Francisco at "one of those quasi-bakeries in the Avenues, where everything is imported from New York." She tried to get them to tell her how to make it, but they admitted it was flown in from the East Coast.

"I couldn't find recipes for it anywhere," she says. "I had to go home and figure it out. I worked on it and worked on it. Everything sucked." A few mistakes and some sleuthing of old photos gave her a couple of breakthroughs, enough so that at one point she went to bed thinking, *It's pretty good. I think I've got, like, a cake.*

Her voice gets more excited as she explains, "I woke up the next morning and shot out of bed and was like: I HAVE THE ANSWER! And I threw away every single scrap of information I had. And I knew. It took me twenty-three tries that day, but I got it."

The cakes she'd had in Prague and the close approximations she found in San Francisco are different from the honey cake she created that day. They were the inspiration, but not the blueprint. "And now, I see my version everywhere."

Does she find the copycats gratifying or infuriating? "I did a therapy about it!" she exclaims. "I'm supposed to accept that my intellectual property is so valuable that people steal it."

She has let it go. "Defending the honey cake would be like a full-time job."

In 2018, Michelle sold the book that would become *Baking at the 20th Century Cafe* to Artisan Books. She rejected the idea of working with a writer and wrote the book herself over nine months, at night and on her days off.

The result is a glorious testament to Michelle's obsessions, with pastry, with Eastern Europe, and with perfection. "I felt like every single recipe had to be special," she says. "I'm not sure if that's how other people do it, but for me, everything in the book needed to have a really good reason for being there."

In late 2019, when she was working on book edits, Michelle posted a photo of the process on Instagram, making light of her editor's choice to cut a section she had written about jam. The crop of her photo made it hard to read the entire quote that was cut, but it boiled down to this: The world is scary and confusing right now, and there is a constant feeling that at any second everything will completely go to shit. You should make jam because when that day comes, when the world implodes, you will be glad that you at least have jam.

At the time, with wildfires raging in California, the advent of Trump's first impeachment trial, and the ongoing fury around cultural and systemic disregard for Black lives and female bodies, I found Michelle's treatise on reasons to make jam somewhat profound. It was also just so *Michelle*, her acerbic wit and blunt fatalism putting itself to use in order to encourage beauty. (It is not lost on either of us, the irony, that when COVID hit and everything *did* go to shit, jam-making became a favorite lockdown pastime. Michelle was a soothsayer with her excised jam treatise.)

Upon reading that Instagram post in 2019, I was unreasonably angry that she'd been asked to cut the jam prediction from her book. The message from her editors and the world seemed to be: Cake lady should be nice. There is no room for a complex cake lady, a cake lady who is sometimes mean and impatient, a cake lady who is tough and a little dark.

It's possible I was projecting. I had recently had an important project disintegrate, in part because my material was too dark and blunt. I saw this rejection as heavily gendered. Male food writers are allowed to be brash and profane, to question the role of America as a toxic (there's that word) cultural powerhouse; I was supposed to be lyrical and uplifting. Even now, even today, even decades after Michelle and I began navigating this testosterone-soaked industry, becoming tougher and savvier and funnier in order to make our way, those qualities were not accepted by the world around us, because that is not what cake ladies—or word ladies—are supposed to project.

At the same time, I'd been thinking a lot about what it took to be a woman who survived in the restaurant industry twenty years ago. And what it means to be someone who, throughout her life, has survived and thrived in part because she is able to be "one of the boys." I have taken a fair amount of pleasure from this distinction and harbored a sense of pride that I was tough enough, that I could roll with the inappropriate humor and pirate ship mentality, that I could do more than fit in, with Dave and the Goldie's crew, with the bad boys of food writing, with the punk guys who went to the various high schools I attended.

I had only just begun to understand how much of that mentality fuels the very problems that hurt all of us in this industry and in culture more broadly. Women, queer people, people of color shouldn't have to climb onto some macho bullshit pirate ship in order to feel comfortable at work or in life. My pride at fitting in is just another excuse, another tool that can be used against people. The idea that if I put up with it, other people should have to put up with it, too, is the same stupid logic that protects the status quo, that makes nothing better for anyone. Just because I could hack it doesn't mean people should *have to* hack it. That kind of thinking is almost as poisonous as the survival-of-the-fittest, abusive model that gave me something to hack in the first place.

I put this idea to Michelle and asked her how she felt, remembering how scary she was to me in my early restaurant days and how much she taught me in the process. We had been talking about the extreme sexual harassment she'd faced in the years between Goldie's and 20th Century Cafe, and the ways we thought we were immune because we had managed to assimilate in spaces where women were generally uncomfortable, and the ways that attitude had served us and also not served us at all.

She said, "The thing about surviving that time period in restaurants, of coming through all of that, is that it makes you really, really, really, really tough. And these days, I don't see anyone who is that tough anymore. No one wants to just do the work. I can let go of the rest, the other bullshit has got to go, but the toughness to get the work done . . . I'm not sure there's a magic way past that."

I ask her if she wants to have to be that tough these days. She does not.

When *Eater* SF ran a story about the eventual permanent closure of 20th Century Cafe, Michelle made it clear to them that she did not want to be portrayed as a victim of COVID. "Instead, the story ended up making me out to be a victim of city regulations," she says, sighing. While neither COVID nor the city's bureaucratic and regulatory labyrinth is completely to blame for the closing of 20th Century Cafe, neither of them helped. The main reason Michelle gives for the closing, though, is fairly simple. "I don't want to be a boss anymore," she says.

On a visit to San Francisco a few years ago, I stopped into the café. When I arrived, the tension in the air among the employees was palpable. I asked for Michelle; the woman behind the counter looked at me as if I were asking her to wrangle a dragon. When Michelle appeared from the kitchen downstairs and asked me to follow her back there— she was working, pulling pastry for strudel that was so thin you could see through it—she was flustered. She'd made someone cry. They had asked for some time off, and she had exploded. The unexpected request impacted plans of her own, downtime that she sorely needed. When I say *flustered*, I really mean "angry." But *flustered* is a more appropriate term for a cake lady, no?

Hayden Ashley, who worked at 20th Century Cafe as a pastry cook, witnessed Michelle's difficulties with managing people. "It was the toughest job I ever held," she told me. "She minced no words, and I always knew where I stood and where I needed to improve." But while Hayden appreciated this directness, she understands that other people struggled with it.

"If you are a woman in the restaurant industry, or any industry, the expectation is that you will be soft," Hayden said. "You're not allowed to have the hard edges and straightforward mannerisms of the men in the same position. So, when you're tough and expect the best from people, they get pissed that they aren't being coddled and treated gently.

"Michelle never made personal attacks, she never talked to me like the men I've worked for with blind, unfocused stress and anger. She gave swift and pointed feedback to bring out the best in me. It was always about the food, but people would take it so personally. I understand why she wouldn't want to do that anymore.

"After working for Michelle, I knew I would never work for a man again," Hayden said. "She showed me that being a force to be reckoned with was not a bad thing."

But for Michelle, it wasn't enough. All the therapy, all the hope and sweat and money she put into trying to create something outside of the old model of abuse and misogyny and purely capitalist ideals, was not enough. In the end, the toughness Michelle talks about as necessary to get the job done is perhaps the exact same thing that makes the industry so poisonous.

She tells me a story about teaching classes recently at a San Francisco culinary school. "All the students are talking about quality of life, about work-life balance. And I'm like: 'Do you want to be excellent at what you do? Then that *is* your life. If the work is your life, there isn't any problem with work-life balance. If that's what you're worried about, then this probably isn't the industry for you.'"

Not the most popular take in the age of Fuck You I Quit.

If someone with her drive and extreme talent and yearning to do things right, someone who will make a cake twenty-three times in one day in order to perfect it (and create a masterpiece in the process), still can't make a go of it in this business, then who can?

What if there were more room for people like Michelle, more respect, more resources? What if women were allowed to be authoritative and men were allowed to be nurturing? What if Michelle were allowed to be weird and dark sometimes and didn't have to be a happy cake lady 100 percent of the time to sell books and fit into the neat narratives that publishers and food critics and the public find so easy to digest? What if we valued the human behind the honey cake, exactly as she is?

The people I know with the most to give, the ones most likely to change the narrative of this industry, are also the ones who are least equipped to turn their passions into a business. And if they do, if they get past the massive strategic hurdles and financial barriers to opening something, it's entirely possible they'll come out of the wringer of running that business thinking that the stress and darkness needed to survive might literally give them cancer.

Ryan's restaurant, John Henry, was open for three weeks before lockdowns forced him to close. He was just starting to gain traction, just starting to break even. I am not convinced that he will ever recover from the grief of that, of putting all that time and energy and money into something so personal and never even getting the chance to see if it might succeed. The loss of John Henry before it really lived is a heartbreak that I fear will ache forever.

COVID also killed the World's Best Restaurants list for *Food & Wine*, as well as my *New York Times* column. I consider both of those things the best work I've ever done, the most rewarding, and the hardest.

I could not have traveled like that forever, and in many ways, my life now, as the senior critic at my hometown newspaper, is far more manageable. But I have my own heartbreak over the things I've lost.

In the restaurant world, as in the rest of the working world post-COVID, there's push for change, for some kind of more humane model. Many restaurants are open fewer days. Here in Melbourne, I've been somewhat inspired by Ngọc Trân, who owns a neighborhood Vietnamese spot, Bao Ngọc, and who changed the hours on the restaurant's Google page to read, "Hi folks! We are no longer participating in capitalism. As such we will be opening when we feel like it."

I spoke to Ngọc about this radical shift, and her story sounded fairly similar to Michelle's. She and her partner had tried for years to run Bao Ngọc in the traditional manner, and the toll was unbearable. Many nights, the couple would sleep in the restaurant, too tired to leave. "I'd be standing there, making pho broth, and crying in the pho," she told me. "When I looked around, there was no humane model."

The idea of a restaurant that operates entirely on its own schedule is antithetical to the idea of customer convenience and the service model upon which the industry is based. But maybe it's that underpinning that needs to change. When Ngọc started posting on social media about the small renovations taking place at Bao Ngọc, people started asking if that meant they'd be opening for regular hours again. "And I'm like, 'No!'" she said. "I really want customers to expect less."

There are other examples—in Portland, Maine, Vien Dobui and his wife, Jessica Sheahan, opened their restaurant Công Tử Bột in 2017 with a goal of paying all employees a minimum of twenty dollars an hour. They practice what Vien calls "consensual scheduling," meaning that all employees actively buy into the week's schedule and do not work any shifts they don't want. ("We spend a *lot* of time on the schedule," Vien told me.) Since having their second child, the couple have also doubled down on their efforts to make the business more humane for themselves, as well as their employees. The Lost Kitchen, also in Maine, operates three days a week, half the year, with a mostly female staff—a setup that wouldn't work for most businesses, but somehow does work there.

As far as I can tell, no one has yet figured out the exact right model. In media, the glorification of the brutality of chef and restaurant life continues via shows like *The Bear*—and to be fair, they wouldn't be depicting anything close to reality unless they showed that brutal side of the business. (Also? No one wants to watch a show about people being nice to one another and having a good, relaxed day at work.)

I'd like to believe—in some ways, I need to believe—that folks like Ngọc and Vien will lead the way toward something better.

These days, I work as a traditional restaurant critic for the daily newspaper in Melbourne. Ryan has gone back to nonprofit work, feeding people who need it. Michelle is teaching some classes and doing honey cake pop-ups in the old 20th Century Cafe space. "Discovering San Francisco's treasured parks in depth, trying to teach myself how to sleep, learning how to read again," she says. She'd love to write another cookbook, but her first book needs to sell more before that's likely.

And, as always, she is keeping me in check.

Ryan and I celebrated our twentieth anniversary during the depths of Melbourne's intensely strict lockdowns, when we weren't allowed to leave the house for months on end. We ordered in sushi and, later, pizza and tried to make the best of it, tried not to think about the trip to Vietnam we had planned to mark the occasion. I posted something about our twenty years together on Instagram. The next day, I woke up to a comment from Michelle:

"Yeah, but what are your intentions??"

Billy II

I t's that magical hour in Los Angeles, when the white haze turns pink-ish, when the hills turn gold and the bougainvillea stands in stark fuch-sia contrast to the gray streets. Bill and I, along with Ryan and Bill's partner, Sundafu, are walking into a trendy new restaurant in the Arts District. Ryan and I are on our way back home to Melbourne after vis-iting his parents in North Carolina. We have two days in LA, and Bill is making sure to fill every waking minute with insanely delicious things.

We started that morning with pour-over coffee that Bill made us at home and about which I can't stop teasing him. When I met Bill, he didn't drink coffee. During his years as national critic for *Eater*, when he was on the road constantly, I often would fly or drive from LA to what-ever city he was covering and act as an extra stomach to absorb all the things he had to eat. During those trips, he cottoned on to my habit of an afternoon macchiato, and now he is the dorkiest coffee dork I know, by a long shot. People: Would you believe me if I told you he drinks his morning coffee from a *wineglass*? All the better to swirl and taste, my dear. I am not shitting you.

"I considered using a mug while you're here," he said to me that morning when my eyes nearly rolled out of my head as he twirled the coffee in his goblet, "just to avoid the ridicule. But then I thought: *Fuck it*. I am who I am. Anyway, it's all your fault."

He's right: I introduced him to coffee, and once Bill falls for something or someone, he is all in. It's what makes him such a good friend, such a good writer, such a good critic. The man is *passionate*.

After coffee, we went and picked up bread and cheese from Cookbook in Echo Park, tacos and burritos from a truck, banchan and noodles from a newish Korean takeout shop, and pumpkin pie from a bake sale on the street that Bill couldn't resist. We went to a park, spread everything out on a long table, and feasted on things I only dream of eating when I'm in Australia, washed down with a prized bottle of Lebanese wine that Bill had saved to drink with me.

Then we napped. And now we're three steps into a restaurant that Bill needs to check out for his annual 101 Best Restaurants list for the *Los Angeles Times*, where he has been the critic for five years. We're about five steps in when I see it: the manager's double take, surprise and delight and concern, before he rushes off toward the kitchen. Bill has been made.

"It's not unusual." Bill sighs as we slide into a semicircular booth. "It's partly his fault." He motions to Sundafu, who, to be fair, could not blend in or go unnoticed anywhere. The man looks like Denzel but . . . better? If that's even possible? They are not a pair you'd easily forget, and Bill describes food and experiences in his reviews so sharply that anyone who might have been there—a waiter, a manager—would easily remember the two handsome dudes who ate and drank those exact things.

Bill and I are ensconced in a continuation of the same conversation we've been having for almost twenty years: What the fuck are we doing? How are we doing it? Do we want to keep doing it? Who are we doing it for?

I gotta say, my boy is a bit despondent. Anyone who followed what happened in the food section at the *Los Angeles Times* in the years after Jonathan passed away will know it was a bad time for all. I wasn't there and don't feel equipped to tell the story, but it reportedly involved a toxic workplace, whispers of sexual harassment, pay disparities, power struggles, several scandal-drenched departures, and a staff left horribly shaken by all of it.

We order cocktails—an old-fashioned with pandan and pineapple, a Collins with Manischewitz, drinks with a kaleidoscope of cultural references, just like the city they represent.

"I can't believe I've been doing this for twenty years now," Bill says.

The trajectory of our careers is so oddly similar, but in many ways, it shows how few people do this as a career, who have maintained that path, who don't burn out. Of that dozen or so people in America, most of them stay in one job, or at least at one publication, for the entirety of their careers. Being a newspaper restaurant critic is a job that people do until they retire, in many cases until they die. Bill and I are oddities—we have wanderlust, but we also only know how to do this one thing. It's made for professional lives that have intersected in so many ways. I followed him into the Atlanta role. I've lost count of the times we've both applied for the same job. He roamed the country endlessly as national critic for *Eater*. I roamed the world as international critic for *Food & Wine*. He followed me into life as a critic in LA, even the utterly bizarre dynamic of replacing Jonathan. Through all these years, our friendship has never been damaged by the underlying competition. If anything, it's been strengthened by the knowledge that someone else understands the intricacies and complications of a life that is so, so weirdly specific.

And now, here both of us are, city critics in the cities that we both love best. And we've both lost some of our idealism. These are the actual dream jobs. And yet they feel somehow small.

"I guess the work I was doing pre-COVID felt vital, different, revolutionary," I say as appetizers start appearing—the ones we ordered and the ones that are "compliments of the kitchen." Bill squirms and tells them it's not necessary, but, like me, he can't make himself be the jerk who sends things back.

"How do you mean?" he asks.

I explain: For *The New York Times*, restaurant reviewing as an act of cultural criticism and exploration of a whole country; for *Food and Wine*, creating a "best of" list—that dreaded beast!—that celebrated the diversity of the whole world, not just a to-do list for wealthy jet-setters. And now, here I am, doing my best in Melbourne to expand the types of places the newspaper covers, but it's hard. They have a rating system that is both convoluted and set in stone, one that rewards fanciness above all else. Because they share this system with the Sydney paper, and because the guide they put out every year uses this system and is written by dozens of reviewers, I can't single-handedly shift the meaning of those ratings. My favorite restaurants in Melbourne don't even make it into the guide most years because they don't score highly enough. I talk about this constantly with my editors, with other writers, and everyone agrees that we need to be more inclusive, more reactive to the way people actually eat these days. But change is slow, and there's still a bias against what the higher-ups see as "cheap eats," a term that usually only serves to devalue immigrant labor and foodways.

Have you noticed a change in me? Here I am, in a position to base my entire life around the Stephanie's of the world, and I find reason to whine about it. But decades of eating in restaurants like that will make you realize how rare the truly great ones are. They exist! And when you find them, the magic is still there! But my time on the road made me appreciate that wonderful food is found at every level, and horrible food is found at every level, and the history and narrative behind the food is often the thing that excites me just as much as the food itself. "Luxury items for rich people" isn't a very interesting narrative.

Bill has more freedom in the things that he can celebrate. And there's so much to celebrate in Los Angeles. In that, he finds great joy. But he struggles, as I did, to live in the shadow of Jonathan, perhaps even more than I did, because he and Jonathan are more alike, as writers and critics. "I have freed myself from the burden of negative reviews," Bill says. "I'm just a guy who wants to lift up the people who are doing cool things, and luckily, LA has no shortage of those people."

But both Bill and I wonder about who should be telling these stories. There are other, vital voices that need to rise, to be given a platform. We worry that those voices will never get the chance, whether or not we stick around for another decade or two. The alt weeklies are as good as dead; there's nowhere for young talent to find mentorship or learn, and the writing seems to always come second to the allure of influence.

It's hard to have a positive outlook on the future of criticism these days. The truly ambitious projects, like the ones I was involved with pre-COVID, aren't returning in the post-COVID world. At least not yet.

Some things do give me hope and inspiration. The review-like newsletter that Helen Rosner has been putting out at *The New Yorker* actually feels fresh. "She's so fucking good," I say, and Bill yelps, "I know!"

"It's funny," I say, "because she's spent so many years declaring that she's a food writer but not a critic, and it turns out: bitch, you a critic."

Helen does what I tried to do with my best reviews, something I struggle to do now when I'm writing to a specific rating that I need to justify: she tackles a topic bigger than the restaurant, bigger than the commerce of the endeavor, and makes the review a piece of philosophy. I want to read her writing about restaurants I will never go to, in a city I do not live in. Part of that is the magic of New York, but part of it is the magic of her and her writing and her brain.

Bill asks me what's the last thing I wrote that I feel that way about.

"It's hard," I say, "but I definitely felt that way about the *New York Times* stuff, even though I was often frustrated with the actual writing process there. They spent a lot of time trying to tamp down my voice, make me more *Times*-ian. But when I look back on my review of Agrarian Kitchen, for instance, I think it did exactly that: it took a restaurant and made it the avatar for something bigger in culture. I used a restaurant review to explore who we are and who we pretend to be and asked if we really want to be that."

Bill shakes his head. "I just don't know if there's space for either of us to do that in our current jobs," he says. He's trying; we both are. But the format and the limitations of the weekly review genre and the needs of our respective publications make it so hard.

"I guess we'll have to write books instead," I say.

We have eaten and drunk ourselves silly, and when the bill comes, the manager delivers it with a flourish. "All of the beverages are on us, compliments of Chef," he says proudly.

"No, no, no . . . ," Bill says, looking desperate. "Please, I need to pay for everything."

The guy looks uneasy, his smile still plastered on his face but faltering, obviously not knowing what to do. Bill launches into a speech I can tell he's given before.

"Look," he says, "first and foremost, this is my job. It's what I do, and it's not my money. Second, that job? The place I work for? It's owned by a billionaire. You are a small business. So why don't you let the company owned by a billionaire pay for the meal that they have budgeted to pay for. Please."

"Okay, I'll check with Chef," the manager says anxiously.

"I'm surprised," I say. "I thought this was kind of a thing of the past . . . like, people were getting the hint that critics don't want free shit even before I left the U.S."

"The influencer economy has fucked everything up again," Bill laments. "There are so few true critics, and so many influencers and semi-critics, and I think this is just the norm now. I hate it so much."

The manager comes back with the full bill and our box of leftovers, and we thank him profusely, and Bill leaves a stupidly large tip.

When we get home to Bill's house, he starts to unpack the leftovers and groans. In the paper bag, they've included a gift—a box of the fancy hand soap they use at the restaurant.

"They won!" I cackle.

"Ughhh, they didddd," Bill moans. He opens and smells it. "I hate this!" he screeches. "It smells like lies, like deceit, like corruption!"

"I'll take it," I say. "I'll take it home to Australia and wash my hands with it, and every time I smell it, I'll think of you and your ironclad integrity. But only if you sign it for me."

Bill takes the box and grabs a pen. With a flourish, he writes, "Bon Appétit!! XOXOX Bill."

REVIEW: THE AGRARIAN KITCHEN EATERY & STORE IN NEW NORFOLK, TASMANIA

First published in *The New York Times*, December 21, 2017

NEW NORFOLK, Tasmania—There may be no restaurant in all of Tasmania as bright and airy, as brimming with good feeling, as the Agrarian Kitchen Eatery & Store. The long room's impossibly high pressed-tin ceilings and white-painted walls manage that elusory meeting of modernity and rusticism—simplicity at its most luxurious.

Sculptural light fixtures, which look like geometric antlers with glowing tips, stand out dramatically. Sunlight streams in through the tall, antique windows, illuminating the farm equipment hanging on the wall. These "artisan garden tools" are for sale, along with a few other well-chosen kitchen and decorative objects. The spade costs $225; the hoe is $113.

The food here is focused on simplicity and seasonality, the kind of pleasure one might derive from a thick piece of dense and springy sourdough bread served with fresh cultured butter. Many things are pickled or otherwise fermented. Fresh farmer's cheese arrives on your polished wooden table sprinkled with tiny, purple garlic flowers alongside chewy pretzels encrusted in caraway seeds.

At one end of the room you can glimpse through to a gleaming kitchen, where hunks of meat are cooked over an open fire, giving the whole dining room a slight scent of wood smoke. Behind the long bar, Adi Ruiz, one of Australia's most accomplished bartenders, shakes and stirs drinks using garden-fresh ingredients.

But there's a stark, almost shocking contrast between Agrarian Kitchen and its surroundings. That room's high ceilings and striking windows are linked to its history, as the infirmary for the women's wing of Tasmania's largest mental hospital. The restaurant is smack in the midst of the ruins of that asylum, a hulking sprawl of old brick and stone buildings that rise ominously from the side of the road as you enter New Norfolk, the town where Agrarian Kitchen makes its home.

The Royal Derwent Hospital operated under several names for over 170 years, from 1827 to 2000. It was an economic driver for the town, and also the alleged site of horrific patient abuse. The grounds are now mostly abandoned, suffering from neglect, vandalism and arson. It is a staggeringly unlikely location for a fancy restaurant.

Agrarian Kitchen is a pleasant 40-minute drive from Tasmania's capital city, Hobart. It is open four days a week—and only two of those for dinner—and seems geared mainly toward day-trippers and tourists. The owners, Rodney Dunn and Séverine Demanet, originally moved to Tasmania from Sydney in 2007 to open a "paddock-to-plate" cooking school and farm in nearby Lachlan. The restaurant, which gets many of its ingredients from its sister farm, opened in June to much acclaim.

The word "agrarian" conjures the kind of fantasy that wealthy urbanites like to indulge, centering on a relationship with nature and food that is full of beauty and wholesomeness. Romantic notions of country life are an important part of Tasmania's, and indeed Australia's, self-image. But despite its stunning natural beauty, the economic and social reality in much of the state is fraught.

Like so many rural communities, New Norfolk, and the surrounding Derwent Valley, is plagued by high unemployment and low high school graduation rates. Recent census information shows the Derwent Valley—and New Norfolk in particular—to be one of the most economically disadvantaged areas in the state. The Agrarian Kitchen represents change for this region, an inkling of Tasmania's bright future—a future with tourism at the heart of its economy. But there is a disconcerting disconnect between the fantasy of country life that the restaurant presents and the sobering reality just outside its doors.

Inside that beautiful room, all seems well. The head chef, Ali Currey-Voumard, is from Tasmania, but honed her skills in some of Melbourne's best-known kitchens. Now that she is back in her home state, Ms. Currey-Voumard is helping to invent a regional Tasmanian variant of new Australian cooking, with produce leading the way.

At the height of spring, the most astonishing thing on the menu was a pile of fresh asparagus, blanched and shocked, and set over kefir cream sprinkled with chives and crumbled bresaola. The accompaniments were nice enough, but the revelation came with the lush green flavor of the asparagus itself. A few weeks later, as spring leaked into summer, the dish was still lovely but not quite as thrilling, the vegetable having lost some of its adolescent charm.

A lot of what is on offer at Agrarian Kitchen resembles wholesome farmers' market-driven home cooking, but with slight cheffy twists. A fat pork chop, cooked just a tiny bit past juiciness, sat in a pool of dark green sauce made from lovage and anchovy. There is always one shareable large-format hunk of wood-fire-cooked meat on the menu, served with a flurry of sides. A Berkshire pork shoulder came with tongs for pulling apart its tender meat and crackling crispy skin, accompanied by boiled pink eye potatoes with bay leaf butter. It made for the kind of meal that felt communal and hearty and nourishing, almost humble. Like getting back to the land, to something that is true and pure.

Despite all this, the contrast between the restaurant's feel-good aura and the surrounding landscape made it hard for me to feel particularly pure about the experience. The dark history of the Royal Derwent hospital, and the dark present of New Norfolk, give the entire operation a haunted quality.

The hope, of course, is that New Norfolk will eventually match the bucolic story that Agrarian Kitchen is selling. Many see it as a beacon of hope, a use for these vast historic buildings, a lure for other like-minded businesses and a way to bring tourists and jobs to New Norfolk. (A significant percentage of the business' employees are from New Norfolk and Lachlan; many of them work at both the restaurant and the farm.)

If Agrarian Kitchen represents the future of Tasmania—its potential tourist economy, its charm, the deliciousness of its food—it also hints at the problematic stories that the moneyed creative class tells itself about the value of its own consumption. Agrarian Kitchen is a lovely restaurant. It is also a bourgeois fantasy, one that trades on some dubious strengths: the sugarcoated romantic charms of rural life; our blasé slavishness to all things artisan; and the precarious thrill of eating a $200 lunch on land that's stained by human misery.

Epilogue

Tony

The stupidest thing I ever did was in the aftermath of a breakup. I was seventeen, and my first long-term boyfriend, my first true love, dumped me. It was inevitable. My mother had moved us from Hartford, Connecticut, to Tarrytown, New York, so she could take a job at *The New York Times*. My boyfriend and I both had a year left of high school, and now we lived in different states. I made plans that we would get through high school and then move to Boston together. He met a cute girl at his part-time supermarket job.

They've now been married for over twenty years.

He could not find the courage to tell me the truth. He was never home when I called. I ended up taking a bus to Hartford and confronting him, and even then, he wouldn't say the words. He made me guess. But the sick feeling I'd had for weeks was full of comprehension I'd refused to face.

I went back to the apartment where I was staying with friends and took all the pills I could find. I'm not sure I blame this act of desperation on depression. I was depressed, in a general sort of way, and I was also seventeen, and I'd moved five times in the previous three years, and two of those moves were across hemispheres. But I mainly did it because I couldn't face waking up to the searing pain of heartbreak and humiliation and loss the next day. And I was so, so, so very angry. I wanted to hurt him as badly as he'd hurt me.

(Do I need to even say this here? It wasn't his fault. In any way. Obviously.)

I didn't think about the other potential hurt, to my parents or siblings. They never crossed my mind. Writing this now is the first time I've ever considered what it would have done to my brother and sisters to lose the oldest among them to something so stupid. . . . It's outrageous how myopic the urge is when it comes.

The next morning, when I did wake up, I was still angry. And now I was angry I was awake, that it didn't work. I got up and walked to the CVS on Farmington Avenue, the same one where the boyfriend and I had stolen cough syrup early in our courtship and taken it to Elizabeth Park on a glorious spring day that exploded with possibility. New love, washed down with Robitussin.

Now, it had come to this: At the CVS, I bought a package of sleeping pills. I thought, for the first time, about writing a note. I was thinking of him; I would address it to him.

But then I thought of my mother, because she was the one who would see it.

I called her. "I'm scared," I told her through gulping sobs.

Two years earlier, when I really had been depressed in an everyday-darkness kind of way, my mother made me promise that if I ever found myself in this kind of danger, all I needed to do was tell her those words: *I'm scared.* She knew how much easier they would be to say than the actual words, which feel so shameful and self-important and hysterical and . . . well, unspeakable.

"Where are you?" she asked from her office in Times Square, at her new job where she was under immense pressure to do well and be competent, at a time where a single mother with four kids was not the norm in the halls of *The New York Times.* (Still isn't.)

I told her. She called her ex, my stepfather, who stayed in Hartford

when we left. He came to get me. The sleeping pills were no longer a
threat; I took two of them and passed out on a small bed at the back of
my stepfather's apartment until my mother arrived. She left work mid-
morning and took the train back to Tarrytown and got in the car and
drove the two hours to pick me up and then drove me home.

I have had deep, dark periods of depression in my life since then.
Days and weeks when I could not make it out of bed, when I felt like a
beast was clawing at my chest. That was not one of those times. And I've
never again come close to the act itself.

There are ghosts in this book. Mainly the ghosts of men who have been
all but sainted in the eyes of the world they left behind but with whom
my relationship is much more complicated.

There is the ghost of Matt, the person I think of when I write. Not
just Matt specifically but all the line cooks like Matt, who work too
many hours, care too much, put themselves under too much stress, die
too often. Matt, who would be the proudest of me, of this, of everything.
Matt who has been gone for more than twenty years, goddamn it all to
hell.

There is the ghost of my father and the things we could have been to
each other, if given the chance.

There is the ghost of Mr. Gold, a man I deeply admired but who disappointed and, yes, hurt me with the pettiness of his dismissal, his refusal
to acknowledge my existence. He didn't owe me anything, and he gave
me one of the greatest gifts and honors I've ever had, that of rising to an
impossible occasion. But my feelings about him will always be fraught.
In the course of writing this book, I reached out to Laurie Ochoa, his
wife, whom I met briefly during that ill-fated interview at the *Los Angeles Times* a year after we moved to Australia. (Originally, in the very
early days of this book's conception, I'd imagined asking Jonathan for
an interview, but then, shockingly, he was gone.) I wanted to humanize
the man, to ask Laurie what it was like for him when he left *LA Weekly*,
to see where that conversation might go. Laurie never responded to my

email, and of course, I don't blame her. Everyone wanted a piece of Jonathan, still wants a piece of him, and I am probably the last person she'd want to give any part of him to. Fair. His entire attitude about me was that I wasn't worth considering—I imagine her trying to honor that. I imagine a lot of things.

But the ghost that haunts this book most thoroughly is that of another posthumously sainted man, one who did consider me, one who haunts so many of us.

It was morning in the United States when the news broke that Anthony Bourdain had taken his own life at a hotel in Alsace, France, but it was late evening in Byron Bay, Australia, where I was sitting at a fancy resort eating a fancy dinner. I was with my sister Grace, who agreed to come with me on this particularly intense work trip, on which I was scheduled to eat fourteen meals in six days. We were on day two and eating our second full dinner of the evening.

The trip was for an assignment I'd taken for a national restaurant guide, to write short reviews of twenty-four or so restaurants, many of which were in Queensland, a two-hour flight from Melbourne. It's the type of assignment that conjures envy in nonprofessional but enthusiastic eaters: take an all-expenses- (or most-expenses-)paid trip to a beautiful location, then eat your brains out at that location's most well-regarded restaurants. But those of us who rely on these assignments for financial and professional reasons know how hard they can be. You are away from your family. You are often alone. You are required to eat beyond gratification, beyond comfort, and often beyond reason. Much of the pleasure of dining is sapped when each bite must be considered as potential source material. And often, the money sucks.

This particular assignment ended up being about four- or five-weeks' work. In the end, I was paid $1,600 for that work. I got a lot of meals out of it, and I took the gig as a way to get to know the Australian food scene better. It was made vastly more bearable thanks to my sister's presence during the research trip, and I don't know how I might have managed if she weren't sitting with me in that fancy restaurant when the fact of Tony's death reached me.

Our waiter was in his midforties, a Brit with bad teeth who looked like Steve Buscemi with an Evan Dando haircut. We appreciated him for his service industry skeevy weirdness. When the news came dinging in through our phones, and Grace and I were suddenly sitting next to each other holding hands and she was crying, the waiter said, "You've had some bad news, have you?"

We told him. "Is that an actor?" he asked. "I've never heard of him." Suddenly, I was furious at this guy for impersonating a lifelong hospitality soldier. How could he not know?

A little later, he came back to the table and told us there was an echidna on the deck near the kitchen, and we should come see it. We walked through the restaurant and out a back door to find a few staff members huddled around the small marsupial, who had buried its head deep into a corner of the wooden deck. You could see its spikes shaking with terror.

Early one morning in the mid-2000s, when I was living in Atlanta, my cell phone woke me with a 917 number I didn't recognize. "Hello, Besha?" a familiar voice said when I answered. "This is Tony Bourdain." I sat up straight in bed like lightning, the way people do in the movies. I was half asleep and a little hungover and completely unprepared.

Two days earlier, I'd called Bourdain's media reps, requesting an interview for *Creative Loafing*. I hadn't heard back from them and had no idea if they were going to agree to the interview. (*Creative Loafing* is a very hard sell as a name for a newspaper that you ought to take seriously.) I guess Bourdain decided he wanted to talk and just went ahead and called me. I stuttered about being in the middle of something and asked if I could call him back in thirty minutes. He agreed. His number is still in my cell contacts as a result.

Is it worth telling you everything Tony meant to me? You've heard it all before. Ryan and I worked in kitchens in New York City and elsewhere in the late '90s and early 2000s. The world Bourdain described in *Kitchen Confidential* was our world. I began writing about food partly because I was frustrated that the voices in criticism and magazines were not voices I recognized. The people I knew who cared the most about food were cooks and waiters and dishwashers and chefs. When *Kitchen Confidential* came out, I was a waitress in New York City going to school for writing and working part-time for a literary agent, dabbling in posting bawdy, pretentious restaurant reviews on eGullet. His voice was our voice. He led the way.

In his years—close to two decades!—as Leader of the Food World, I grew jaded. I, too, am an old punk who can't shake my disdain for the sell-out. His theater tours, his more ill-advised TV ventures, all gave me the ugly jealous impulse to write him off. That he was so integral to the tenor of the bro culture that bruised me, in ways both personal and professional, certainly added to this urge to be sick of him.

But it was impossible. Every time I spoke to him, every time I read something he wrote or watched one of the better shows, I had to swallow my misguided desire to proclaim (if only to myself) Bourdain's time as over. He was so present, so thoughtful, so willing to self-examine. During that first conversation (after I woke up enough to get my shit together to call him back), he was promoting one of his theater tours. He had just released a book. He was talking to multiple journalists a day. And you could tell he had the answers to everything in his pocket— pulled from the material, always Bourdain-ian and funny and profane, but canned nonetheless. Even so, when you pushed to get past those rehearsed responses, when you asked questions that were unexpected, you could feel him ticking open on the other end of the line, and all of a sudden, he was *engaged*, and thrilled to be engaged, and the conversation was real, and he was smarter than anyone else on whatever topic you threw at him. What a fucking mind!

Years later, when I was working for *LA Weekly*, I went to the set of *The Taste*, the cooking competition show that many people see as Bourdain's lamest project. I was told I'd have ten minutes to interview him after his taping was done. We'd met a couple of times briefly, and I'd interviewed him on the phone, and he'd tweeted appreciation for some of my work at *LA Weekly*. But we did not know each other. We settled down to talk outside his trailer, and we just . . . kept talking. For well over an hour. Every ten minutes or so, at first, a PR handler from the show would stop by to try to call time, but he waved her off. Eventually, he just said, "Look, I'm fine. We're talking, and we're gonna keep talking."

Even on the set of the glitziest, silliest thing he ever did, he was infinitely more real than any other celebrity I've ever encountered. You know this, though, right? Everyone knows this.

When I made the gut-wrenching decision to leave a job I adored in Los Angeles and move back to Australia, the reasons boiled down to this: I wanted to center my life more around a personal identity and less around a professional identity. The 2016 presidential election threw me into a massive, soul-searching, existential quagmire. *What is the fucking point? What am I trying to achieve?* Every decision I made up until then in my adult life was about advancing my career, about ambition, about ego. I was so sick of American ego; I wanted to squash my own.

And then, the opportunity arose to write for *The New York Times*. It seemed too good to be true. I could have my ambition and my low-key Australian lifestyle and my sister and brother and father. It would be the best of all worlds.

Things are never that easy, folks. So much of my identity *is* centered around my professional life and the food world community. That community is now very far away.

If it was hard on me, it was harder on my husband. And it was hardest on my son. I upended his life in a way that felt monstrous. In the wake of that, I could not have picked a worse time to be spending weeks on the road, which is what my new reality required. It also required eating and drinking and doing amazing, fun things. I was never not awestruck by my luck. But I was anxious and worried, too. I was depressed a lot of the time. I missed my kid and my husband terribly when I traveled. I missed my autonomy and the adventure of the road when I was home.

The imbalance was not sustainable. A life of eating and drinking and traveling is a life of overwhelming privilege. There's nothing else I want to do with my life, no job I'd rather have. But it's also hard. I've spent a lot of time feeling like a bad parent. I've spent a lot of nights lonely in hotel rooms.

On the other side of COVID, I downshifted hugely. I wanted a life where I could go to pub trivia with my family and friends on Tuesday nights, where I could swim in the pool up the street from my house every day, where I could reliably be there for my son when he needed me. I still eat amazing things, almost daily. But now I do it mostly in Melbourne. I miss the travel, the adventure, the discovery, the wildness of a life on the road. But I don't miss the loneliness.

Tony's travel didn't just support himself and his family and his identity. It supported hundreds of people, friends, coworkers; a whole industry built around him.

It's a refrain that came up constantly in the weeks after his death, in tweets and articles and conversation: We wanted to *be* him. We wanted to be his friend and sidekick, but mostly we thought of his life as the best life, the perfect life. That's a lot of pressure to put on one man—all these millions of people sending the message both literally and also through the ether of our collective consciousness: *You have the life all of us want.*

Imagine everyone you meet saying that to you. Imagine still feeling like shit.

In the days after Bourdain's death, when I was still deeply entrenched in a life on the road, I projected my own experiences onto his tragedy: my struggle with the gift of the work I do juxtaposed with the difficulty of doing it and still being a good parent and partner, my struggle with the endless nights in hotels, my struggle with the shame of feeling bad when everything in my life looked (and was!) like a dream.

I even projected my own lovelorn desperation all those years ago, taking the bait from tabloids that maybe this was an act of passion in the wake of an obsessive love affair gone wrong. (It should go without saying that this type of speculation is both human and grotesque, and that none of us could know what he was going through, and that it is an ugly fallacy to pretend that we might.) Even in his death, I shoved my own bullshit onto him, onto his memory.

My own psychological struggles are the least interesting parts of me. They don't make me tragic or cool or fascinating. If talking about the strain of mental illness saves lives, we should do more of it. But there's a fine line between destigmatizing mental illness and romanticizing it, especially when you're dealing with someone as mythical and beloved as Bourdain.

I'm unreasonably angry that this death is one of the main things history will remember. It's possible that it inspired some folks to get the help they needed. It also had the potential to drive other people deeper into an identity that is so entwined with darkness, disentanglement becomes almost impossible. I think I can say with confidence that if you are a person who identified strongly with Bourdain and are struggling, you should know that he would prefer the former for you and not the latter.

Like so many things, this book was waylaid by COVID. It should have been the opposite scenario—I was trapped at home, stuck in Melbourne's lockdowns, which were some of the harshest and longest in the world. I had nothing else to do. But my brain would not, could not do it. I was bewildered, unmoored, coming off two years on the road for World's Best Restaurants and my work for *The New York Times*, two years of extreme adventure, and then two years of intermittent lockdowns where, for months on end, we weren't even allowed to leave our homes other than to go to the store, weren't even allowed to sit in the park. I started writing, but I got very, very stuck. Instead, Ryan and I took up gin rummy. We learned to make the perfect piña colada. I sat on the roof in the afternoons so I could hang out with my friend Brooke, who lived across the laneway. She sat in her backyard, and we basked in the privilege of a distanced social connection that was impossible for most people in Melbourne at that time. I was lucky. But I could not find it in me to create anything at all.

I was listening to a lot of Liz Phair for a while in there, and in particular her album *Exile in Guyville*, a brilliant and very female album that also happens to be a song-by-song response to / reckoning with the Rolling Stones album *Exile on Main St.*

In those months, I also was reading a lot of food memoirs and books, trying to get myself inspired. And I picked up *Kitchen Confidential* for the first time in decades. Something started percolating in the creative part of my brain, the very thing that I'd been missing when trying to sit down to write. I saw the opportunity for a dialogue of sorts, a response to the brash and testosterone-soaked text that inspired all of us, all those years ago.

This book is not a chapter-by-chapter response to *Kitchen Confidential*. But I did let it inspire me in that way when I needed it most. There are echoes, themes, riffs, borrowed or answered or something. I allowed his worship for chef and kitchen culture to inspire and frame some of my own experiences and thoughts about this world. I am not a chef, and I am not a man, and this world has been hard for me to navigate, and I have been dismissed more times than I've been welcomed.

But Tony? Tony always welcomed me. And he helped me immensely, from beyond, with the writing of this book.

On the night of Bourdain's death, after my sister and I left the fancy resort with the clueless waiter and the scared echidna, we went into town and tried to find an appropriate bar. I'm not sure what I was hoping for. I think I wanted to find a line cook with grief to match my own. I wanted to buy that cook a drink.

Instead, all we found were empty tourist bars with a few sad kids trying to make spring break last forever. We gave up. Heading out of the last bar, the worn-down heel of my worn-out boots slipped on a step, and I went down hard on the staircase. It hurt, a lot.

I stayed up half the night, reading the things people had to say about Bourdain, feeling far away from everyone—my community, my family, and most of all him, this person I barely knew but to whom all of us felt intimately connected. I fell asleep for a few short hours and woke again to scroll through the disbelief, the sadness, the cries for us all to look out for one another more. My ass hurt from the tumble, enough that I thought I should take a look.

The reflection in the mirror in the dawn light made me gasp. My entire ass was covered in a giant, angry, heart-shaped bruise, the darkest bruise I'd ever seen. It looked like I'd sat in blue-black ink.

The bruise was still there as I wrote an early draft of this epilogue, an essay, at the time, a week after his death. I could feel it—it made writing hard, because to write, you have to sit, and sitting was painful. Writing is painful. Life is fucking painful. And darkly, wickedly comical. And because of that, the pursuit of connection and pleasure, be it at a table or in the pages of a book or over a glass of whiskey, is vital.

The bruise left a shadow that lingered for almost a year. And at the risk of further projecting, it comforts me to think that Bourdain might get a kick out of it: his shadow in my book; his shadow in the form of the black heart on my ass—in his honor—that hurt like a motherfucker. And reminded me, always, to live the hell out of this glorious, messy, miraculous life.

Acknowledgments

I'd like to thank every person, named and unnamed and fake-named, who makes an appearance in this text, even the ones who kinda suck but especially those who don't suck at all: You all made me who I am and gave me a story to tell. I love (most of) you a lot.

So many acknowledgments start this way, and now I know why: This book would never have come about if not for my agent, Kitty Cowles, who pushed me and supported me and never let me give up, who has championed me for years and years, who cares about the actual writing and the person doing the writing. The same is true for Randi Kramer, the editor who saw this book through all the hard parts and left Celadon before all the fun parts, but who believed in it always. If not for her passion for the project—and for Deb Futter, who supported Randi's enthusiasm and took the manuscript over the finish line—*Hunger Like a Thirst* never would have seen the light of day.

About that title: I want to extend my deepest gratitude to Liz Phair, who graciously allowed me to use her lyric to name my book. *Hunger Like a Thirst* comes from the song "Strange Loop" on the album *Exile in Guyville*. As mentioned in the epilogue, that album has been a huge inspiration to me over the years and especially as I was writing this book, and the generosity of Ms. Phair to allow me to use her words for my title still makes me giddy.

I need to thank my editors over the years, in particular Richard Hart, Ken Edelstein, Mara Shalhoup, Debbie Michaud, Damien Cave, Mark Josephson, Ardyn Bernoth, and Roslyn Grundy. Every one of you has made me a better writer; a couple of you have made me a better person.

Mel Hansche, Hunter Lewis, and Jacqui Gifford entrusted me with World's Best Restaurants, for which I am eternally grateful. It wasn't just a career-defining assignment, it was a life-defining experience.

Thank you to my parrot, Chobi, for keeping me company during the writing of this book, literally sitting on my shoulder for much of it—the ear nibbles weren't that helpful, but the *Squee-squee-squaw!!*s really lifted my spirits.

Thank you to Mary Gillen Blythe, for your long-standing unconditional love and support, and for following me around the world even though you didn't really mean to; your friendship is among my most precious assets. There are so many women who have been ports in the storm for me over the years, who keep me sane and pull me up when I'm full of shit, who care deeply about the work and, through their friendship, have inspired me to be worthy, in particular, Osayi Endolyn, Aubrey Zinaich, and Jennifer Zyman, I can't imagine my life without you in it; I hope I never have to.

I am who I am because of my mother, Susanna Rodell, who encouraged me to always be fiercely true to myself, who is the reason I am a writer, and who showed incredible good sportsmanship (womanship?) in understanding why I write about her in such candid (and one-sided) terms. I also owe infinitude to my father, Ian Siggins, who taught me how to think; my stepfather, Peter Anthony, who taught me how to argue and laugh and fall down and get up; and my siblings Fred Siggins, Grace Anthony, Ruby Rodell, and Georgina Siggins, who taught me how to love. (Fred gets extra thanks for being my first and best reader, always, and Grace for being my first and best cheerleader, always. Everyone deserves a Grace.)

Bill Addison! What would I be without you? Your influence is self-evident in these pages, obviously, but officially: thank you, thank you.

Thank you to Trish and Duane Stewart, my in-laws, who got me to that very first Association of Food Journalists awards ceremony (in a pretty dress, at that), who are my second home, who raised my Ryan.

And finally, thank you to my husband, Ryan, who has given up almost everything, over and over again, in order to support my career and encourage me to follow my happiness. I hope I've given you half of what you've given me in this life. Let's go to bed.

ABOUT THE AUTHOR

Besha Rodell is a James Beard Award–winning food writer, editor, and restaurant critic who has been obsessed with eating out since she was a child. Born in Australia, in a bungalow on a farm her father dubbed Narnia, she moved to the United States as a teenager. She has been writing professionally for more than two decades, and her work has appeared in numerous publications, including *The New York Times*, *Food & Wine*, *Saveur*, *Bon Appétit*, *Travel + Leisure*, *Punch*, *Eater*, *Gravy*, and many others. She was the restaurant critic at *LA Weekly* and was a critic and columnist for *The New York Times*, where she is still a regular contributor. In 2019, Rodell was tapped by *Food & Wine* to be its global critic, traveling solo to pick the world's best restaurants for an annual list. She is currently the chief restaurant critic at *The Age*, a daily newspaper in Melbourne, Australia. Rodell moved back to Australia in 2017 and lives in Melbourne with her husband, Ryan; her parrot, Chobi; and a rotating menagerie of foster cats.

CELADON
BOOKS

Founded in 2017, Celadon Books, a division of
Macmillan Publishers, publishes a highly curated list
of twenty to twenty-five new titles a year. The list of
both fiction and nonfiction is eclectic and focuses
on publishing commercial and literary books and
discovering and nurturing talent.